The Creation of Reality
in Psychoanalysis

The Creation of Reality
in Psychoanalysis

A View of the Contributions
of Donald Spence, Roy Schafer,
Robert Stolorow, Irwin Z. Hoffman,
and Beyond

Richard Moore

THE ANALYTIC PRESS

1999   Hillsdale, NJ   London

Published by The Analytic Press, Inc.
101 West Street, Hillsdale, NJ 07642

Set in Palatino 10/12 by Laserset, Inc., New York, NY
Index by Leonard Rosenbaum, Washington, DC

Library of Congress Cataloging-in-Publication Data

Moore, Richard 1936–
    The creation of reality in psychoanalysis : a view of the
contributions of Donald Spence, Roy Schafer, Robert Stolorow,
Irwin Z. Hoffman, and beyond / Richard Moore.
        p.   cm.
    Includes bibliographical references and index.
    ISBN: 0-88163-303-8
    1. Reality—Psychological aspects.   2. Psychoanalysis.
I. Title.
BF175.5.R4M66   1999   98-52181
150.19'5—dc21   CIP

Printed in the United States of America
10 9 8 7 6 5 4 3 2 1

That the present in general is not primal but, rather, reconstituted, that it is not the absolute, wholly living form which constitutes experience, that there is no purity of the living present—such is the theme, formidable for metaphysics, which Freud, in a conceptual scheme unequal to the thing itself, would have us pursue.

Jacques Derrida

Our individual and collective sanities rest on a certain poetic license, a necessary illusion that the world we discuss is there to be experienced.

Christopher Bollas

Contents

Acknowledgments

$\mathcal{T}$his book is the product of a long chain of events, none of which would have been possible without the participation of certain key people. First, I want to express my gratitude to Jake Keenan, who loves to play catch with ideas, for helping me get started. I am also very grateful to the faculty and the administration at the Center for Psychological Studies in Albany, California for giving me the freedom, as well as the support, to find my own way with the dissertation that eventually became this book. I particularly want to express appreciation to Helena Herschel, Ph.D., not only for her helpful suggestions about the dissertation on which this book is based, but also for being the first to envision its potential as a book. I also want thank my knowledgeable friend Steven Galper, L.C.S.W., for wading through a very early version of this manuscript, and my cousin, Sylvia Levine, for volunteering her editing skills for the final proofreading. Also genuinely deserving of credit is Susanna Bonetti, Senior Library Assistant at the Erik Erikson Library at the San Francisco Psychoanalytic Institute, for her professionalism and kindness. Gratitude is also particularly due to Paul Stepansky, Ph.D., of The Analytic Press, for his careful reading and many invaluable suggestions and observations. Indispensable to the completion of this project has been John Kerr, also of The Analytic Press. From his initial receipt of my manuscript, through a final line-by-line reading, and all the myriad clarifications and discussions in between, his clarity, understanding, and humor are deeply appreciated. I also want to thank a few special people who, though they are not necessarily involved with the subject nor sufficiently fluent in the language of psychology to immerse themselves fully in this book, know me like a book and were vital to me in completing this project. These include my friends and confidants of many years, Robert Wendlinger and Daniel Gottsegen, my mother and father, Esther Kassoy and William Moore, and, most of all, Linda Sanford, who managed to love me through all the times when my preoccupation with the ideas expressed in the following pages made a faraway look my most common expression.

Introduction

*W*hat follows is a psychoanalytic discussion about the relationship between subjectivity and external reality. This discussion covers a variety of different positions on this matter. While many of these positions are quite complex, both their range and some of their central tenets can be foreshadowed with a simple story. Unlikely as it may seem, this story concerns three baseball umpires talking together about their work. The first umpire says, "I watch the ball really closely, I don't let anything or anyone distract me, and I call each pitch exactly as it is." The second umpire, more humble, says simply, "I call 'em as I see 'em." Then the third umpire declares, "They ain't nothing till *I* call them." We will discuss analogues to each of these views as they exist in psychoanalysis today. We will also attempt to elaborate a version of the position held by the third umpire which might contribute to psychoanalysis in the future. To introduce the discussion, it is important first to make a few statements about the broader psychoanalytic discourse in which this discussion occurs as well as to mention other significant aspects of the current social context which bear on it in direct and indirect ways.

Historical Context

The fact that Freud first put forth many of his ideas a century ago did not save him from having to deal with many of the same complexities that confront today's psychoanalytic theorists. Nevertheless, it must be acknowledged that the world, particularly the intellectual world, was significantly different from the one in which we now discuss his work. When Freud first put forth his ideas, the nature of reality in psychoanalysis was almost a given. This conception of reality was given by the complete dominance of the positivism of the 19th century[1] in the scientific circles to which Freud belonged when he began to propose what would become psychoanalysis. It is in this context that we must note Freud's own highly articulate and public championing of psychoanalysis as a new *science*. It was as a science that psychoanalysis had to confront and describe an objective and verifiable reality. Though it has since been pointed out in some philosophical, as well as in some recent psychoanalytic, circles that Freud's method often strayed from any grounding in an objective reality, his explicit statements about the existence of such a reality never did. The existence of an objective and ultimately empirically verifiable reality was not a matter about which Freud publicly entertained doubts. Wolman (1984) states clearly that "according to Freud, objective and verified observation is the sole source of knowledge" (p. 71).[2]

But for Freud's psychoanalysis, a reliance on objective and verified observation included a high degree of reliance on patients' reports of observations about their own past. Freud considered this past reality to be the foundation of a patient's current complaints and the basis of psychoanalytic understanding. Essentially Freud's approach became, in practice, dependent on his patient's memory, and it was in regard to this conception of memory as the custodian of historical reality that psychoanalysis may be said to have suffered its most severe setbacks. Under Freud's tutelage recent memories began to

---

[1] The term positivism has a long and complex history beginning in France in the 19th century with August Comte and including a group of philosophers called the Vienna Circle early in the 20th. Currently it is associated with a variety of meanings in the hands of various philosophers (Lacey, 1976, pp. 183–186). It is used here to refer to the belief in an external world existing independently of human perception which eventually might be completely understood by objective observers using the scientific methods of the time.

[2] Wolman (1984) also convincing portrays Freud's philosophical position as *epistemological realism* rather than positivism. Epistemological realism denotes a position in which the existence of an objective reality is self-consciously and pragmatically assumed rather than held as a belief. That is, although Freud personally reserved final judgment concerning the nature of reality, he consciously chose to act and write in accord with the basic assumptions of his day about such fundamental matters. However, Freud typically expressed both his conclusions and his observations with a certainty that conveyed belief.

yield to earlier ones that required psychoanalytic intervention to become conscious, and earlier ones sometimes yielded to dreams and Freud's own reconstructions of what he believed had occurred but could no longer be recalled. Eventually Freud also found some cause for current psychological problems in his patient's genetic and even phylogenetic past.

Over the course of his career, this effective use of the past as an infinitely receding source of causation opened the doors to several things. One was a complementary concept of the present that was less and less an independent reality and more and more merely the face of a personal past. Second was the tendency to explain his increasingly historical understanding of his patients with an ever more sophisticated and complex theory delving further and further back in time. The third was a complementary degree of related ambiguity about the final determination of causation in psycho-analysis (Freud, 1939, p. 85). That is, as the historical ground under Freud's understanding slid further into his patients' personal past, the apparent certainty surrounding the technique by which each succeeding determination of causation was derived also suffered continuing erosion. This ambiguity is, to judge from the many highly disparate theoretical approaches that continue to thrive within psychoanalysis, never to be resolved, and perhaps never even reconciled. It is that ambiguity which also may have helped lead some psychoanalysts to attempt to abandon at least that particular chase through time and to propose a central role in both theory and clinical practice for a subjectivity not dependent on any knowable context in external reality. These psychoanalysts, several of whose approaches to this problem form the focus of this book, will be grouped in the discussion that follows under the rubric of the narrative camp in psychoanalysis.

Contemporary Context

The difficulty in establishing the validity of long-term autobio-graphical memory, particularly when the memory in question involves incestuous experience, is the most concrete example of this difficulty in identifying the "actual" or "true" cause in psycho-analysis. It is not an accident that this issue has dogged psychoanaly-sis almost since its inception. Even the specific patients on whose recollections Freud founded his pioneering work and based various stages of his own internal debate in this theoretically crucial area are arguably no less controversial now than they were at the turn of the century (e.g., Crews et al, 1994; for a somewhat sensationalized example, see Masson, 1984). In recent years, however, this debate has actually widened in two important directions. Within psychoanalysis, the focus of this debate has shifted away from the validity of any particular memory and toward the much more basic issue of the psychoanalytic view of the reality from which memory is derived. With this shift has come intrinsic challenges to the most basic premises of psychoanalysis. These premises, which until recently, were accepted as a given, are the foundations of its metapsychology. They include, at least, an assumption of, and often an explicit conviction about, a context of an objective and potentially empirically verifiable social and material reality. This book is an effort to explore and elaborate in detail some of the strengths and weaknesses of the challenges to these premises and, it is hoped, to contribute toward the formulation of a more integrated and more solidly grounded metapsychological response.

At the same time that the interest in such questions has intensified within psychoanalysis, the context for those questions in the culture as a whole has also shifted in important ways that add potential relevance to our inquiry. One highly visible example is the general public interest in the validity of recollections about past reality that recently gained unprecedented coverage in the popular news media. I refer, of course, to the recent spate of public interest about the authenticity of reported memories of childhood sexual abuse. At this writing, such public interest has barely just subsided. It is not unreasonable to speculate, however, that in this age of relativity and intensifying postmodernism, the same ambiguity involving un-examined assumptions about the relation of subjectivity to external reality lay beneath the recent public uproar and contribute to the enduring insolubility of the debate surrounding it. The pervasive presence of such concerns is also reflected in academia, where a river of publications relating even more directly to the nature of reality continues to flow through virtually every field of scholarship. A particularly striking and illustrative example is the explicit defense of positivism against postmodernism by Alan Sokol, a physicist at New York University. Sokol was reportedly moved to prove that those "who spoke of science as a 'social construction' didn't know what they were talking about" (Fish, 1996). According to Fish and others, he did this by publishing a professional journal article purporting to link quantum mechanics and postmodern thought, and another article in another journal boasting that the first article was a hoax. This dramatic defense is particularly interesting not only because it suggests the perceived power of such postmodern forces, but also because its underlying logic reveals that Sokol has already absorbed a basic tenet of the social-constructivism he opposes. The polemic impact of his action relies heavily on the premise that the validity of a thesis is associated with the sincerity (i.e., the internal experience) of the person who advances it. No empirically based position would allow the contention that publishing a persuasive article advocating a thesis that the writer opposes in any way invalidates that thesis.

Between the public media and the professional journals there has also risen an influential popular psychology literature about the basis in external reality of recovered memory. These publications have almost consistently served less to clarify this debate than to amplify it. Such books, though often well written and informative, are typically written explicitly to play a partisan role (see Loftus, 1993, p. 525, for her critical comments on the "incest book industry," as well as Tavris, 1993). Many of these partisan texts offer uncritical support to all those who believe they were victims of sexual abuse against any and all doubts concerning the historical basis of their claims. Alice Miller (1990) whose widely sold books emphasize such uncritical support, states that "a child *will never invent traumas.*" (1990, p. 74). Unusual in that she was previously a psychoanalyst, Miller accompanies her current stance with frequent specific denunciations of psychoanalysis (pp. 61, 64, 153 for example). Similarly, though professionally untrained, the authors of the often-noted *The Courage to Heal* (Bass and Davis, 1988) write, "If you think you were abused and your life shows the symptoms, then you were" (p. 22) and if "you are unable to remember any specific instances like the ones mentioned above but still have a feeling that something abusive happened to you, it probably did" (p. 21). This widely read book has been implicated in many court cases (Loftus, 1993, p. 525).

One salient common feature of this literature seems to be extreme faith in the historical validity of any narrative that includes experiences of sexual abuse of children—regardless of the narrative's form or derivation. A complementary posture of virtually no faith in any narrative involving disavowal of such experiences by either the accused adult or even the purported victim is also common. These two stances—that subjective experience is definitive and that it can be almost completely disregarded when it disavows abuse—clearly represent a smorgasbord approach to the nature of reality. Taken together, these stances appear to suggest understandably strong feelings, but no single tenable perspective about reality. Certainly such a mixed view cannot provide the basis for a clinical perspective or a theoretical resolution of the sort pursued here. Unfortunately, psychoanalysis, despite (or perhaps because of) almost a century of concern with this issue, has not been able to unify around an effective alternative perspective about the meaning of such memories. Rather, the partisan view just outlined has increasingly been influential in virtually all arenas. In the courts and in various legislatures laws have recently been specifically designed with the lawmaker's own view of the psychotherapeutic process in mind. An increasing number of laws press all psychotherapists to break confidence to report suspicions of possible abuse whenever the person suspected might still be active (for example, see the statement of the Office of the Attorney General in 1987, quoted in Leslie, 1990, p. 15). In addition, a growing number of states (19 by 1993, according to Bower, 1993a, p. 184) have removed the previously existing statute of limitations on prosecuting accused abusers in order to allow as evidence such memories that arise decades after the possible fact (for a view of the legislative basis for these changes, see Taylor, 1994).

It is important to note in passing that there is also an opposite pole in this polarized and politicized public controversy. We refer not to advocates and apologists for incest (for discussion of those age old positions, see Demause, 1991, pp. 131, 132). There is a current partisan literature for the victims of the "false" memories of children, memories that contain images of incest without basis in historical fact (see Coleman, 1992; Ofshe and Watters, 1993); there is also a controversial national organization (The False Memory Syndrome Foundation) established to supply supportive contacts, literature, and reprints. The FMS Foundation has been accused by 17 prominent research psychologists, writing in the newsletter of the American Psychological Society, of inventing the "syndrome" with no supportive data (Carstensen et al., 1993, p. 23), and by many others, of leading a backlash against gains in public acceptance of the real plight of child abuse victims (Bower, 1993a, p. 186). The organization also has received support and participation from within the fields of psychology, psychiatry, and even psychoanalysis. For example, the Foundation lists Donald Spence, whose work is referred to elsewhere in these pages, on its 1994 board of advisors. Most important, those in support of the FMS position are able to draw on a growing body of empirical studies suggesting that false memories do sometimes occur and can even be implanted (see Loftus, 1993). Moreover, there are increasingly some jurists inclined to agree. Some recent court decisions have failed to validate traumatic recollections: one involved (Hatfield, 1996) a woman whose memory in a related instance had been specifically authenticated by the psychoanalytically identified psychiatrist Lenore Terr (1994, pp. 32–60). These court cases have relied on generally accepted evidence (such as DNA) to demonstrate that not all such memories are authentic.

Obviously, it is impossible to weigh precisely the profound effect that all the media attention to concerns about the relation among perception, recall, and the external world has both on the mental experience of patients in psychoanalysis, most especially those who carry or discover images of incest in their own memories and on the minds of the psychoanalysts who listen to them. Certainly no exhaustive evaluation is sought here. However the recent public reevaluation of memory and its impact on psychoanalytic practice form an undeniable part of the context of the discourse examined here. Consequently, we remain mindful of the public controversy over "false" memories as we focus our attention on many of the metapsychological ramifications underlying similar issues in psychoanalysis.

The Discussion

We begin by exploring Freud's basic position on historical truth in psychoanalysis, and also his famous archeological metaphor in that regard. To illustrate this position requires a discussion of Freud's allegiance to the philosophy of the physical (particularly the biological) sciences; his investment in the "kernel of truth" metaphor, with its implicit faith in the power of invoked historical truth to promote psychodynamic change; and his overall perspective of psychoanalysis as a path through defensive improvisations to the goal of personal historical truth.

To Freud's explicit historicism we contrast Freud's own implicit reliance on narrative truth (a story that is experienced as true independent of its origins) and also his explicit development of the concept of *Nachtraglichkeit* (Freud, 1896; Modell, 1990). The latter concept, while intrinsic in many other key psychoanalytic concepts (such as transference; see Modell, 1990, p. 17) refers directly to the possibility of the continual reworking of memory to accommodate current needs. Freud refers to it as a successive "retranslation of psychic material" and also as "a retranscription" (letter to Fliess, December 6, 1896, in Masson, 1985, p. 207). In any case, the concept represents Freud's realization that memory may not function simply as a custodian for historical reality. The concept also represents an admission that the reality of our memory may never be, and perhaps should not be, merely a reflection of the reality of our past. This explicit perspective, with its prescient disparity from the proclaimed view of virtually all the legal and social institutions in our society, also brings Freud into surprisingly close range of the narrative camp in psychoanalysis.

It is, of course, possible to take the position that Freud's apparent adherence to the philosophic views prevalent among natural scientists of his day was never more than a superficial concession (see Habermas, 1972, pp. 214-273). In this view, Freud really built his work on subjective and hermeneutic grounds, which various writers are only now bringing more clearly into focus. I hold, however, that those grounds are comprehensible only within the context of an objective reality overall. For example, Freud's emphasis on psychic reality can no more be understood without the contrast of a verifiable external world than an airplane's flight can be understood without a conception of gravity. Yet various writers, and particularly those four writers discussed in the following pages, have begun to suggest the possibility of a psychoanalysis with which the concept of an objective and verifiable world cannot logically co-exist.

The third, fourth, fifth, sixth, and seventh chapters of this book contain an exploration and evaluation of some of the seminal contemporary psychoanalytic figures contributing to the current discourse on narrative. The third chapter offers an overview of what we describe as narrative approaches in psychoanalysis in general, and ends with a more intensive discussion of the contribution of Donald Spence. The fourth, fifth, and sixth chapters present explorations of the contributions of Roy Schafer, Robert Stolorow, and Irwin Z. Hoffman respectively. Each of these writers derives his view of narrative from his particular perspective on mankind's relation to an ambiguous reality. To introduce them each in the most general terms, one could say first that Spence (1982, 1993) forces us to share his painfully unresolved confrontation with an unavoidable element of subjectivity in all perception and expression. Schafer (1992) provides a less conflicted view of subjective perception and expression as simply the only reality that has ever been available. This view, while sophisticated in its conception, appears to have minimal impact on most of the traditional aspects of Schafer's psychoanalytic practice. In contrast, Stolorow (Stolorow, Brandchaft, and Atwood, 1987; Stolorow, 1988) places the unconscious mutual articulation of existing subjective reality at the center of his practice, but he does so under the aegis of a structural model that often seriously undercuts, if not actually belies, the process he describes. Hoffman (1987, 1991) also speaks of the possibility of the full acceptance of the mutual creation of reality as the central focus of his work (see also Keller, 1994) and often chooses to embrace uncertainty rather than a prespecified theoretical understanding. However, he also invokes the traditional structure of psychoanalysis by simply reconceptualizing the meaning of the traditional words naming its individual parts without examining the structure implied in their sum. At other times he appears to use traditional formulations reflexively without the benefit of such reconceptualizations.

To provide a stepping-stone from the work of all these writers to the ideas presented here, chapter seven is devoted to a brief comparison of these writers and their commonalties. As these positions are compared they are evaluated with regard to their internal theoretical consistency and clinical utility. Through a discussion of their explicit and implicit characterization of truth and reality within the psychoanalytic hour, a spotlight is thrown on the contradiction within each of these approaches between their proclaimed subjectivist, and often constructivist, theoretical perspective and an increasingly tenuous clinical base in traditional psychoanalytic reality. It is a major thesis of this book that the tension between the premises of psychoanalysis and the direction taken by this growing narrative discourse is reflected in the work of each of these writers as a basic logical discontinuity appearing in many of their central concepts.

The eighth and final chapter offers a preliminary exploration of a constructivist synthesis of the opposing perspectives presented earlier. The chapter attempts to elaborate a more unified metapsychology congruent with the subjectivist perspectives of Spence, Schafer, Stolorow, and Hoffman, but also one significantly less fettered by traditional assumptions about external reality. The chapter draws on several writers not previously discussed, but especially on the work of D. W. Winnicott and Christopher Bollas. It presents an approach that elevates the process of construction itself to a central psychoanalytic concern, rather than any of the results or behaviors that may flow from that process. While obviously extremely speculative, the ideas presented here are seen as having the potential to move the constructivist discussion one step further. This approach proposes major changes in the concept of normalcy and also in the way in which the role of the unconscious is viewed in the context of a consciousness that constructs. It also suggests major changes in how we see trauma. In particular, it considers a definition of trauma as damage to the process of construction itself. This view of trauma potentially shifts clinical emphasis from the nature of the original traumatizing event toward repair of that process of construction.

Many of the ideas presented, particularly in chapters devoted to those who have pioneered in charting a new course for psychoanalysis, may be seen as deconstructive. However, that is not the intended brunt of this work. The goal of this work is to contribute meaningfully to a broader psychoanalytic discourse. It is not to deconstruct, or decenter, or even simply critique, existing psychoanalytic theory. The aim is to help recenter psychoanalytic metapsychology in a way that might provide a more solid platform from which to address the issue of a constructivist reality at the level of clinical theory.

_____ 2

Freud's Realities

*T*he circle of interpretations rippling from Freud's great splash in the intellectual world of late 19th- and early 20th-century Europe continues to widen even today; there is no way it can be reversed. Although almost all the original documents remain, our own changing world continues to carry us further from the point of view from which they were originally launched by their author. In addition, nothing illustrates the difficulty in recovering the past more clearly than an attempt to resurrect a single aspect of the thinking of a complex man whose thought was constantly evolving, inherently controversial, and sometimes even contradictory at its inception. Specifically, with regard to the topic of this book, the basis of Freud's beliefs regarding an objective and potentially verifiable past necessarily lay partly in his more general commitment to an objective and potentially verifiable material reality overall. Freud, at least in this intellectual sense, was committed to such a reality. Questions remain, however, about the exact nature of his commitment. Then there is a second question: what was the size, nature, and consistency of the role of that commitment in shaping psychoanalysis? With even the simplest attempt to answer these questions a drift toward competing assessments arises almost immediately and quickly becomes almost too powerful to resist. Grünbaum (1984), Wolman (1984), Habermas (1972), Sulloway (1979), Masson (1984), Ricoeur (1970), Sachs (1989), and Popper (1963), as well as several somewhat

11

disparate statements by Freud himself, offer just a few among the many current interpretations.

In these varied evaluations of Freud's views on reality, several standards have been used. Historically, the significance of the issue was most often linked with the desire either to include or to bar psychoanalysis from the esteemed status of science (as opposed to the more recent desire of some to distinguish the roots of psychoanalysis from today's spreading hermeneutic branches). Consequently, it is understandable that virtually all these standards for measuring psychoanalysis's commitment to the possibility of an objective view of an objective reality are drawn from the natural sciences. Freud's own efforts to construct a reductionist theory in a manner consonant with 19th-century physics and biology fall seriously short of their mark (Grünbaum, 1984; Sulloway, 1979). Robinson (1993) expresses a less demanding, though also widely held position. Robinson's position is noteworthy here because it potentially leads to a recognition of Freud's commitment to history as a central issue in the evaluation of psychoanalysis as a science. Robinson's view is that psychoanalysis need not model itself on physics to be a science. He proposes that "science is in fact a continuum, with psychoanalysis occupying an honored place toward the Darwinian end" (pp. 262–263). Darwin's work, which holds an indisputably hallowed place in the history of science, was largely theoretical speculation based on uncontrolled observations in the field. Robinson's position honors the more speculative metapsychological approach to observed data often taken by Freud and his followers and suggests the more realistic analogy of field observation—rather than the more pristine, hypothesis testing laboratory procedures once envisioned as the sole basis for physics—as an acceptable standard of scientific rigor for the psychoanalytic session. More specifically, if we accept Robinson's view, Grünbaum's (1984) description of Freud's failure to empirically validate psychoanalytic treatment (the "tally" argument) and Popper's (1963) concern with the refutability of Freud's hypotheses move from potentially devastating to the scientific status of psychoanalysis to merely interesting critiques. Center stage in evaluating psychoanalysis's membership in the scientific community is then left to establishing that psychoanalysis shares physic's most basic commitment—to an ultimately objectifiable reality—and the eventual goal of its empirical verification of its observations and hypotheses.

Although psychoanalysis almost immediately began to deal with the intangible "psychic reality" of the mind, it did so only in the constant context of a real daily world that existed independently of the minds that perceived it. The concept of psychic reality did not challenge the notion of an independent reality. As suggested earlier, Freud's psychoanalysis remained as dependent on the notion of an objective reality as the flight of an airplane is on gravity. The requisite commitment to the existence of material reality in the present, along with psychoanalysis's currently challenged faith in the ultimate fidelity of the mind's ability to record, form the twin pillars of psychoanalysis's commitment to historical reality. Freud's psychoanalysis, with its ubiquitous archeological metaphor, largely presented itself to the world as a science based on accurate "traces" of a real past. It is the invocation of a past material reality that left those "traces"—or "historical truth," as the term is currently used— that is arguably the final ground of its claim to be a science. More relevant here, this invocation of a past material reality is also the major basis for distinguishing it from more current narrative conceptions of the psychoanalytic process and thus forms the nub of the current controversy about recovered memory, at least within psychoanalysis itself.

Freud's (1933) statements about present objective material reality were typically unequivocal. Consider the following surprisingly current polemic. Here Freud, at 76, tears into those whose views might today be characterized as constructivist. To Freud such views are "a counterpart to political anarchism"; about their adherents, he comments, "Just now the relativity theory of modern physics seems to have gone to their head."

According to the anarchist theory there is no such thing as truth, no assured knowledge of the external world. What we give out as being scientific truth is only the product of our own needs as they are bound to find utterance under changing external conditions: once again they are illusion. Fundamentally, we find only what we need and see only what we want to see. We have no other possibility. Since the criterion of truth—correspondence with the external world—is absent, it is entirely a matter of indifference what opinions we adopt. All of them are equally true and equally false. And no one has a right to accuse anyone else of error.

A person of an epistemological bent might find it tempting to follow the paths—the sophistries—by which the anarchists succeed in enticing such conclusions from science. No doubt we should come upon situations similar to those derived from the familiar paradox of the Cretin who says that all Cretins are liars. But I have neither the desire nor the capacity for going into this more deeply. All I can say is that the anarchist theory sounds wonderfully superior so long as it relates to opinions about abstract things: it breaks down with its first step into practical life. Now the actions of men are governed by their opinions, their knowledge; and it is the same scientific spirit that speculates about the structure of atoms or the origin of man and that plans the construction of a bridge capable of bearing a load. If what we believe were really a matter of indifference, if there were no such thing as knowledge distinguished among our opinions by corresponding to reality, we might build bridges just as well out of cardboard as out of stone, we might inject our patients with a decagram of morphine instead of a centigram, and might use tear-gas as a narcotic instead of ether. But even the intellectual anarchists would violently repudiate such practical applications of their theory [pp. 175–176].

Freud also expresses the same monolithic faith in an independent reality at the clinical level. This time he uses psychoanalytic structural language rather than his ample rhetorical skills to drive home his views. The statement that follows is also important here because it explicitly links the perception of objective reality with the fidelity of the engraving of that perception in "memory traces."

The relation to the external world has become the decisive factor for the ego; it has taken on the task of representing the real world to the id. . . . In accomplishing this function, the ego must observe the external world, must lay down an accurate picture of it in the memory traces of its perceptions, and by the exercise of the function of "reality testing" must put aside whatever in this picture of the external world is an addition derived from internal sources of excitation [p. 75].

This particular text will be considered more fully later, but in the immediate context of this investigation the question arises: what is the basis of this certainty by Freud about his position? Obviously, the times in which he lived and his training as a physician must be heavily considered. As Peter Gay (1988) has noted, "His attempt to establish psychology as a natural science on the solid basis of neurology fits the aspirations of the positivists with whom Freud had studied, and whose hopes and fantasies he now worked to realize" (p. 79; see for a related point Otis, 1993). Clearly, even if Freud had not been trained in the shadow of some of the renowned scientists of his day, he, like anyone seeking public acceptance for a new discipline, would have found great comfort under the umbrella of science. In fact, it would not be completely unreasonable to suspect Freud of publishing his sometimes extensive defenses of science (i.e., 1933), with relatively meager accompanying presentations of his actual psychoanalytic methods, as a way of insuring that comfort.

Also, because we are discussing a psychoanalytic framework, Freud's personal motivations need not be excluded. Consider this statement:

As Lichtenberg says "An astronomer knows whether the moon is inhabited or not with about as much certainty as he knows who was his father, but not with so much certainty as he knows who was his mother." A great advance was made in civilization when men decided to put their inferences upon a level with the testimony of their senses and to make the step from matriarchy to patriarchy [Freud, 1909b, p. 233n].

Even without availing ourselves of what is known about his feelings toward his young mother and his early questions about his sister's paternity (Gay, 1988, p. 6), a current view of the foregoing comments might suggest that Freud harbored some pertinent oedipal associations—as well as his oft-noted gender biases. In addition to Freud's identification of science with masculinity, he also clearly identified it with adulthood (and the triumph of the reality principle). It is not unfair, then, to suppose that more than a little was at stake for Freud when he put forth his formal views concerning objective reality.

Unfortunately, consideration of Freud's possible mental states, however valuable to our understanding of Freud, can ultimately tell us very little about the optimal resolution of current theoretical disputes in psychoanalysis. Arguments, like formulas or medicines, should not lose or gain force because of a particular psychological environment in their origin. Any search for guidance from Freud in questions about the objective nature of reality which currently concern us here probably must end with our interpretations of his ideas as he wrote them down. Although in practice many of the currently dubious-sounding inferential arguments he used to support his clinical conclusions about his patients obviously no longer seem illustrative of any commitment to objective evidence, there is no indication in his theoretical writings that he ever questioned his own intellectual position on this matter. That he lived and worked at a certain time in the history of science, his training as a medical researcher, the formal demands of the reality principle, and some of his own personal issues—all may well have pressed him to maintain that position. Clearly such a position must be questioned today.

Freud's View of the Perception of Material Reality

The issue of Freud's view of the ability to perceive the objective reality of whose existence he was convinced requires additional attention. In this regard, a statement by Freud in 1927 warrants our interest. In this statement Freud focused exclusively on that theoretically distinct issue of our ability to perceive objective reality, rather than any question of its existence, and he also attempted to push the logic of his position considerably further than he did in the more polished and less defensive 1933 statement quoted earlier. Unfortunately, although the arguments he used (published slightly earlier, in 1927) remain relevant, they currently appear, at least to me, markedly less solid than the tone of certainty he marshaled to support them.

[A]n attempt has been made to discredit scientific endeavor in a radical way, on the ground that, being bound to the conditions of our own organization, it can yield nothing else but subjective results, whilst the real nature of things outside ourselves remains inaccessible. But this is to disregard several factors which are of decisive importance for the understanding of scientific work. In the first place, our organization—that is, our mental apparatus—has been developed precisely in the attempt to explore the outer world, and it must have therefore have realized in its structure some measure of expediency; in the second place, it is itself a constituent part of that world which we set out to investigate, and it readily admits of such an investigation; thirdly, the task of science is fully covered if we limit it to showing how the world must appear to us in consequence of the particular character of our organization; fourthly, the ultimate findings of science, precisely because of the way in which they are acquired, are determined not only by our organization but also by the things which have affected that organization; and, finally, the problem of the nature of the world without regard to our percipient [sic] mental apparatus is an empty abstraction, devoid of practical interest [Freud, 1927, pp. 55–56].

These arguments, by themselves, although ticked off with military precision, can no longer (if they ever could) carry the day. After all, there is nothing at all inherently accurate about a system simply because it has been developed in the general context to which it is to be applied; most individual mental dysfunction, for example, has arguably been developed in attempts to explore the outer world. Similarly, that a mental apparatus is a constituent of the world says virtually nothing about its perceptual accuracy. The third argument simply assumes that our perceptions, idiosyncratic as they may or may not be, somehow have a consistent relation to an admittedly only apparent version of reality. The fourth argument, involving the concept of the ultimate findings of science, is circular because if there is no objective reality there are no ultimate findings. And, finally, the problem of the nature of the world has increasingly been based less and less on "our perceptive mental apparatus," at least in the physical sciences. This is particularly true since Einstein was able to use symbols to comprehend the natural world far beyond anything yielded by its appearance to our perceptual apparatus (and beyond the grasp of many people's overall intellectual apparatus). Freud's arguments here, while historically interesting, incorporate the assumptions about reality and perception he seeks to prove and do not appear to have stood the test of time.

An entirely different problem in regard to Freud's ideas about the observation of objective reality also cannot be brushed away. It arises from within the psychoanalytic framework itself. Freud (1933, as quoted more extensively earlier) states that it is the ego that "puts aside whatever . . . is an addition derived from internal sources of excitation" and represents "the real world" to the id (p. 67). Most of psychoanalysis, however, can be seen as trying to understand the conscious ego's failure to perform just that task. Specifically, near the end of his life Freud (1939) arrived at the rather blunt conclusion that

> [I]t has not been possible to demonstrate . . . that the human intellect has a particularly fine flair for the truth or that the human mind shows any special inclination for recognizing the truth. We have found, on the contrary, that our human intellect very easily goes astray without any warning, and that nothing is more easily believed by us than what, without reference to the truth—comes to meet our wishful illusions [p. 129].

Additionally, just a few pages earlier, Freud suggests that the intrinsic design of the human mind makes it intrinsically poorly suited to really comprehend the complexity of the real world. He notes:

> [A]n important discrepancy between the attitude taken up by our organ of thought and the arrangement of things in the world, which are supposed to be grasped by means of our thought. It is enough for our need to discover causes (which, to be sure, is imperative) if each event has *one* demonstrable cause. But in the reality lying outside us this is scarcely the case . . . [p. 107].

Perhaps Freud's commitment to our ability to perceive and record an objective reality pertained most strongly to some period after the development of the ability to reality test and prior to the accumulation in the unconscious of sufficient amounts of repressed material to distort our views. Basic to Freud's views is that it is the search for expression by such repressed material which tends to distort realistic perception. It is unclear, however, when such an objective vista might obtain. Freud (1915a) hypothesized that, even in the earliest formation of personality, innate instinctual material was present that is denied the consciousness it seeks by repression (p. 148). Although a form of this theoretically necessary early "primal" repression can play a significant role (for example as "fixation" in Freud's (1911) essay on paranoia in the Schreber case (p. 67), it probably was not, in itself, considered sufficient to cause significant distortion in most other people. In any case, within the psychoanalytic view, other repressions are not long in coming, nor is their domain later easily avoided. Thus it is difficult to find much solid ground, even within psychoanalysis, where the ego might reliably perform this critical role of putting "aside whatever . . . is an addition derived from internal sources of excitation" and representing "the real world" to the id.

Not withstanding these difficulties, throughout Freud's psycho-analytic career the basic premise on which he based his clinical approach was that an objective material reality is initially directly and consciously perceived and simultaneously fully recorded in memory "traces," whose fidelity is essentially that of a contact print. One fact must not be ignored, however, if Freud's relation to the past is to be understood. It was never the past per se, but always exclu-sively mental representations of that past that were psychologically operative in his patients; and these key faithful representations were also necessarily unconscious. Even in 1896, when "The Aetiology of Hysteria" proclaimed his view that early sexual abuse was at the root of hysteria, Freud (1896) held that

> the matter is not merely one of the existence of the sexual experiences, but that a psychological precondition enters as well. The scenes must be present as *unconscious memories*; only so long as, and in so far as, they are unconscious are they able to create and maintain hysterical symptoms [p. 211].

Freud had realized from the start that the complete understanding of an initial perception, no matter how accurate it or the resulting memory may be on the sensory level, is limited by the maturity and capacity for comprehension and acceptance by the perceiver. Later he began actively to distrust conscious recollection generally and moved his focus more toward what he considered direct mani-festations of the unconscious. By 1914, Freud (1914a) held that mere "remembering in the old manner" (p. 153) was not sufficient. Repetitions of patterns of behavior also became a primary source of information about the patient's past. "As long as he is under treatment he never escapes from the compulsion to repeat; at last one understands that it is his way of remembering" (p. 149). Similarly, dreams also became not only a "royal road to the unconscious," but a major highway to the reality of his patients' past. Freud (1918) wrote:

> It seems to me absolutely equivalent to a recollection if the memories are replaced (as in the present case) by dreams, the analysis of which invariably leads back to the same scene, and which reproduce every portion of its content in an indefatigable variety of new shapes. Indeed, dreaming is another kind of remembering, though one which is subject to the conditions which rule at night and to the laws of dream formation. It is this recurrence in dreams that I regard as the explanation of the fact that the patients themselves gradually acquire a profound conviction of the reality of these primal scenes, a conviction which is in no respect inferior to one based upon recollection [p. 51].

In this way, Freud apparently began to treat dreams explicitly as a more persuasive record of the past than conscious memory and, implicitly, the techniques of free association and interpretation as at least as precise as recall.

In 1915–17, while lecturing at the University of Vienna, Freud made his shift from reliance on conscious verbal recollections of external or "material" reality even more explicit by introducing his concept of an internal, psychic reality. Speaking of a hypothetical patient, Freud (1917) said:

> If we begin by telling him straight away that he is now engaged in bringing to light the phantasies with which he has disguised the history of his childhood (just as every nation disguises its forgotten prehistory by constructing legends), we observe that his interest in pursuing the subject further suddenly diminishes in an undesirable fashion. He too wants to experience realities and despises everything that is merely "imaginary." If, however, we leave him, till this piece of work is finished, in the belief that we are occupied in investigating the real events of his childhood, we run the risk of his later accusing us of being mistaken and laughing at us for our apparent credulity. It will be a long time before he can take in our proposal that we should equate phantasy and reality and not bother to begin with whether the childhood experiences under examination are the one or the other. Yet this is clearly the only correct attitude to adopt toward these mental productions. They too possess a reality of a sort. It remains a fact that the patient has created these phantasies for himself, and this fact is of scarcely less importance for his neurosis than if he had really experienced what phantasies contain. These phantasies possess *psychical* as contrasted with *material* reality, and we gradually learn to

understand that *in the world of the neurosis it is psychical reality which is the decisive kind* [p. 368].

In any case, the lack of any currently compelling rationale by Freud for his commitment to an objective reality, and the suggestion of considerable doubt even in his own writing about patient's ability, or desire, to perceive such an objective reality, reliably, make it difficult to place much weight on his intellectual arguments for it. Clearly, in his own work it was primarily subjective reality that increasingly occupied his attention and on which, perhaps paradoxically, he tried to base his own controversial claims for objectivity. It is important to note that Freud did not go so far as to say that reality is socially constructed, merely that the human capacity to perceive the objective is very often tenuous. Nevertheless, it was on that capacity for objectivity, particularly about the impact of the past, that psychoanalysis came to rely.

The Objective Past as Intrinsic in Psychoanalysis

Even when we accept Freud's intellectual views on objective reality, and his most optimistic accounts of our potential to perceive it, and focus directly on the role of past reality within psychoanalytic theory, Freud's position remains complex. To assess the impact of past reality within psychoanalytic theory, we need to rely on more than just Freud's scattered statements. We need to look directly at the psychoanalytic theory he produced. When we do, we, without exception, encounter the formative imprint of both the external and the "psychic" past inseparably at the core of every psychoanalytic concept. For example, consider the theory of repression, which Freud (1914b) alluded to as "the corner-stone upon which the whole structure of psychoanalysis rests"(p. 16). Repression itself is held to function in a far less stolid manner than that metaphor initially suggests. Its dynamic function is actually that of a weapon against conscious instinctual expression. Since the instincts are themselves old, even in a phylogenetic sense, and their expression includes derivatives in thought and behavior over at least the lifetime of an adult patient, repression effectively becomes a weapon against the past. The concept of repression is a theoretical rendering of the process by which selected material from, or relating to, the past is blocked, buried, and kept buried.

Something similar can be said about the critical concept of regression. It literally "denotes the subject's reversion to past stages of his development" (Laplanche and Pontalis, 1973, p. 386). Speaking of the history of the concept of regression, Freud (1914b) notes that "it appeared that psychoanalysis could explain nothing belonging to the present without referring back to something past" (p. 106). It was not in these and other critical dynamic concepts, however, but in the foundation of Freud's conceptualization of the basic structure of personality that Freud's deepest commitment to the past may be most clearly seen. Freud's structural model, which he introduced in 1920, uniquely illustrates the essential and intrinsic role of the objective past in psychoanalysis. Nowhere is his view of history more fully realized than in his concept of the three major agencies, id, ego, and superego, that populate this model of the mind's functioning. With the structural model, the unconscious is no longer the relatively simple repository of repressed material that it was. Its roots in history far exceed that of its recollected images. Its very structure is the past directly embodied in the present.

Consider the ego, the structure that, of the three, is conceptualized most as a creature of the present. The ego is originally derived from the unyielding id's friction with the reality of the relatively recent past, including primary body sensations and eventually the experience of lost object choices. It is essentially a record of the personal past transformed into the psychic present. Originally "the mental projection of the surface of the body" (Freud, 1927, translator's note, p. 31), the ego's development proceeds by introjection of past "sexual" objects as well as the energy first invested in them. Freud (1923) writes, "[T]he process, [introjection] especially in the early phases of development, is a very frequent one, and it makes it possible to suppose that the character of the ego is a precipitate of abandoned object cathexes and that it contains a record of past object-choices" (p. 29).

The roots of the superego lie deeper. The superego, while directly derived from the personal values of parents who embodied particularly powerful forces in that recent history, is actually a hand-me-down with theoretically infinite roots in the past.

> Thus a child's super-ego is in fact constructed on the model not of its parents but of its parent's super-ego; the contents which fill it are the same and it becomes the vehicle of tradition and of all the time-resisting judgments of value which have propagated themselves in this manner from generation to generation [Freud, 1933, p. 67].

It is with the id, however, with its timeless instincts, that Freud (1933) revealed what is arguably the phylogenetic past incarnate.

> There is nothing in the id that corresponds to the idea of time; there is no recognition of the passage of time, and—a thing that is most remarkable and awaits consideration in philosophical thought—no

alteration in its mental processes is produced by the passage of time. Wishful impulses which have never passed beyond the id, but impressions, too, which have been sunk into the id by repression, are virtually immortal; after the passage of decades they behave as though they had just occurred. They can only be recognized as belonging to the past [p. 74].

And, again: "Thus in the id, which is capable of being inherited, are harbored residues of the existences of countless egos. . . ." (Freud, 1927, p. 38).

Although it is largely ignored today, Freud was clearly committed to his concepts of a genetic and even older phylogenetic past. References to them are generously sprinkled in many of his writings. However, he was understandably cautious about what, in current terms, appears to border on attributing the causes of current behavior to past lives. He was obviously aware of the dangers of acknowledging such easily asserted and impossible to verify factors and was reluctant to allow them a major role in psychoanalysis. Speaking of such phylogenetic considerations, Freud (1918) specified, "I consider that they are only admissible when psychoanalysis strictly observes the correct order of precedence, and after forcing its way through the strata of what has been acquired by the individual, comes at last upon traces of what has been inherited" (p. 121). Nevertheless, one who could arguably be said to predicate his entire work on the belief that the present is the face of the past could not ignore the sheer immensity of history. Consequently, for Freud, the phylogenetic past, like the repressed personal (genetic) past, must retain its power to override objective memory. "Wherever experiences fail to fit in with the hereditary schema, they become remodeled in the imagination" (p. 119).

Our emphasis here on Freud's beliefs concerning the hereditary past may be legitimately subject to the objection that this concept no longer plays a significant role in psychoanalysis. This objection does not, however, take into account the possibility that his ideas about the inheritable racial and phylogenetic past are developments that are intrinsic to his overall view of the past. As extreme aspects of its development, they may reflect more clearly its central nature and thereby help illuminate those parts of his relation with the past which do continue to be influential in current debate.

Overall, the more we examine the role Freud assigned the individual past, the less it appears as a seed from which a given personality sprung and the more it rises in our vision almost like an uncharted mountain, immeasurably larger than the small area we initially sought to explore. Such a past obviously demands a powerful and reliable (and perhaps equally mythic) means of exploration. Freud employed his concept of truth for that purpose. Perhaps it was to be expected that he would define even that concept in such a way that it ultimately also relied for its credibility on the existence of the very kind of objective past Freud sought to use it to verify and explore.

Truth as a Bridge to the Past

As the formidable silhouette of the role Freud's theory assigned to the past emerges, it becomes clear that a counterbalance is required: a basic psychoanalytic construct independent of the past; a separate theoretical ground on which to stand for viewing, understanding, and even counteracting the past as Freud understood it. This ground must be solid enough to support his techniques for detecting the past and grappling with its negative influence. In this central role Freud placed not the present—which, after all, he viewed only as an embodiment of the past—but what he called *truth*. Like his assumption of an objective reality, and the centrality of the past as a determinative force, truth about the past runs through Freud's theory like a thematic chord. Whether in the foreground of his theory or the background of his assumptions, it is always present. In Freud's early clinical work he felt that it might be sufficient for him to offer his patients a few correct words describing the truth that had been repressed; later more labored "constructions" were often required. And these "constructions," even when successful, sometimes proved to represent "only a preliminary labour" (Freud, 1937, p. 260).

By truth, Freud usually meant words whose meaning corresponded to a past objective reality whose traces were objectively recorded in his patients' minds. Freud (1923) did attempt to elaborate a theory about this verbally initiated reconstitutive process. After first asserting that things become preconscious before they become conscious, he presented the following brief dialogue: "How does a thing become preconscious?" And the answer was: "By coming into connection with the verbal images that correspond to it" (p. 20).

"Correspond" is a critical word in Freud's lexicon of truth. He steadfastly remained certain that the unconscious mind contained truth. Therefore, what "corresponded" to it was also the truth. The corollary was also held to be correct. That is, what failed to correspond was not true. In fact, what failed to correspond not only lacked the cutting edge of truth and its power to cure, it usually lacked, in Freud's estimation, the power even to affect his patients. Even late in his career, in the article in which he may have been at his most sophisticated about the necessity for truthful recollection in treatment Freud (1937), remained convinced that "no damage is done if, for once in a way, we make a mistake and offer the patient a wrong construction as the probable historical truth." He added: "What in fact occurs in such an event is rather that the patient remains as though he were untouched" (p. 261).

Despite his apparently ingrained commitment to the past of his patients, and very possibly because his commitment drove him to seek it beyond his patients' own reports of their recollection, Freud appears to have eventually been forced by his clinical experience to reappraise the role of accurate or complete recollection by his patients. In fact, Freud was to spend much of his career, and gain extremely fruitful results, exploring the infidelity of conscious memory. It is important to note that this gradual reevaluation of conscious awareness of the past does not at all appear to have reflected a diminished view of the power of the past per se. It represented only a reappreciation of conscious memory. Conscious memory increasingly became only the trailhead of a path to truth about the past, and not the truth itself. Rather than simply a search for a precise correspondence between an external objective experience (such as trauma) and its symptoms, Freud's task became to bring to bear on the symptoms a more evolved, distinctly psychoanalytic understanding. Essentially, Freud attempted to go even more deeply into the past of the mind than before. Still, the basic task remained: "Our first purpose, of course, was to understand the disorders of the human mind, because a remarkable experience had shown that here understanding and cure almost coincide, that a traversable road leads from one to the other" (Freud, 1933, p. 145).

Some of the concepts that Freud relied on and developed to traverse that difficult road are of major interest here. As the search for the historical "reminiscences" referred to in Breuer's and Freud's (1893–1895) appealing diagnosis of hysterics evolved into the pursuit of the often elusive "kernel of truth," Freud's notion of what coincided grew more complex and its hallmarks more inferential. Three concepts, in particular, deserve discussion here. Each appeared in some published form fairly early in his career and then grew in importance. They are: first, Freud's important, but misleadingly labeled, concept of "historical truth"; second, screen memories; and, third, the notion of *Nachtraglichkeit* or deferred memory, as it was somewhat misleadingly translated by Strachey (Laplanche and Pointalis, 1973). Each of these concepts refers to a mental representation of the past which shares an indirect and deceptive relation to past external reality. Each consequently focuses clinical attention on the elusive, but theoretically anticipated, past that it attempts to clarify, and diverts attention away from present reportable mental representations. By "historical truth" Freud (1937, pp. 261, 267–269; 1939, p. 129) meant something quite distinct and, in fact, almost directly opposite, from the way in which the term is currently used here and elsewhere (as for example, Spence, 1982). Rather than using the term to refer to the accurately rendered objective past, Freud used it to refer to the "kernel of truth" in distorted subjectivity; the element of causal symbolic connection between some actual past event stored in the unconscious and what is, currently and erroneously, consciously thought to be the past or present material truth (e.g. a child's early experience with the father as the basis of a later belief in a living God, or an early psychic trauma as the objective source of a later delusion). He used this understanding of the failure to discriminate between experience derived through an unconscious connection and that derived from current sense data as an explanation for mistaken assessment of reality and for what might currently be called "false memory" as well. This concept of historical truth also contains both genetic and phylogenetic implications that may apply to every case history. That is, within any memory that surfaces may lie a kernel of "historical truth" from the personal or from the racial past. The existence of this possibility adds major implications for the uncertainty of personal memory. For example:

> When we study the reactions to early traumas, we are quite often surprised to find that they are not strictly limited to what the subject himself has really experienced, but diverge from this in a way that fits much better with the model of a phylogenetic event and in general, can only be explained by such an influence. The behavior of neurotic children towards their parents in the Oedipus and castration complex abounds in such reactions, which seem unjustified in the individual case and only become intelligible phylogenetically—by their connection with the experience of earlier generations. It would be well worthwhile to place this material, which I am able to appeal to here, before the public in a collected form [Freud, 1939, p. 99].

Given the difficulty in collecting convincing data for such a hypothesis, one might be forgiven for doubting the persuasiveness of the data, which never appeared, on which he based these remarks.

A second concept, that of a screen memory, describes a form of memory that can be even more deceptive. A screen memory is an unusually sharp, and apparently trivial, recollection that has replaced a more traumatic memory through the mechanism of displacement.

Its distinctness is a result of the energy displaced to it through a compromise between the unconscious force exerted by the repressed memory of the actual traumatic event and the conscious ego that is willing to accept the milder substitute. As with all internally modified perceptions, there may also be an element of "historical truth" in screen memories. To the extent that they are screen memories, however, their meaning is most fruitfully sought not in their own repressed content, but in those memories whose place they have taken. Freud distinguished between positive and negative screen memories, as well as screen memories that replaced memories that predated, came after, or were contemporaneous with the memories they replaced (Freud, 1899; also 1901, pp. 43–51; Laplanche and Pontalis, 1973, pp. 410–411).

With this concept, Freud explicitly established a framework for potentially disqualifying the vividness of memory as a criterion for inferring the importance of the contents of a memory; in fact, it reversed that criterion. It appears to have shifted the evaluation of validity further away from the conscious experience of the patient and closer to the theoretical expertise of the analyst. While the concept of screen memory is not intrinsic, or formative, in Freud's view of personal history, it is indicative of a direction of development within that view. It is worth noting that, although screen memories may be a sophisticated tool in the search to comprehend the past, they are also potentially subject to unsophisticated use. The elevation of the possibility that a patient's keenly recalled memory, whose content does not seem important, can safely be disregarded would seem to present at least an inexperienced analyst with greater opportunities for error in appraising a patient's past.

Nachtraglichkeit was first mentioned by Freud in 1896: "I am working on the assumption that our psychic mechanism has come into being by a process of stratification: the material present in the form of memory traces being subjected from time to time to a rearrangement in accordance with fresh circumstances—to a retranscription" (quoted in Masson, 1985, p. 207). In the same paragraph, Freud continues by suggesting that such retranscription "must take place" between successive "epochs" of life, and he even explains what he calls "the peculiarities of the psycho-neurosis by supposing that the translation has not taken place in the case of some of the material. . . ." This latter, epistemologically potentially more positive, view of *Nachtraglichkeit* did not receive emphasis in Freud's later writings, but it remains a potential wild card in a psychoanalysis based on objective truth as a bridge to the past. The concept of retranscription did not attain full importance in Freud's writing until the publication of the case of the Rat man.[1] Here is how Freud (1909c) applied it in that report:

> If we do not wish to go astray in our judgement of their historical reality, we must above all bear in mind that people's "childhood memories" are only consolidated at a later period, usually at the age of puberty; and that this involves a complicated process of remodelling, analogous in every way to the process by which a nation constructs legends about its early history. It at once becomes evident that in his phantasies about his infancy the individual as he grows up *endeavors to efface* the recollection of his auto-erotic activities; and this he does by exalting their memory-traces to the level of object-love, just as a real historian will view the past in the light of the present. This explains why the phantasies abound in seductions and assaults, where the facts will have been confined to auto-erotic activities and the caresses or punishments that stimulated them. Furthermore, it becomes clear that in constructing phantasies about his childhood the individual *sexualizes his memories*; that is, he brings commonplace experiences into relation with his sexual activity, and extends his sexual interest to them—though in doing this he is probably following upon the traces of a really existing connection [pp. 206–207].

When such memories are recalled, they can be visualized as lying in layers, growing more reflective of their cumulative modifications, and less an imprint of their original source with each succeeding layer. While it does not technically contradict Freud's more usually quoted view of the original memory as a perfectly preserved virtual contact print of reality, this perspective allows for so many inaccurate copies, and locates them in such easily found locations, it possesses the potential almost to reverse Freud's more frequent treatment of memory as veridical. Even more explosive to Freud's commitment to memory corresponding to an objective past, it seems ineluctably to hoist the petard that recall and modification might be one process. It suggests that therefore conscious memory might never be historically correct and that even (or especially) Freud's painfully executed reconstructions might be (and probably were) retranscriptions in the interest of present needs.

Another, much less dramatic concept that also bears brief mention here is that of the family romance (Freud, 1909a). This concept,

---

[1] Though it is mentioned clearly at the end of Freud's (1899) initial article on screen memories: "Our childhood memories show us our earliest years not as they were but as they appeared at the later periods when the memories were aroused. In these periods of arousal, the childhood memories did not, as people are accustomed to say, *emerge*; they were *formed* at that time" (p. 322).

though similar in several aspects to the three noted earlier, has less significance here because, although it may be powerfully evocative, it functions within the boundaries of consciousness. A person, to whom this concept refers, may, for example, repetitively imagine that his "real" parents were blue-blooded royalty rather than the shopkeepers who raised him, but manages, if only reluctantly, to maintain his awareness that his fantasy is only that. Nevertheless, the fantasy does represent an attempt to repair and compensate for unconscious needs and undoubtedly has its own "kernel of truth" in the person's infantile idealization of his parents. The concept raises questions about which events induce processes leading to inaccurate memories and which only trigger fantasies. Clearly, with regard to the former, autoerotic fantasy in this perspective is often less admissible to consciousness than are erotic seductions or assaults (see earlier quote from Freud, 1909, pp. 207–208). But, with regard to the latter, one also wonders to what degree external (social) credibility is a factor in admission to consciousness—it is hard to persuade most friends that one is an actual prince—and what other worldly concerns the ego might take into account.

Freud clearly regarded only memories relegated to the unconscious as the immediate source of psychoneurotic symptoms, and thus the focus of his method. All the concepts discussed here can be said to locate in the unconscious such authentic counterparts to corresponding conscious manifestations of the past which are false. The use of these concepts (except family romance) makes the authenticity of conscious memories both less trustworthy and much more significant to psychoanalysis; and they do this without yielding psychoanalysis's view of the omnipresent role of the unconscious. Each represents a significant retreat from a reliance on the fidelity of personal memory; and, with the glaring exception of *Nachtraglichkeit*, they all achieve this retreat by extending and enlarging the faith of psychoanalysis in the power of the past.

Another observation is worth making. These three concepts (again, excluding family romance) all ultimately appear to put any obvious basis for direct internal verification just out of reach. The concept of a symbolic relation between unconscious memories and conscious memories involved in both "historical truth" and screen memories, as well as the additive modification involved in *Nachtraglichkeit*, all make the connection between truth and memory somewhat tenuous. Freud certainly advanced a number of inferential clinical techniques, including free association, as sources of verification. However, unless individuals can almost continuously and consciously discriminate between direct and symbolic relations with stored material, the probability that a given meaning might have only a symbolic, or even a partially symbolic, relation constitutes a significant uncertainty regarding the basic nature of our ability to know. Freud's primary response to this ambiguity seems to have been his continual attempt to make such connections conscious. His ultimate answer to such limitations within the psychoanalytic method itself was, of course, his version of the scientific method; the subjectivity of which he may have significantly underestimated.

A final major concept that requires discussion arises in the context of Freud's battle to make elusive, repressed early memories conscious; the issue involved is not theoretical, but technical. It is the concept of a construction. A construction is a conjecture, advanced by the analyst, about what has been forgotten by the patient so as to stimulate or, if necessary, replace the theoretically essential early memory that the patient is unable to recover. This concept refers to a practice that was clearly not new when Freud published a full discussion of it in 1937. Many of the earliest cases he presented in the service of the trauma theory—the view that all hysteria originated in actual abuse—can be seen as constructions without their being identified as such (Freud, 1896). With this concept, Freud concedes much about the road to the unconscious. In his discussion of his work with the "Wolf Man," Freud (1918) noted:

> All I mean to say is this: scenes, like this one in my present patient's case, which date from such an early period and exhibit such a content, and which further lay claim to such an extraordinary significance for the history of the case, are as a rule not reproduced as recollections, but have to be divined—constructed—gradually and laboriously from an aggregate of indications [p. 51].

Even when correctly "divined," constructions may not manage to bring complete success, "Quite often we do not succeed in bringing the patient to recollect what has been repressed" (Freud, 1937, p. 265). That is, Freud concedes that analysis may often fail ever to bring the patient into direct or conscious contact with the repressed memory of the past that is the very center of the psychoanalytic approach. The entire treatment often culminates in inferred accuracy. However, "if the analysis is carried out correctly, we produce in him an assured conviction of the truth of the construction which achieves the same therapeutic result as a recaptured memory" (pp. 265–266).

Overlooking the psychoanalytic question of how a construction can be therapeutically effective and not release the relevant memory, Freud here substitutes faith in his theory for any independent evidence (although he lists several clinically congruent indications that a construction is "correct"). He ultimately leans heavily on his commitment to the past; the actual repressed past is the cause of symptoms, and constructions that affect the symptoms must therefore correspond to the actual past even if memories do not.

Some of what we have said about Freud's concepts of "historical truth," screen memories, and *Nachtraglichkeit* can also be said of constructions. Constructions, of course, originate from the analyst's side of the analytic couple. They are, at least in Freud's view, fully conscious in origin and intentional. Like the concepts previously mentioned, however, they too finally rely on correspondence with an unconscious truth that may never be manifest and is consequently often not directly verifiable. Ultimately, they also share a faith, grounded in perceived clinical experience, that either change or maintenance of present symptoms can only reflect a connection to the past. Again, Freud's commitment to inferred history replaces, and parades as, a commitment to a past objective reality. One broad and centrally located avenue for further exploring this specific issue, as well as the overall role of memory in Freud's thought, is to chronicle changes he made in the course of his repeated use of the metaphor of archeology to describe his therapy.

The Archeological Metaphor

In evaluating Freud's use of this apparently overdetermined metaphor, it is perhaps relevant to know that archeology was very much in the public eye throughout Freud's life (Gamwell, 1989, p. 22). Newspapers published such exploits as the recovery of the ruins of Troy much as the media would later cover moon walks. Archaeologists were (like astronauts almost a century later) public heroes. This was particularly true of the archeologist Heinrich Schliemann, whose book Freud bought and very much enjoyed, as he related to Fliess in 1899 (Masson, 1985). Freud's own penchant for collecting antiquities (Gay, 1988, pp. 170–171, has called it an addiction) first appears in the historical record in 1896 when he reported to Fliess his "invigoration" at purchasing two plaster casts of Florentine statues (letter of Dec. 6, 1896, in Masson, 1985, p. 214).[2]

---

[2] Freud's word *erquickung* has been variously translated to convey various heightened positive states, see Gamwell, 1989, p. 25. Over his life he collected more than 2000 objects. He is reported to have fondled them, occasionally to have set them in front of his plate at dinner to contemplate (Spitz, 1989, p. 155) and otherwise to have cloistered all of them in his office where he spent his work days. He admitted to his own wishful misreading of signs over other kinds of stores as advertising "antiquities" (Freud, 1901, p. 110, added by Freud in 1907). The literature about the

Because of the role of antiquities as an analogue for memories in the overall archeological metaphor, it is worth noting that, according to his dealer, Freud would not tolerate fakes, although he was occasionally willing to accept well-made models admittedly constructed as copies (interview with Lustig, September 5, 1988, cited in Gamwell and Wells, 1989, p. 23). While his increased purchasing power later in his career made the purchase of copies increasingly unnecessary, however, his power to uncover memories apparently did not grow correspondingly.

Overall, the power of the archeological metaphor in the history of psychoanalysis is so great, one is tempted to reverse fields and seek an additional psychoanalytic metaphor from the unconscious to explain the archeological metaphor's widespread and enduring popularity. An obvious relational candidate is the lost sense of intrinsic preciousness that fortunate infants experience and may, as adults, later hunger to recover. In any case, the image of excavation of the precious lingers not only in the public mind, but also in the current psychoanalytic literature and in the reports of Freud's patients long after their analyses were over. The Wolf-man (1971) recalls Freud explaining to him that "the psychoanalyst, like the archeologist in his excavations, must uncover layer after layer of the patient's psyche before coming to the deepest, most valuable treasures" (p. 139).

The archeology metaphor also appears in Freud's correspondence in connection with his exuberant success with a patient—"It is as if Schliemann had once more excavated Troy" (letter of Dec. 21, 1899, Masson 1985, p. 391)—in his accounts of work with several other patients, and sprinkled through his theoretical writings. It may represent something akin to psychoanalysis's own family romance. More profoundly, as has been suggested (Spence, 1982), it may have helped shape the evolution of psychoanalysis.

One could arguably say that the archeological metaphor is most accurate when it is understood as a metaphor that served Freud to reconcile his scientific aspirations with his technique. As his focus became invisible to the outside observer, he needed a perspective

---

source of Freud's literal object relations includes, among other, more complex ideas, suggestions that his interest was due to: his maintenance of his relation to his father (Gamwell, 1989, pp. 25–26); his denial of his oedipal victory over his father (Spitz, 1989, p. 159); his denial or search for his Jewish roots (Gay, 1988, p. 172; Spitz, 1989, pp. 155–157; Bergmann, 1989, p. 174); his loneliness (Gamwell, 1989, p. 26); and, of course, his residual anality (Gay, 1988, p. 170). Whatever the psychodynamic source, his interest facilitated the selection and embellishment of an archeological metaphor to conceptualize, inspire, market, and perhaps even model his method of treatment.

that supported the application of a protracted scientific technique to a reality that could rarely be immediately validated. However as Freud's creation quickly grew more uniquely complex, the metaphor appears increasingly less apt to describe psychoanalysis. This increasingly incongruent complexity, which continues to the present, makes several questions about the continuing use of this metaphor seem unavoidable. Freud himself finally came to deal with several such issues in his 1937 article on constructions.

While earlier in his career his use of the metaphor could be seen to reflect his desire for psychoanalysis to bask in an established archeological limelight, in *Constructions in Analysis,* Freud (1937) seems to claim a superior role for a more complex and sophisticated psychoanalysis. After reasserting the basic similarities between the two disciplines, particularly that between "construction, or, if it is preferred, of reconstruction" and "an archeologist's excavation" he adds that "[t]he two processes are in fact identical, except that the analyst works under better conditions and has more material at his command" (p. 259).

He then goes on to list six other differences. They include the fact that the material is still alive, all the essentials are perfectly preserved, psychic material is more complicated, there is less information about what to expect, reconstruction is not done in sequence, and the reconstruction is "only a preliminary labour" (p. 260). In this way he maintains his commitment to the mind's faithful recording of an objective past, places constructions in the most favorable light, and takes top billing for psychoanalysis.

However, many questions about the use of this metaphor remain. Spence (1987) has sharply and comprehensively attacked this metaphor from his particular hermeneutic perspective. He emphasizes the problems inherent in Freud's failure to take into account the contribution of the observer to what is observed (p. 112), attacks the misleading metaphor of depth (p. 30), and puts forth his own view that "there are no clinical specimens which convincingly support the archeological metaphor" (pp. 78–79).

In the context of current disputes about the validity of patients' memories, two of the most problematic aspects of the archeological metaphor lie with the archeological role of the analyst as a validator of "finds." When the analyst is assigned the professional responsibility for assessing the actuality of the patient's reported personal experience, he or she, unlike an archeologist, never actually visits the site of the experience, geographic or psychic, and typically has no outside information. An archeologist can not only hold an object in his or her hand but may subject it to infinite outside tests. In contrast, once analysis began, Freud actively avoided seeking any potentially validating supplementary information from relevant family members:

[I]t may seem tempting to take the easy course of filling up gaps in the patient's memory by making inquiries from the older members of his family; but I cannot advise too strongly against such a technique. Any stories that may be told by relatives in reply to inquiries and requests are at the mercy of every critical misgiving that can come into play. One invariably regrets having made oneself dependent upon such information; at the same time confidence in the analysis is shaken and a court of appeal is set up over it. Whatever can be remembered at all will anyhow come to light in the further course of analysis [Freud, 1918, p. 197n].

Even in Freud's own terms, what is the basis for describing what he reported doing with his patients as somehow excavating the unconscious? Even with the most careful pursuit of associations, the intrinsic inaccessibility of the unconscious forever blocks the patient from consciously gaining actual entrance into his own unconscious. The legitimacy of the analyst's using the analytic process to represent a final authority in the evaluation of the accuracy of retrieved memory does not seem to go beyond drawing inferences from the patterns of behavior and descriptions provided by the person who merely has occasional access to material possibly from the unconscious. The point is not that such inferences are not formidable, or that some inference is not also present in archeology, but that psychoanalytic inferences do not parallel, or even approach, the relative certainty of the archeological dig. Perhaps it is more as if Freud had found a method analogous to sonar to locate and provide a rough outline of buried memories and then help the patient (or himself) make a facsimile that seemed sufficiently familiar and could be worked with as though it were the original. This metaphor, while less dramatic, arguably fits the technical data Freud has recorded about his cases. With the archeological metaphor Freud seems to have confused his faith in an accurately recorded objective past (psychic and external) with his critically limited ability to contact it.

There is one other major aspect of the metaphorical concept of the analyst as validator of psychic finds that may well be exercising an important negative influence in current disputes about recovered memories. It lies with the relative worth assigned in archeological research to "finds" that originated at the time their appearance and location would suggest, and those contrived to share that appearance, but actually made much later. The latter are called "fakes" and are scorned and eventually discarded. A person who creates such a fake is regarded similarly. Consider the patient who creates a "fake" memory of sexual abuse. A patient who accuses a family member of sexually violating him or her when no such behavior could possibly have actually occurred clearly demonstrates severe psychic damage, which clinically is in no way necessarily less deserving of care and respect than the more sympathetically received psychic damage of an incest survivor. The symptoms may be psychodynamically distinct, but the psychic damage is indisputably authentic in both instances. Without the archeological metaphor, the discrimination of "false" from "real" memories with psychoanalytic patients is more easily reduced to a knotty technical consideration. To be sure, this is clearly not the position of the courts (or much of the public), who, implicitly in tune with psychoanalysis's own archeological model, support clinicians willing to assume the mantle of authorities who can validate such finds.

It is important to mention that the archeological metaphor, while critically beleaguered and deprived of much of its former resonance, retains some applicability and possible value as an educational tool. Spence (1987) has suggested that the archeological model, with its idea of many layers, may have been the inspiration for Freud's topographic model (p. 13). A similar, but less clearly defined concept of layering pertains in relation to dreams, in reference to which Freud often spoke of layers of meaning. This valuable clinical concept allows interpretations of dreams and associations with logically incompatible meanings to be acceptable simultaneously because they originate at different "depths." *Nachtraglichkeit,* probably Freud's closest approach to a theoretical construct consonant with a narrative approach, also paradoxically serves the archeological model well. Layers, each distinctly preserving the subjective recollection existing at the time of its creation, can conceivably coexist with the deeper storage of the original images of historical reality. It is worth noting, however, that *Nachtraglichkeit* is unlike any current view of memory as narrative, in that it results in a distinct series of layers and not a continuous process, and the deepest layer remains forever potentially recoverable.

Overall, however, the archeological metaphor seems itself to endure mainly as a residue of the past of psychoanalysis. With regard to its current value, one is tempted to quote Freud's (1933) disarmingly blunt appraisal about another, less memorable, of his metaphorical comparisons: "analogies, it is true, decide nothing, but they can make one feel more at home" (p. 72). To appraise Freud's commitment to the past fully we need to look beyond his metaphors.

Freud as Theory Builder

Our attempt to understand Freud's position on historical truth through either his archeological metaphor or his theoretical concepts has intentionally been limited. It has been conducted almost solely from a psychoanalytic perspective and is based directly on his writings. In short, it shares much with a primarily hermeneutic inquiry. Methods based on more external views can and do see Freud and his view of history differently. For example, Freud can be viewed not as the archeologist he sometimes felt himself to be, but as primarily a builder of theory in a particular time and place. It is, for example, quite reasonable to expect that the actual construction, care, and marketing of his theory in the climate of fin de siècle Europe could conceivably have been a powerful influence in shaping Freud's general views as well as his view of memory and its relation to the past. In particular, both Freud's seduction theory and his subsequent change of course have probably been even more heavily debated in regard to Freud's ability to handle outside pressures than on their respective theoretical merits. Consequently, no appraisal of Freud's treatment of history should fail to include some consideration of the day-to-day social context in which Freud labored.

Jeffrey Masson's 1984 book *The Assault on Truth* has achieved prominence, not to say notoriety, among what Gay (1988) has referred to as the "avalanche" of secondary literature about Freud, of which "an astonishing share is malicious or down right absurd" (p. 741). While not absurd, Masson's opportunistic depiction of Freud's early trauma theory as congruent with current feminist positions and his depictions of Freud's historic change of course as a failure of courage do seem to rely heavily on Masson's personal attack on Freud's character for their appeal. While apparently impeccable in his research, Masson is less controlled in his journalistic conclusions. He repeatedly details very circumstantial evidence, admits that he has no proof, and then proceeds to use his conclusions to color other ambiguous evidence. For example, he extensively quotes August Tardieu (a professor of legal medicine in the 1860s) extensively both in English and in French, and accompanies his remarks with that gentleman's full-page picture, because Freud *may* have read Tardieu's accounts, "which catalogued in horrifying detail the brutal abuses suffered by children at the hands of their caretakers, often their own parents" (Masson, 1984, p. 15). These data are apparently reported to increase the reader's sense of Freud's culpability when Freud later changed his mind about the role of abuse in hysteria and obsessive-compulsive disorders. Yet Masson's apparent bias for the "seduction theory" and against Freud appears paradoxically to distort his interpretation of Freud's report of his original data in the same manner in which Freud apparently distorted it. As Israels and Schatzman (1993, p. 272) have pointed out, Freud's patients never came to him bearing the reports on which Masson says Freud was later to turn his back. These reports are clearly what Freud would later describe as constructions. Although he explicitly regarded the following behaviors as proof of the authenticity of his hypothesis, Freud (1896) says unequivocably:

> Before they come for analysis the patients know nothing about these scenes. They are indignant as a rule if we warn them that such scenes are going to emerge. Only the strongest compulsion of the treatment can induce them to embark on a reproduction of them. While they are recalling these infantile experiences to consciousness, they suffer under the most violent sensations, of which they are ashamed and which they try to conceal; and, even after they have gone through them once more in such a convincing manner, they still attempt to withhold belief from them, by emphasizing the fact that, unlike what happens in the case of other forgotten material, they have no feeling of remembering the scenes [quoted in Masson, 1984, pp. 264–265].

Clearly, if Freud is to be accused of later ignoring his patients' heartfelt reports, these are not the ones. In any case, Masson could hardly avoid knowing that it would not be theoretically significant for hysterical patients to bring Freud such reports already formulated because "[t]he scenes must be present as *unconscious memories*; only so long, and in so far as, they are they unconscious are they able to create and maintain hysterical symptoms" (Freud, 1895, in Masson, 1984, p. 272).

Whatever his success in casting doubt on Freud's integrity as a scientist, Masson does succeed in creating a picture of incredible intellectual foment at the turn of the century; when explanations of behavior that would be laughable today often captured and stimulated respectable minds. Without major surprises in otorhino-laryngology, it is unlikely that anyone will soon criticize Freud for deserting his best friend's "nasal reflex neurosis" (Masson, 1984, p. 74). Similarly his abandonment of the psychological dangers of masturbation has caused no stir (Masson, 1985, p. 41). That Freud publicly proclaimed one theory and later changed his mind says nothing definite either about his character or the correctness of any of his views.

In a different but related vein, Israels and Schatzman (1993) present compelling evidence that Freud misrepresented his success with his patients in the interest of promoting his own seduction theory: "in some eighteen cases of hysteria I have been able to discover this connection in every single symptom, and, where the circumstances allowed, to confirm it by therapeutic success" (Freud, 1896, in Masson, 1984, p. 260). Yet, if Freud was slow to disclaim his theory and his results publicly, he was not long coming to a different view privately. Within a year of his first publication he privately conceded to Fliess that, among his many reasons for discarding it were, "[t]he continual disappointment in my efforts to bring any analysis to a conclusion; the absence of the complete successes on which I had counted" (Masson, 1984, p. 108). Israels and Schatzman contend that the tangled web spun by Freud's initial deception about his therapeutic success resulted in Freud's needing thereafter to obfuscate the true reason for abandoning his seduction theory—it didn't work. This view (like those offered in various less measured attacks on Freud's character such as Esterson, 1993) raises direct questions about Freud's personal integrity (as well as the professional standards operating at that time), and indirectly about psycho-analysis as his creation. While it is obvious that no statute of limitations pertains to unearthing flaws in Freud's character, there must be some point in the development of a discipline when questions about its founder no longer bring the whole structure into doubt. The discovery of dishonesty in Darwin's reports would pose little threat to modern zoology. Certainly nowhere in the literature is the suggestion made that Freud's own mental health constitutes a fair test of his method or that the power of psychoanalytic technique, even as he described it, is in any way exemplified by self-analysis as he performed it.

Putting issues of Freud's character to one side, then, one may reconsider Freud's proposal and retraction of the seduction theory in terms of his commitment to both sexuality and history throughout his career. Without attempting to explore the deeply intertwined relationship of the two factors it is possible to suggest that, for Freud, sex and the past were aspects of the same history-shaping force. Initially, he began in both cases with the relatively immediate—that is, shame and anxiety about a relatively recent event such as a sexual assault (Freud, 1895). Throughout the development of his theory, however, he constantly extended and internalized the influence of both of these two inseparable factors. The past became phylogenetic, sex became all pleasure. Freud's commitment to these pillars never changed. He adjusted their placement; putting them deeper in the unconscious and farther back in time, but he never doubted his certainty about their importance. In this sense it might be possible to view Freud's early commitment to his seduction theory, as well as his moving on, as an almost inevitable step in his ever-widening search to ground psychology in these forces of history.

Final Comments

It is clear that Freud's commitment to a verifiable material present pales in importance next to his commitment to the past. It was his commitment to the past which allowed him to construe his observations of current clinical phenomena in such a way that he was able to construct psychoanalysis. By midcareer, he seems to have largely put his theoretical dependence on any external validation of material reality behind him. Psychic reality, repetitious behavior, and the content of dreams all became their own proof of the past. It is not within the focus of this discussion to debate whether with the adoption of such sources of verification Freud actually redefined or merely extended the connection of his work to external reality. It remains virtually impossible to deny, however, that Freud's overwhelming reliance on the past would not have been possible without an underlying assumption that an objective past existed. It is relatively simple to disregard pragmatically the precise form of this connection between behavior and history to support specific interpretations or constructions—as Freud was apparently increasingly willing to do. However, to disregard totally either the existence of the material past or a direct relation between human nature and a material past would make Freud's overall conception, particularly as exemplified in his structural model, inconceivable. The issues of whether human beings can individually and consciously grasp their personal relation with an objective past, or even whether this is a relevant task for psychoanalysis, are issues about which Freud himself raised increasingly serious questions. These are the subject of discussion in subsequent chapters.

Perhaps it is, as much as any other single factor, the perceived correctness of Freud's view of the past on a popular level that bears significant responsibility for Freud's emergence from his small, antique-lined office to an enduring place on the world stage. Much has been made of 17th century mankind's reluctance to accept Galileo's findings and move its conception of itself from the center of the celestial universe. A similar case has been made about Freud's ideas prompting a reluctant humanity to concede a loss of control of its own consciousness. There are significant differences, however. Mankind was afforded no subjective hint that its loss of status lay in the stars until Galileo's discoveries made it unavoidable. In contrast, human beings have always had moments when their own behavior seemed unreasonable or out of control. It seems possible that Freud's views (though upsetting to official doctrines of the time) might initially have even been soothing in some respects. They traded the darker images of a soul tormented by a devil, evil spirits, and raging gods for the relatively domestic image of an ego astride a spirited horse, a horse that incarnated spirits of lives past and personal history forgotten. And they relocated that mount, not in some antic predatory nether world in the far reaches of the universe, but in the more familiar backyard of each individual's own mental history. In a sense, they moved mankind back toward the center of its own universe.

In general, for Freud, the past always has the first and the last word. It appears in the cause and reappears in the effect. While this is implicit in every aspect of his work, it is rarely made verbally explicit and is never explicated adequately. Freud's archeological model may have reflected his early enthusiasm for exploring the past, but it clearly failed to reflect either the complexity of his techniques or the breadth of his commitment. Often, it seems that Freud's commitment to the past is synonymous with his commitment to causality itself, and that he will accept no explanations which do not rely on it. As mentioned in the preceding pages, when he does not find the needed explanation at first, his reaction is always to go deeper into the past. When Freud pauses, as he increasingly does in midcareer (Freud, 1913, 1927, 1930), to view the historical plight of mankind, it is as if the whole of humanity's past functions, for him, as its unconscious.

Overall, it is difficult to escape the conclusion that Freud's relation to history per se was the major force in shaping his theory. The monolithic immensity of Freud's unyielding commitment to history as he saw it makes it possible to see him as a kind of Sisyphus in reverse. He attempted the frustrating task of pushing human awareness further and further back down into contact with its unconscious past. The degree to which he succeeded in making that past more conscious to mankind as a whole, regardless of what the historical and personal limitations of his view of the specific contents of that past may prove to be, is an undeniable tribute to his greatness. As Freud (1939, referring to the power of certain ideas) summarized his position most succinctly: "in so far as it brings a return of the past, it must be called the truth"(p. 130). No commitment to history could be more complete.

Freud's legacies to our conception of memory and its psychoanalytic context are rich and varied. He pursued the objective past he first glimpsed in his own and his patients' dreams and parapraxes until he sometimes lost sight of it in the increasingly deeper forests of patients' memories, and he was finally forced to rely on only his theory to guide him in constructing the reality he had hoped to find. It might be said that within Freud's view such an external past reality, whether currently available in memory or only inferred, remained as intrinsic to the structure of both the conscious and the unconscious psyche as a hypotenuse is to the other sides of a triangle. It is ironic that his speculations about why the trail to that reality sometimes grew cold, manifest in such concepts as *Nachtraglichkeit*, or in what he called historical truth, may prove more enduring than his findings.

Even more ironic is that, in his search to ground psychoanalysis further and further back in the past, he, perhaps more than anyone else, seems to have increasingly undermined the faith that the present could be objectively perceived and the past accurately remembered. It is in the context of such undermined faith that the narrative views presented next may be seen as a logical extension of Freud's work.

3
Narrative Views
The Challenge of Donald Spence

$\mathcal{T}$he long and highly evolved narrative tradition is virtually as old and as broad as that of communication itself. Whenever it first transpired that one piece of information modified the meaning of another, narrative can be said to have begun. Polkinghorne (1988) has elaborated a modern definition of narrative as:

> a scheme by means of which human beings give meaning to their experience of temporality and personal actions. Narrative meaning functions to give form to the understanding of a purpose to life and to join everyday actions and events into episodic units. It provides a framework for understanding the past events of one's life and for planning future actions. It is the primary scheme by means of which human existence is rendered meaningful [p. 11].

In portraying that tradition, Polkinghorne includes Descartes' idea of images in the brain like "inner ghostly snapshots" (p. 24), Wittgenstein's belief that a socially derived language could not provide a neutral means by which reality "as it is in itself" (p. 26) could be described, and Wilhelm Dilthey's attempts to comprehend historical accounts by empathy (as well as his attempts to differentiate social from objective knowledge, p. 39). It is beyond the scope of this work to do more than offer a brief homage to these early thinkers with their mention here. It is important to note, however, if only in passing, that many of their ideas, first struggled with at an earlier time in history without the benefit of the insights of modern social science in general and psychoanalysis in particular, have obvious resonance in the current debates in psychoanalysis explored here.

When psychoanalysis first entered the narrative tradition is a subject of some controversy. It has been argued that Freud's work overall, despite his own "scientific self-misunderstanding" (Habermas, 1972, p. 214) to the contrary, was basically a hermeneutic process founded on narrative. Specifically, such a "hermeneutic application is concerned with *completing* the narrative background of a general interpretation by creating a narrative, that is a narrative presentation of an individual history" (pp. 265–266). This is not the position explicitly taken by Freud or the overwhelming majority of his followers, and it is not the perspective offered here. It *is* held here, however, that, despite Freud's constant and explicit commitment to a real past as the foundation of psychoanalysis, his own complex and changing views of the authenticity of autobiographical memory manage to contain explicit antecedents for almost every current narrative perspective on that topic in psychoanalysis. Additionally, Freud was certainly more than aware of the narrative dimension in his patients' reports (most of Freud's work on transference can be seen in this light). Also, and most important here, he was aware of it in connection with his later interpretations (see Freud,1918, pp. 238–239; 1937). Finally, as many have argued (sometimes with defamatory intent), he was undoubtedly aware of that dimension when he reported on his cases to the scientific community of his day (for a distinctly positive elaboration of Freud's skill with narrative, see Mahoney, 1987, 1989; Spence, 1982, particularly p. 32).[1]

Nevertheless, nothing in Freud's writing or his behavior anticipated what has proven to be the immense impact on psychoanalytic

---

[1] Perhaps nothing illustrates Freud's commitment to his own narrative (in both positive and negative regards) more concretely than the following editor's note from the National Institute of Mental Health's (1935) *Abstracts of the Standard Edition of Freud*: "It was Freud's practice throughout his life, after one of his works had appeared in print, to destroy all the material on which the publication was based. It is accordingly true that extremely few of the original manuscripts of his works have survived, still less the preliminary notes and records from which they were derived" (p. 68).

thinking of the advocacy of a narrative approach as the primary orientation toward psychoanalytic material. This advocacy is exemplified in varying degrees and ways in the work of the four men whose work is described in this and the next chapters. The work of Donald Spence, Roy Schafer, Robert Stolorow, and Irwin Z. Hoffman, along with the work of a growing number of others, threatens to shake loose much of the soil from psychoanalysis's roots in both biological and personal history, and to reground those roots more deeply in the personal meaning of that history in the present, particularly as it is reflected in the meanings exchanged in the psychoanalytic hour itself. In so doing, these writers threaten to change the very meaning of both truth and memory in psychoanalysis and perhaps, ultimately, in our society at large. They also may prove to be among the founding fathers of what might be termed a genuinely post-Freudian psychoanalysis, post-Freudian not in the sense of simply abandoning Freud's perspective, but in the sense of being actually based more on developments within psychoanalysis since Freud's death than on its roots in Freud's original contributions. They are not chosen for discussion here either because we contend that they are the only persons working in this currently very active arena, or even that they consistently maintain leadership in theoretical innovation there. Considered in their selection are the facts that they have published a sufficient body of clearly expressed, significant, pertinent, and original work to allow extensive exam- ination of their ideas and that these ideas have been and often have remained correspondingly influential, even seminal, within psychoanalysis over an extended period of time. Most of all, they have been selected because of their relevance for this discussion. Their well-articulated ideas remain basic and indispensable to the questions we wish to raise about truth and memory within psychoanalysis.

Context of the Discussion

The decision made here to place the relevant work of these innovative men specifically in the narrative tradition is itself, when viewed from within that tradition, a decision to construct a narrative. As is almost always the case when a narrative is constructed, many other plausible narratives are simultaneously possible. Generally speaking, the origins of the thought of the writers to be discussed might be as illuminatingly traced to a variety of roots within philosophy. Less generally, those origins might be traced to the relativist camp of the almost infinitely faceted and long-standing philosophical debate between objectivists and relativists (see Bernstein, 1983). Specifically, in this regard the trail can be, and has been, read as leading backward to the work of the philosophers classified as hermeneutic, such as Habermas (1972), Ricouer (1970), and especially Gadamer (1960), and before them Heidegger (1927) and Wittgenstein (1953).[2] While some reviewers may tend to use the work of one or another of these philosophers to measure the validity of one or another psycho-analyst's thought by a particular philosophic standard, that is not our goal here. Here the present implications of various ideas for psychoanalysis are the major focus—and not the philosophical sources of those ideas or even their current relative standing in philosophy.

As with the possibility of a narrative rooted in philosophy, it is worth noting that, despite the ostensible break with the methodology of the natural sciences that some of the work of Spence, Schafer, Stolorow, and Hoffman is often held to represent, the work considered here could also legitimately be seen as a result of the impact of the methodology of post-Newtonian physics on the social sciences.[3] Even more particularly, it could be seen as part of the intellectual fall out from Heisenberg's uncertainty principle or Stephen Hawking's (1988) more recent conjectures about the irreversible loss of the history of the universe into black holes (see also Folger, 1993). The Heisenberg principle is of particular interest because, although it is usually described as a statement that the momentum and the position of an atomic particle cannot be determined with a single observation (see Weinberg, 1994, p. 74), it can be plausibly stated that, at this most basic and physical level, the act of observing changes what is observed. Such a restatement implies that ongoing observation of an independent reality is (increasingly) impossible. Hence, we are confronted with a funda-mental indeterminacy of the world. It is relatively easy to establish a plausible narrative connecting the impact of such a perspective on

---

[2] See Grayling (1988) for more detailed discussion of these philosophers' potentially relevant contributions; also see DiCenso (1990). See Spezzano (1994) for a discussion of Spence's hermeneutic standing or Spiro (1976) for a comprehensive philosophic evaluation of Schafer's proposal for a new psychoanalytic language.

[3] Schafer (1980) has noted how Freud's view of the mind as "mental apparatus" is based on Newtonian physics "as transmitted through the physiological and neuroanatomical laboratories of the nineteenth century" (p. 32). Kohut (1984) made a similar point in more detail (pp. 36–42) and concluded that "[t]he relationship between traditional analysis and analytic self psychology may be seen to parallel the relationship between the physics of Newton . . . and the physics of Plank" (p. 41).

the work considered here (see Schwartz, 1995, particularly pp. 46–48, for a contrasting view). How could psychoanalysis, or any evolving social discipline with a history as a stepchild of the natural sciences, ignore the ripples from this potentially radical perspective emerging from the most traditional of our natural sciences? Nevertheless, although the role of such possible roots may or may not be critical in the development of the ideas discussed in these pages, no attempt is made here either to authenticate that role or to elaborate further narrative about it. The possible existence of such antecedents to the questions we raise here will receive further consideration here solely in proportion to their ability to clarify and advance our discussion.

It is also worth noting that ultimately the sheer impact of these writers may make it more accurate to describe them in terms of their part of what may eventually prove to be the beginning of a true paradigm shift within psychoanalysis, in the sense communicated so well by Thomas Kuhn (1962). Their work has already contributed to the growth of a distinct framework within psychoanalysis. More grandly, but still very plausibly, the work considered here might be seen by some as one small manifestation of the Western culture-wide sweep of a postmodernism whose deconstructionist attack on all certainty is difficult to deny as the intellectual *Zeitgeist* of our age (Spence, 1993, p. 3; Schafer, 1994, p. 257).

Most important within the constraints of the present work, we view the writings to be considered here, and the extensive additional body of work they have stimulated in turn, as a response to a deep and ongoing need to clarify the theoretical ground of psychoanalysis. Obviously, those who locate psychoanalysis's roots in narrative may see and welcome this clarification as the only change the writings discussed here represent. However, it is less important whether this change is a long-awaited clarification of an existing body of thought or the result of new burgeoning from seeds previously only scattered incidentally at the periphery. What is truly important is that the change may, in fact, eventually propel psychoanalysis into a much different space than the one dreamt of in Freud's philosophy. We consider this possibility in our final chapter.

Some of the present need for clarification may legitimately be traced to Freud's attempted emulation of other sciences. For entangled with Freud's attempt to fit psychoanalysis under the umbrella of the natural sciences was a tendency—and more than a tendency—to confuse kinds of truth and also the kinds of validation needed to establish those truths. It is hoped that this section will help elaborate some of the reasons why, for psychoanalysis, the classically pursued objectivity about subjectivity as the basis for an empirical truth has proved so elusive.[4]

While our focus on the work to be considered here must be relatively narrow, the work itself must be recognized as touching on issues both enduring and vast. Even simply raising the issue of the nature of truth within the discipline of psychoanalysis is inseparable from calling into question virtually all the broader assumptions that form its metapsychological ground (see Rapaport and Gill, 1959). The concept of truth intrinsically carries within it key notions about the nature of relationships people can and do have with the world, including with other people, as well as the nature of both humanity and reality in general. The concept of truth may be taken to imply, for example, that people can actually know themselves, each other, and the world, as well as determine when additional information is required to achieve that knowledge. Such ubiquitous and yet elusive notions, in metapsychological form or otherwise, must continually be faced within psychoanalysis. They are part of both its context and its essence.

Organization of the Discussion

Each writer's work will be approached in the same way. We will examine the writing of each of them from the perspective of his potential to contribute to the answers of just three very basic general questions and two much more specific questions concerning the psychoanalytic session. Such examination, because of the nature of the problem at hand, must touch on metaphysical issues (D. B. Stern, 1991, p. 56). All the questions are to be understood as being asked in the context of an interest in the basis of communication within the psychoanalytic hour.

The first question through which we will seek each writer's perspective is the most unabashedly metaphysical: what is the nature of reality? The second question is, what is the nature of the human

---

[4] Even with most scientists' continuing profession of complete confidence in empirical rigor for exploring physical reality, the distinctive relation between the concept of subjectivity and the concept of truth is simply not a problem that even physicists can continue to fail to note. The 20th century's most prominent physicist succinctly commented, "It is difficult even to attach a precise meaning to the term 'scientific truth.' Thus the meaning of the word 'truth' varies according to whether we deal with a fact of experience, a mathematical proposition, or a scientific theory" (Einstein, 1954, p. 261).

experience of reality? The third, what is the nature of human communication of the experience of reality? Implied in the third question is the question of what is the nature of human reception of human communication of the experience of reality?

In addition to the first three questions, there are two more specific questions whose answers should be consistent with the answers to the first three. One, what kind of knowledge can reasonably be acquired on the basis of information about the past acquired in a psychoanalytic session; and two, what kind of action can reasonably be taken on the basis of such knowledge acquired in the psychoanalytic session? These latter questions are asked with both psychoanalytic participants, the patient and the analyst, in mind.

Unfortunately, because these simply expressed questions are often not raised directly by the authors themselves, the answers distilled here are often considerably less simple than the questions. The complexity of the answers is also at least partly due to the capacity of these questions to illuminate key contradictory and inconsistent positions that are not otherwise readily apparent. In the following chapters, different answers to these same questions are considered.

The discussions presented here are not intended to constitute a basic introduction, nor can they serve as more general expositions of the thinking of these four authors. Every effort has been made to keep the presentation as accessible as possible and to quote extensively from each author's own work. However, this presentation inevitably emphasizes and interprets aspects of each author's work relevant to the particular questions about the nature of reality in psychoanalysis raised here. Consequently, some general familiarity on the part of the reader with these authors' overall contributions is assumed, and readers who are totally unfamiliar with the work in question are asked to consult the original texts.

The chapter concludes with a discussion of the work of Donald Spence. Comparable discussions of the work of Roy Schafer, Robert Stolorow, and Irwin Z. Hoffman will comprise chapters 4, 5, and 6. In chapter 7, following the completion of the exploration of each writer's work individually, there is a brief summary and discussion of some aspects of their work taken together. We conclude this first section with Donald Spence because, arguably, it is Spence who has returned the issue of reality to the psychoanalytic table in recent times, or, as it might be said, reopened the "Pandora's box of ambiguity," which, as he notes, Freud first opened (Spence, 1982, p. 288). We begin with the first of the five questions with which we have chosen to organize the discussion.

Donald Spence

1. What is the nature of reality as seen from the perspective of Donald Spence?

Our analysis of Spence's perspective centers on his landmark book, *Narrative Truth and Historical Truth* (1982). Though further reflections on and elaborations of the views expressed in this influential and often-referenced text appear throughout his writings, it is with this book that Spence opened the debate. In it he thoroughly and squarely addresses the questions we wish to consider here. As the title of his book suggests, reality for Donald Spence is of two main types, and it is the question of their respective roles and importance within psychoanalysis that Spence raises so forcefully. First for him is traditional external and material reality, which he contrasts with the psychic reality of the narrative. This external reality is the reality about which historical truth is told. This is the reality that Freud once held that the infant's nascent ego first learns to distinguish by its responsiveness, or lack of responsiveness, to motor action. Likewise, it is the reality that Freud felt he recognized when it appeared in more complex forms in his patients' recollections. This external reality exists as either a physical object or a series of events, which are, at least theoretically, available for perception to any observers who are present.[5]

In his book, Spence does not question either the existence or the basic underlying primacy of this material reality. He does not question the objective external basis of historical truth about material reality (or of present external reality), and he similarly does not concern himself with its possible boundaries except as a perceptual matter. In the main, things for Spence are materially real or not; however our ability to perceive them is, unfortunately, often much more ambiguous than we realize. His efforts are designed to sound the alarm about this problem and to begin to seek a remedy. He calls our attention to the necessity of using time and place as landmarks in evaluating historical truth. Historical truth must, at least potentially, be fitted by more demanding standards than those which fit

---

[5] It is "external" in that it usually exists outside of the mind of the observer or observers. However, since the internal organs of the brain of either the observer or another person so unfortunate as to have them revealed for visual inspection also undoubtedly constitute external reality, what we are referring to is not really a spatial differentiation (see Schafer, 1972, for a complementary perspective on an analogous process—internalization) but obviously involves a totally different realm.

narrative into its coherent story. Spence states that historical truth is, in fact,

> time bound and is dedicated to the strict observance of correspondence rules; our aim is to come as close as possible to what "really" happened. Historical truth is not satisfied with coherence for its own sake; we must have some assurance that the pieces being fitted into the puzzle also belong to a certain time and place and that this belonging can be corroborated in some systematic manner [p. 32].

Spence admittedly does not strike a strong chord when he suggests the use of time and place in psychoanalysis as significant means of distinction between kinds of truth. Time and place are very seldom corroborated systematically in psychoanalysis. Within most analytic hours, the analyst is usually persuaded of authenticity, if he is concerned with it at all, by very general contextual clues. Where Spence makes his most compelling arguments, and his greatest impact, is with his severe questioning of the ability of either analyst or patient to perceive historical reality, recall it, and, finally, communicate it. He places such questioning squarely within the psychoanalytic tradition when he comments that

> [i]t was one of Freud's signal achievements to make clear the illusory quality of memory and to show how the mechanisms of displacement and condensation apply to memory as much as they apply to dreams. Although the memory has the feeling of being closer to the real experience, it was Freud's genius to show how this sense is often illusory and how memory and dream belong to the same group of wish-determined phenomena [p. 59].

Spence also notes later in his book that "Freud opened for us his Pandora's box of ambiguity, but he was somewhat optimistic about the extent to which the treatment method would discover the 'true' meaning of any piece of behavior" (p. 288). It could reasonably be added that what Spence has done is add the illusory qualities of perception and communication to memory and dreams. That said, he may still be too optimistic about recovering "true" meaning. This is so even though he bravely raises the question of whether the reality underlying psychoanalysis can ever be retrieved. If we use the metaphor of Humpty Dumpty to illustrate the almost constant precariousness of the classical psychoanalyst's mediating position between psychic and historical truth, we can say that Spence may have given it the fatal nudge. Despite admirable concepts like "naturalizing" transcripts by providing essential contextual data and "unpacking" texts by including the internal processes of the writer,

Spence has, by his own hand, established that these wishful tasks are infinite and can never even approach completion. Historical truth, even that of the psychoanalyst's own session (see p. 132), cannot be put back together again. In a follow-up statement Spence (1987) is willing to state this a little more firmly than in his earlier work: "To search for historical truth is to live out the metaphor of analyst as archeologist" (p. 78). He then goes on to quote Max Black about the possibility of every science moving from metaphor to (the specificity of) algebra and concludes: "It is one of the main themes of this book that no signs of this algebra exist" (p. 78). On the other hand, in the same book, Spence says that theory cannot be built "on narrative truth alone" (p. 167) and at one point seeks to explain to the reader how "true understanding" of the patient or text can be achieved (p. 49).[6] [Spence is least compelling when he attempts to set standards to bring psychoanalysis into maximum alignment with the historical truth whose elusiveness he portrays so much more effectively.] One problem in looking for such "true understanding" may be that Spence's search for paths to objective historical truth ultimately demands an objectively discriminating perceiver who can identify them. He also seems to assume that the identification of narrative truth requires less discernment than does historical truth. It is clear that in each instance there are theoretically many more narrative truths available for explanation in what Spence calls "the vast, uncharted region of approximate matches" (p. 153) than the single historical truth held to be preferable. However, there does not seem to be any compelling evidence that separating the almost suitable narrative truths from those which can be seamlessly inserted requires less objectivity. It is that very objectivity which receives Spence's most telling blows. Yet both terms, historical truth and narrative truth, intrinsically presuppose discernible reality that requires just such objectivity on which to base their objective categorization.

Ultimately Spence must raise the pragmatic question of whether psychoanalysis's preoccupation with external reality, particularly past reality, may not prevent it from fully appreciating what may be more truly the currency of the psychoanalytic realm: the truth patients and analysts create, accept, and remember—narrative truth. Consequently, this is the kind of truth Spence (1982) increasingly finds himself focusing on:

---

[6] Bruner (1993, p. 11), who wrote the foreword to Spence's 1982 book, has since good naturedly noted that "Don Spence . . . gets homesick for the old positivism he has left behind even before it disappears over the horizon" (p. 11). As we shall see, Spence is not alone in this nostalgia.

> Narrative truth can be defined as the criterion we use to decide when a certain experience has been captured to our satisfaction; it depends on continuity and closure and the extent to which the fit of the pieces takes on an aesthetic finality. Narrative truth is what we have in mind when we say that such and such is a good story, that a given explanation carries conviction, that one solution to a mystery must be true. Once a given construction has acquired narrative truth, it becomes just as real as any other kind of truth; this new reality becomes part of the psychoanalytic cure [p. 31].

Unfortunately, Spence never quite convinces us (or, it seems, himself) that such psychic reality is just as real. He obviously does not mean that psychoanalysis no longer need concern itself with the difference between narrative and historical truth. He means that such a narrative is only "just as" real within the mind of the person who believes it. The realm of such reality, when it does not overlap external reality, or even the narrative reality of anyone else, is relatively small. Although he also uses narrative in the larger, socially overlapping sense of all stories or explanations, the brunt of Spence's book seems to revolve around the smaller, personal use that could be construed as error from the perspective of historic truth. It is this kind of pragmatic narrative, as opposed to historic truth, for which Spence finds that psychoanalysis typically needs to settle. He believes that psychoanalysis needs to face the degree to which it is settling, and to make a virtue of that necessity when possible. Yet he continues to urge an unending battle to regain as much of a material basis for psychoanalytic work and communication as possible and to "separate the singer from the song" (Spence, 1993, p. 7). He asks, perhaps wistfully, "In the light of all that has been said, can we ever return to the original 'text' of reality?" (Spence, 1982, p. 54). His answer to this key question is, "Probably not. But we can identify some of the conditions that make possible a reasonable reconstruction" (p. 54).

This allegiance to the search for even an approximately verifiable material reality over any simply narrative reality demonstrates Spence's roots in the history of the psychoanalysis that preceded him. It equally well, as we shall see, distinguishes him from some psychoanalytic writers who have followed him. In his 1982 work, he also tends to deal with narrative reality as primarily an individual construction, and not a mutual or truly social construction. This individual approach changes modestly in his later writing. In 1987 he goes so far as to argue for a social construction of psychoanalytic theory modeled on the process used in the judicial creation of case law, but with regard to the patient–analyst relation he demonstrates an individually based perspective when he states that "meaning is supplied by the listener" (p. 67). In seeking the limitations of Spence's enormous contribution to current discourse, it is important to note that he makes virtually no explicit attempt to ground the appeal of one narrative over another in any conception of psychic reality at an unconscious level. The primary understanding he advances of the effectiveness of any narrative remains at the level of evaluating its capacity to enhance cognitive understanding.

2. What is the nature of the human experience of reality from the perspective of Donald Spence?

With the raising of this question we are, of course, immediately dealing with the experiential basis for both of Spence's types of reality. It is precisely the similar subjective basis of validation, along with the fact that both are largely only verbally represented in the analytic hour, that makes narrative truth and historical truth identical for psychoanalysts in important respects. It is the difference in the two experiences, however, for which Spence initially searches hardest. Spence attempts to distinguish narrative truth as exclusively based in verbal behavior, whereas historical truth is grounded in more concrete, external reality. This distinction serves to differentiate narrative truth theoretically from historical truth, but in psycho- analytic practice that difference is typically not in evidence. Spence acknowledges that a constant struggle over meaning takes place within each analytic hour. Spence sees that that struggle can sometimes be resolved by differentiating the experience of the analyst and that of the patient. By this differentiation he means that interaction between the analyst's psychoanalytic theory and (what can be seen as) the patient's transference (or the analyst's counter- transference for both) influenced perspective can be viewed as a conflict between competing verbal narratives to define the nature of the experience of relation between the patient and the analyst. Essentially, Spence treats both kinds of truth as verbal in the psychoanalytic session; both become fully integrated into the per- spective of the perceiver, and neither one is, practically speaking, verifiable. Both become psychic reality and, as Freud (1917) noted, "In the world of neurosis it is psychical reality which is the decisive kind" (p. 368, quoted by Spence, 1982, pp. 176–177).

That he sees narrative as founded at the level of language leads to an interesting contradiction in Spence's weighing in of his two truths because Spence raises strong doubts that the actual experience of historical truth can be conveyed in language. He quotes Viderman (1979): "The archaic experiences have no structure, no figurable shape. Only interpretative speech can shape them" (quoted in Spence, 1982, p. 173). As Spence sees it, this means that: "[i]n making a formal interpretation, we exchange one kind of truth—historical truth—for the truth of being coherent and sayable—narrative truth" (p. 173). It is hard to avoid the conclusion, in the context of this more extreme formulation, that narrative truth is the *only* kind that ever makes it into speech.

Similarly, Spence sees clearly that all experiences require a mental context. He quotes Arendt: "No experience yields any meaning or even coherence without undergoing the operations of imagery and thinking. Seen from the perspective of thinking, life in its sheer thereness is meaningless" (p. 162). This is tantamount to saying that there is no such thing as reality (in the same sense in which Winnicott, 1971, so famously noted, in reference to the reciprocal creation of each other's roles by mother and child, "There is no such thing as an infant"). There is always a context supplied by the perceiver which gives material reality its significance. Thus, even the faithfully recorded experiences of reality that Spence believes lie waiting "to be expressed" (p. 41) in the unconscious require context at least twice: once when they are recorded and again when they are recalled. What is the total impact of these intrinsic mental supplements on our experience? Typically, Spence sees additional context as supplying undesirable additional narrative for which he can never completely correct. Spence seeks to minimize these functions that distort, while at the same time sharpening, the functions that organize and give meaning to our perception. This clearly seems contradictory if, as Spence's quote of Arendt seems to suggest, it is the same human functions that do both. Also, if all experience is intrinsically even partially narrative, then perhaps it would be most appropriate, even from a materialist perspective, to speak of a narrative spectrum rather than a dichotomy between kinds of truth of the sort Spence puts forth.

Despite the fact that Spence has put considerable effort toward elaborating various ways to help differentiate between the experience of narrative truth and that of historical truth, most of those ways require a high degree of objectivity and vigilance, and none approach being definitive. Many are, at best, signs for the consumer to beware. For example, Spence notes that regardless of its validity, "if the same explanation can be used more than once, it acquires added credibility" (p. 141). He also notes that, if one explanation, no matter how unlikely, can account for many things, it has great narrative appeal: "Notice that generality tends to compensate for improbability. . . . even if it [the import of the generality] seems preposterous or improbable" (pp. 144–145). These, and others, are important considerations, but they are clearly secondary cognitive evaluative considerations and not a direct part of experience of reality.

The fact is that in Spence's two-truth framework the same idea or image can, at least hypothetically, pass with amazing rapidity from "unwitting interpretation" (that is, an interpretation made without conscious awareness) to interpretation consciously offered to the patient as narrative, to acceptance by the patient as narrative truth, and, finally, even to possible outside verification as historical truth. Therefore, differentiation could sometimes be purely a matter of timing. Until a piece of information is also definitively located in its time and place in the context of the analytic process, its truth status cannot be known. Therefore, the act of locating can itself become a potentially major determinant of status of the idea or image. Viewing truth status as a process even suggests the operation of a kind of psychoanalytic uncertainty principle. Once the location of an idea or image in the process is observed by either party—for example, seen by the analyst as an unwitting interpretation—the process is changed and that information is less likely to be offered as an interpretation for the patient's consideration.

Two different ways of categorizing the experiences of narrative that Spence explores are aesthetic and pragmatic. For example, referring to aesthetic experiences, he speaks of the truth of a painting as separate from its truth as a representation of the "real world" (p. 274; see Gadamer, 1960, for more extensive consideration of this possibility) and attempts to equate aesthetic experience with clinical impact (p. 168). Similarly, and more important, he sees a valid place in psychoanalysis for interpretations made for pragmatic effect rather than their "inherent (historical) truth or falseness" (p. 275). For Spence, these are instances where "the analyst commits himself to a belief in his formulation, but not necessarily to a belief in its referent" (p. 273). This means that the experience of the truth of a statement might intentionally be very different for analyst and for patient. Here Spence raises an ethical issue he does not adequately address. He provides ample pragmatic justification for the use of narrative. Also he cites Freud's use of constructions and makes (possibly unfortunate) apparent similarly motivated reference to use of narrative by politicians in campaigns (p. 271). The question remains, however, can an analyst ethically construct a reality for his patient which the analyst privately knows is not the truth?

It should be noted that this issue exists so harshly only when the narrating analyst himself remains grounded in historical truth. When truth is held to be always subjective, then it seems more reasonable to u narrative as a psychoanalytic tool. Any concept of dishonesty exi only in relation to a particular concept of truth. It may be the pat nt's concepts, not the analyst's, however, that are ultimately de rminative here in terms of ethical outcome, and more needs to be aid about this issue than is appropriate here.

Overall, as a practical matter in psychoanalysis, it is often virtually ir possible to separate the experience of narrative truth from that of h torical truth. The organization of information and experience that e her kind of truth offers as reality depends on the acceptance of t at truth. Theoretically, narratives sometimes have a waiting (or aluation) period before they become accepted as truth. Since storical truth is theoretically always historical truth, any period of valuation prior to acceptance as historical truth is seen not as etermining its truth status, but only as a delay in recognition. Even or the clinically discerning and hypothetically objective observer, however, the two waiting periods typically cannot be distinguished. Therefore, although for Spence, as for Freud, historical truth lies in each psychoanalytic patient's mind—"a set of experiences waiting to be expressed" (p. 41)—this reality too must await ratification whenever it is said to appear.

The problem and the strength of narrative is that it enters awareness already at the level of verbal expression, and its acceptance immediately ends the period when it can be experienced as distinct from a report based on an objective and historical reality. This view of the experience of reality is for Spence what a more limited version of it became for Freud (1937) in his late consideration of "constructions"—simultaneously the basis of a frankly narrative based technique and an ongoing search to minimize its domain. Despite his specific advocacy of narrative technique, Spence remains grounded in his preference for the experience of the historical reality to whose sparse availability he is trying to adjust.

3. What is the nature of human communication
    of the experience of reality?

When we ask, What is the nature of human communication of the experience of reality? we come to what may be Spence's most radical contribution. Noting Ricoeur's statement that psychoanalysis concerns itself exclusively with what is "capable of being said" (Spence, 1982, p. 65), Spence goes on to make some of the limits of that exclusivity painfully clear. He again quotes Viderman (1979): "The archaic experiences have no structure, no figurable shape. Only interpretative speech can shape them . . ." (quoted in Spence, 1982, p. 173). Spence deduces from this that actual experience is often lost when represented in speech. He notes that "[l]anguage is both too rich and too poor to represent experience" (p. 49) and, more dramatically, that "to put a picture into words is to run the risk of never seeing it again . . ." (p. 62). Such is the predicament faced by patient and analyst alike in formulating thought: "He must continually translate from the private language of experience into the common language of speech" (p. 82).

At times Spence sees language as a poor vessel indeed. Its very widely applicable structure makes it particularly suited for individual misrepresentation. He believes that a drawing is more easily described than a photo, and a screen memory is more easily described than an actual memory. Essentially, in Spence's view communication typically equals the destruction and remodeling, to fit speech, of the historical truth psychoanalysis claims to seek. Spence does not pause to consider the potentially troubling overall view of a social fabric woven of the misrepresentation that such tenuous communication implies. As he does elsewhere, he occasionally holds out slight rays of almost incongruous hope. For example, he characterizes the work of skillful authors of fiction in terms of "gifted" representation. Similarly, he notes, without pursuing the methodological questions entailed, that a good interpretation "can often result in a clearer sense of the original experience, much as a good critic helps us see the painting in more detail" (p. 62).

Unfortunately, the chances of the analyst's hearing the patient's expressions as the patient expressed them are probably no greater than those of the patient's expressing himself in "gifted" verbal representations of his actual preverbal (or nonverbal) experience. The analyst's conscious biases and his "unwitting interpretations," which are held to be particularly dangerous because they occur outside awareness, are both constantly operative. In addition Spence sees a failure to provide helpful information about context to the analyst built into the prescribed free association process,[7] and he sees the analyst's evenly hovering attention as similarly designed to avoid supplying such information. Altogether, these factors seem to make a meeting of the minds in a psychoanalytic session an appointment very likely to be missed.

---

[7] Spence also sees "no reason to assume that associations—no matter how free— will necessarily lead us back to the original image"(p. 79).

4. What information about the past can reasonably be derived
   from a psychoanalytic session as represented by Spence?

The only possible response to this question may be that there seems
precious little which we can be certain is "historical reality" and no
way to identify those times when we can be certain. Essentially the
analyst is on his own in evaluating a patient's reports. Moreover, he
definitely cannot rely on his own sense of the matter. Spence (1987)
has cautioned, "The more we feel that we truly understand the text
or patient and the more it becomes part of our world view, the more
likely it will happen that significant misunderstanding is taking
place" (p. 49). Certainly the analyst's own narrative of the psychoanalysis, buoyed by an unknown mix of narrative truth and historical
truth that informs both the patient's reports and the analyst's
perception of the patient's reports, must float uncertainly on these
shifting seas. Overall, it is probably a wise patient who does not ask
too much about the basis for his analyst's interpretations.[8] What
remains in the wreckage, if Spence's critique of the possibility of
knowing in the psychoanalytic hour is taken seriously, are only the
analyst's and the patient's respective memories, impressionistic notes
about the process, and discouragingly dim prospects of either one's
reconstructing the whole process in a helpful way on the basis of his
own or the other's reports.

   Although his more recent efforts do not continue to bear as directly
on our topic here, it is important to note that Spence has no intention
of giving up this fight. In a yet more recent book, Spence (1994) shifts
some of the onus for the mass of uncertainty he has unearthed in
psychoanalysis to the shoulders of Freud himself. Spence finds
Freud's graceful rhetoric too often to have been a hollow triumph of
style over substance. Similarly, Freud's authoritarian tone when
making references to data that never appear, and his presentation of
his clinical work in what Spence sees as the Aristotelian tradition of
the single case illumined by the gifted researcher, are seen by Spence
as totally incongruent with Freud's claims to membership in the
scientific community even of his own day and blatantly to belie his
supposed adherence to the scientific method.

---

[8] In this light, one could almost say that interpretations emerge from this
framework as the analyst's transitional objects. They emerge in the analyst's mind as
both real and not real, and they eventually either are transformed into more socially
based experience or are relinquished.

Looking at the current situation in psychoanalysis, Spence (1994) finds that Freud's legacy of placing the authority of theory before data still prevails:

> The result is a barren literature filled with theoretical clichés, anecdotal observations, and bad science masquerading as explanation. Homage to the status quo degrades the standard of reasoning and the quality of argument. We have abandoned such inductive principles as the importance of reasoning from a large sample and the need for cross-validation of any hypothesis, no matter how attractive, and have fallen back on the fascination with the single specimen that corrupted science before the Baconian revolution [p. 158].

While Spence's strictures can only increase awareness about the use of self-serving, highly selective data, and the unsupported conclusions offered in many case presentations, it seems unlikely that blaming Freud and making efforts to be more rigorous in the application of scientific method to psychoanalysis will solve the underlying problem that Spence himself has helped uncover: that is, the continual flow of subjective interpretation that continues to comprise every aspect of the psychoanalytic hour. From Donald Spence's perspective, this problem may prove something of a postmodern Augean stable. No matter how many manifestations of that continual flow are removed, it is simply not one that any new broom, no matter how vigilantly wielded, will be able to sweep clean. Had Freud somehow successfully opted for the slow, carefully crafted series of experiments necessary to begin psychoanalysis on an empirical foundation, psychoanalysis would be very different today. Even if that could be imagined to have occurred, however, it would not, could not—and, I believe, should not—have saved psychoanalysis, particularly psychoanalysis, from the rising awareness of both uncertainty and the role of subjectivity that seems increasingly to mark our age.

5. What action can reasonably be taken on the basis of information gathered in the psychoanalytic hour?

It would be hard to find a solid basis for any action outside an analytic hour such as Spence describes. If one actually takes Spence's (1982) critique to heart, even the educational possibilities of sharing "naturalized" texts of a session in consultation seems more credibly based on the desire for a shared interaction about a session than an attempt actually to share a session. Possibilities for generating appropriate suggestions from others on the basis of such a derivative report seem at least equally chancy. Generally, there seems little on which to base a feeling that one is qualified to take any specific action outside the psychoanalytic hour on the basis of what is thought to occur within it. Probably the most reasonable type of actions are actually those corrective actions to which Spence devotes much of this and his later books. Those include actions that aid the analyst in continuing to explore his own reactions in the interest of minimizing "unwitting interpretation" as well as Spence's more recent efforts to reduce the excessive ambiguity now traditional in psychoanalytic methodology. In his pioneering framework, bounded by two truths, it is ironic that it seems to be so much easier for Spence credibly to identify unsought narratives in advance than to differentiate either category of reality once it is accepted. Minimally, it can be concluded that any narrative justifying legal action based solely on an image or thought occurring within a psychoanalytic session understood in this way would, and should, probably be suspect far beyond a reasonable doubt.

Overall, Spence seems to have dropped a kind of depth charge into psychoanalysis from which neither he nor psychoanalysis has been able to recover. By succeeding so well in casting doubt on the ability of analysts and patients to perform the basic tasks that connect truth and cure, Spence has raised doubts that neither he nor anyone else has been able to completely quell. His attempts to begin to propose a way of conducting psychoanalysis within the shadow of those doubts have for the most part only unearthed more uncertainty. Narrative truth cannot plug the hole in the dike for Spence any more than constructions could permanently replace Freud's inability to unearth the memories his theory required. Although narrative truth may provide a vital opening toward a new direction for psychoanalysis, the positivistic ground on which Freudian metapsychology was built has begun to fall away, and Spence has called it to our attention. Analysts (and patients) who take Spence's work seriously cannot ever again definitively establish an underlying truth or positively identify it if they do. To a decidedly uncomfortable degree, the objective domain of psychoanalysis is reluctantly reinstated as narrative. For psychoanalysis to accept this uncertainty as the norm, it must temper its claims as a traditional science and modify its foundations. Spence, of course, cannot either be faulted or receive credit for this problem. He presents his efforts as an attempt to repair the traditional structure. It seems increasingly likely, however, that it is for his irrefutable identification of the problem and his highly influential pointing in the direction of narrative for the solution for which he will be remembered.

Roy Schafer's Versions

$\mathcal{R}$oy Schafer has made significant contributions to the field of psychoanalysis for more than 35 years. Here we are mainly concerned with his more recent work pertaining to hermeneutics, narrative, and the nature of knowing. Once again, we will attempt to find answers to our five basic questions.

1. What is the nature of reality as seen from the perspective of Roy Schafer?

Early in the introduction to *Retelling a Life,* Schafer (1992) distinguishes his view of narrative from that of Spence. "It is especially important to emphasize that narrative is not an alternative to truth or reality; rather, it is the mode in which, inevitably, truth and reality are presented" (pp. xiv–xv). He then proceeds to outline succinctly his answer to our first question about his view of reality or, rather, in his case, the absence of any certain view about it: "We have only versions of the true and the real. Narratively unmediated, definitive access to truth and reality cannot be demonstrated. In this respect, therefore, there can be no absolute foundation on which any observer or thinker stands; each must choose his or her narrative or version" (p. xv).

That is a statement to which we will refer again. Schafer concludes the same paragraph by introducing both the subject of context as a differentiated aspect of narrative and the critical role he assigns language, both critical topics about which Schafer will have much more to say: "Further, each narrative presupposes or establishes a context, and the sentences of any one account attain full significance only within their context and through more or less systematic or consistent use of the language appropriate to the purpose" (p. xv).

This relatively dense, yet characteristically precise, sentence manages to convey Schafer's idea that both the experience of the "full significance" of a "version" of reality (the focus of our eventual second question) and the communication of it (the subject of our third question) are simultaneous creations through language. In fact the role of language in psychoanalysis is a major focus, and perhaps even the major focus, of Schafer's almost panoramic spectrum of contributions to psychoanalytic thought throughout his career.

The foregoing quotations may serve as an introduction for our discussions of certain parts of Schafer's thought. There are important additional questions and comments, however, that should be added. For example, with regard to Schafer's view of the nature of reality, things grow somewhat more complex when he speaks of narratives as versions without specifying what he thinks they are versions of. Even if we accept that there is something out there which must remain forever moot, however, we must pause when we encounter Schafer's special treatment of psychic reality as a version. Schafer neither uses nor defines psychic reality as all that which is experienced as real by the analysand. Despite the occasional use of vague qualifying terms that suggest, but never specify, other, perhaps broader possibilities, Schafer uses the term generally to refer only to those narratives of an analysand's own experience that do not correspond to the analyst's version of consensual or psychoanalytic reality (e.g., Schafer, 1992, p. 206). More specifically, Schafer uses the term to refer to a child's narrative, maintained unconsciously within the adult, which it is the analyst's primary job to replace with one derived from Freud. Psychic reality is, for Schafer, a kind of misguided and immature version. It is what exists only before the analyst's version allows the former child's narrative to be "modified" so that it may better serve the adult. Schafer in this way effectively maintains the Freudian distinction between material reality and psychic reality. In other words, he focuses on what needs to be corrected and manifests no apparent interest in the overall integrity, or value, of the analysand's narrative as a totality. Also, despite his ostensible humility regarding the lack of an absolute foundation for his views, in Schafer's narrative perspective the analyst wields no less authority than he did as a supposedly more objectively grounded classical analyst. Consequently, from Schafer's somewhat parochial narrative perspective, it is still the analysand's world that is to be modified under the analyst's direction.

> [T]he point is that the psychoanalyst constructs this world through those aspects of interpretation that implement the Freudian strategy of defining significance, interrelatedness and context. By means of this strategy one also makes of psychic reality something more than, and something different from, what it has been. Among other things, one establishes for the analysand a perspective on it as primarily a child's atemporal, wishful and frightened construction of reality and as such a construction that is in principle modifiable. To accept this modifiability is itself a new action and one of the most important a person can ever perform [Schafer, 1989, p. 21].

Schafer (1989) has succinctly defined his limits by stating that "the analyst can only be empathizing with the analysand as he or she exists in this [i.e. the analyst's] constructed model" (p. 39). Further, he states, "I am saying that the psychoanalyst interprets, not raw experience, but [his own] interpretations" (p. 27). Despite his having said these things, it is somewhat puzzling that Schafer appears to proceed with his newly constructed foundation for psychoanalysis without any of the caution or humility one might anticipate of an analyst who views himself as one person without any absolute foundation viewing another whose plight is similarly precarious. Nor does he merely offer to help, or share, in an alternate "construction of, a personal past" (p. 16), which "is not *the* personal past, but *a* personal past" (p. 16) in the hope that it will be more helpful. Schafer simply proceeds to identify those portions of the analysand's subjective experience of life and the world that are based on narratives identified as misconstructed in childhood and thereby initiates a process that will change them. Essentially, the subjective reality with which the analyst is in accord is not defined as psychic reality. Basically, one narrative is used to invalidate another. Thus the author of a highly articulate constructivist viewpoint, which concedes an inability to know any reality directly or definitively,[1]

---

[1] Schafer (1994) pragmatically acknowledges that although the analyst enters "as best one can into what gets defined jointly as the patient's psychic reality. . . . we must allow that we cannot directly grasp or unambiguously define the patient's psychic reality" (p. 282).

often does not seem to allow his impeccable constructivism to concretely impact his technical considerations.[2] Schafer writes as though the psychoanalytic narrative allows him to transcend his own lack of an objective foundation and definitively distinguish one "version" of his analysand's subjectivity from another.

Schafer makes similar claims for the analyst's ability to keep track of the influence of his or her own unconscious. Hoffman (1991) virtually reads Schafer out of the psychoanalytic constructivist community for Schafer's reference to "continuous scrutiny of the countertransference" (quoted in Hoffman, p. 81) as a technique for purification of the analyst's personal influence. Hoffman adds, "The very fact that Schafer seems to believe that 'continuous scrutiny' is possible, not to mention what he implies such scrutiny can accomplish, gives his view of the process the stamp of positivism rather than constructivism" (p. 81). In the same volume to which Hoffman refers, Schafer (1983) acknowledges the wide range of serious emotional problems that even analytically competent analysts may manifest in their personal lives (p. 37), but he maintains that "[r]emaining within the fairly strict limits required by neutrality, they will tend to work honestly, bravely, patiently, and nonjudgementally" (pp. 47–48). These are virtues prevalent in the psychoanalytic narratives of an earlier historical period. What can being nonjudgmental mean to a person whose views are admittedly only a version? While certainly still possessing a degree of validity in a traditional context, such constructs, like that of analytic neutrality, can no longer, be considered adequately revealing tools for evaluating countertransference in a narrative context.

Another problem with Schafer's (1989) view of reality also has roots in his version of psychic reality as determined through language. On one hand, his view of narrative designates language as both creator and mediator of meaning. On the other hand, his view of psychic reality as derived from childhood implies the possibility of a key role for what might be described as preverbal narrative.

> The material itself is organized around personal versions of the major and typical sexual and aggressive conflicts of early childhood. The idea of conflict implies the infantile danger situations, such as loss of

---

[2] For examples of such technical discussions see Schafer (1990, p. 209), where he writes under the heading "Working Outside of Psychic Reality," or Schafer (1980, p. 38), where he identifies such nonverbal behavior by a patient as bodily rigidity or lateness as constituting narratives for the "competent" analyst.

loved persons and loss of their love, and the anxieties and defences that are features of these situations. And the idea of danger situations is conceived subjectively; that is, it refers to the child's view of itself and its world, to what it experiences emotionally and unconsciously. Further, one understands the child to be defining this experience largely in the terms of primitive bodily awareness and conceptualization—one might say in terms of infantile categories of understanding. The child's categories are based on organs (e.g. mouth, anus, genitalia), substances (e.g. faeces, urine, milk, blood), movements (e.g. kissing, clinging, hitting) [p. 7].

That quotation borders on the puzzling because once we conceptualize the infant as having primitive bodily awareness, Schafer's perspective forces us to abandon his perspective on the role of language for some experience (perhaps as in Ogden's, 1988, autistic-contiguous mode). Consequently the basis of the child's initial narrative interpretation becomes a little murky. How does primitive (preverbal) conceptualizing of narrative work? It seems to involve a storage and sequencing of sensations on which to base something like a nonverbal interpretation. There may be an important difference between body-based knowing and verbally based knowing (although, if so, they obviously are present simultaneously at times). This distinction may be critically important as an indication of the nature of narrative and the role of language, as well as the nature of knowing itself.[3] Schafer (1989) himself does not express specific concern with this issue. He does, however, raise the related and equally important question of how the analyst knows such categories exist:

To return to whether the fateful bodily categorical principles are found or applied, one must answer that they are both: The facts are what it

---

[3] An adult analogue of this distinction between different mixes of these two kinds of narrative may possibly be exemplified in a personal account received from an acquaintance who reports the existence of two kinds of lines that people stand in in contemporary Russia. One is for money changing and involves long hours of grim, silent strangers standing in closely packed lines that wind around the block. Everyone in such a line supplements the narrative they share about the meaning of the line by maintaining a constantly vigilant appraisal of their position based on clear physical data. The other kind of line is exemplified by the neighborhood line to receive milk delivery. This line involves only one person at a time. Each person arriving at the line replaces the sole person standing there until he or she is, in turn, replaced by a new arrival. Each person is required to remember only the person whom he or she replaces. When the milk delivery arrives, the line, which had existed purely as a shared verbal narrative until that moment, assembles in perfect order and its actual composition and length is concretely revealed to everyone for the first time.

is psychoanalytically meaningful and useful to designate, and what is meaningful to designate is established by facts; one looks for idiosyncratic versions of what has been found and one finds the sort of thing one is looking for. Plenty of room is left for unexpected findings and new puzzles. Like the historian, the analyst works within this interpretative or hermeneutic circle [p. 20].

So facts are what one finds when one is looking for them. As we change what we look for, we change what we find. When we find something unexpected (it is not clear where the basis for finding something "unexpected" originates), we change what we are looking for until our narrative accommodates it. This perception is summed up even more succinctly by Schafer (1994): "[q]uestions and evidence are regarded as correlatives rather than, as Freud and most analysts have assumed, independent variables" (p. 263).

In relation to the conception of categories of primitive experience referred to earlier, Schafer (1987) states:

[e]ven to render an action in an extremely terse description may be viewed as the expression of a choice that is in accord with an implicit narrative design. Nevertheless, in each instance of minimal description we are left with the question "What are we to see it as and why?" It is the regulative and generative influences of the description that are minimal. We are left with many degrees of freedom even if not, under the prevailing conditions, with total freedom. There are constraints, even though it is characteristic of psychoanalytic interpretation and some kinds of interpretation in the humanities to show that the constraints are far fewer than the conventional narrator would feel comfortable with (e.g., some kissing may be retold as an attack that is close to hitting and some hitting may be retold as a sadistic form of loving that is close to kissing) [p. 331].

The result of this line of reasoning is not, for Schafer, that the classical categories of psychoanalysis are now subject to new questioning. Rather, they now appear ensconced in new validity as narrative.

As distinguished from Spence, who questions psychoanalytic knowing as a preliminary to a somewhat desperate search for new ground, Schafer seems to repeatedly to use his new "hermeneutic" context to provide a new rationale for established practices in psychoanalysis that may be proving increasingly indefensible on positivist grounds. He states:

In contending that psychoanalytic questions, facts, evidence, and conclusions are effectively inseparable, I am taking a constructivist and hermeneutic position. I believe that position is the one that most aptly characterizes the day-to-day work of the psychoanalyst.

Technology has no place in this conception [Schafer, 1994, pp. 263–264].

Thus he disowns the embattled metapsychological context of psychoanalysis while largely endorsing the present practices that sprung from it. What he seems to propose is that psychoanalysis be accepted as valid under new rules and even that psychoanalysis really was a product of this different epistemology all along (although, to say the least, the concept of an entire discourse's contributing to the development of a master narrative such as psychoanalysis, and proceeding along lines largely alien to the language used by the participants, raises additional questions about the role of language in narrative). This idea of an unrecognized basis in narrative has, of course, distinguished philosophic credentials (for example, see Habermas, 1972, pp. 214–273).[4]

Some aspects of the statement by Schafer (1992) quoted earlier may now be explored. "We have only versions of the true and the real. Narratively unmediated, definitive access to truth and reality cannot be demonstrated. In this respect, therefore, there can be no absolute foundation on which any observer or thinker stands; each must choose his or her narrative or version" (p. xv).

This statement appears to mean that, since there is no absolute reality, where we thought material reality was narrative has always been. Where truth was now stands a choice. The validity of that choice is reassuringly described as heavily circumscribed by factors requiring "careful consideration." Referring to the psychoanalytic narrative emphasizing "repetitive recreation of infantile, family centered situations bearing on sex, agression, and other such matters" (p. 50) as a second reality distinct from a "positivistic telling" (p. 49), Schafer (1980) notes that "Validity, it seems can only be achieved within a system that is viewed as such and that appears, after careful consideration, to have the virtues of coherence, consistency, comprehensiveness, and common sense. This is the system that establishes the second reality in psychoanalysis" (pp. 50–51).

What is the nature of this "careful consideration"? If we concentrate harder, do we have some significantly greater contact with some underlying reality? Can we then bring some measure of objectivity to this second reality and thereby really know coherence, consistency, comprehensiveness, and common sense and apply them with confidence? Apparently not, because "[i]n our discipline, as in

---

[4] Schafer (1983), in relation to a related point, pays credit to Habermas: "My discussion owes much to Habermas's penetrating analysis of the linguistic and narrative aspects of psychoanalytic interpretation" (p. 234).

the historical, there are no *absolute* grounds for deciding what is real or who is right or who is morally "good"; each well-developed school is sufficiently self-enclosed and self-validating to fend off the criticism of others to its own satisfaction" (Schafer, 1994, p. 258). The bottom line of this line of argument is that reality is whatever we believe it is. Consequently, for purposes of psychoanalysis, psychoanalytic interpretation is reality. Not the only reality, but the one intrinsic to psychoanalysis. This is equally true for each separate school of psychoanalysis.[5] Thus Schafer does provide a clear view of his working conception of reality. Reality is psychoanalysis as he narrates it. Perhaps one of the lesser innovations Schafer (1980) introduces to the actual practice of psychoanalysis is his technique for introducing analysands to this reality.

> One may say that *psychoanalytic interpretation tells about a second reality.*
> . . . Only superficially does the analytic construction of this second
> reality seem to be crudely reductive; it is crudely reductive only when
> it is performed presumptuously or stupidly, as when the analyst says,
> "This is what you are *really* doing." The competent analyst says, in
> effect, "Let me show you over the course of the analysis another reality,
> commonsensical elements of which are already, though incoherently
> and eclectically, included in what you now call reality. We shall be
> looking at you and others in your life, past and present, in a special
> light, and we shall come to understand our analytic project and our
> relationship in this light, too. This second reality is as real as any other.
> In many ways it is more coherent and inclusive and more open to
> your activity than the reality you now vouch for and try to make do
> with. On this basis, it also makes the possibility of change clearer and
> more or less realizable, and so it may open for you a way out of your
> present difficulties" [p. 50].

Once he has cast this special light on the analysand, the psychoanalytic narrative can proceed. However, considering the extreme comprehensiveness of the change potentially undergone by the analysand,[6] and the fact that there is no way for the analysand to

---

[5] Schafer (1997) has recently manifested interest in the Kleinian narrative. In his introduction to a collection of writings, *The Contemporary Kleinians of London,* he describes the collection as written as though "inviting their readers to enter into provisional imaginative apprenticeship in the Kleinian version of psychic reality" and says "its exploration in depth cannot fail to be rewarding" (p. xiv).

[6] Schafer (1989) notes: "[T]hree interrelated theses concerning the nature of the clinical psychoanalytic enterprise: (1) that it constructs a personal past of a certain kind; (2) that it constructs a present subjective world of a certain kind; (3) that both of these constructions require a relatively systematic transformation of the terms in

anticipate the extent of that change, one wonders about pursuing it not on the basis of any truth claims at all, but largely because "it may open for you a way out of your present difficulties." This rationale tends to put psychoanalytic intervention on approximately the same metapsychological ground as mood-altering pharmaceuticals, that is, pure pragmatism.

Schafer's conception of truth occupies a position close to, but distinct from, Spence's narrative truth. For Spence, narrative truth is psychically based narrative that is substituted for an account based on material reality. For Schafer, narrative truth is also a psychically based narrative, but, perhaps more nihilistically, it is the only kind of truth we can know. And, for Schafer, this truth about the nature of truth entails a clarification of the previously misunderstood nature of psychoanalysis more than it suggests or necessitates a basic change of its course.

2. What is the nature of the human experience of reality?

When we shift from a consideration of Schafer's view of reality to his view of the experience of reality, we must note once again that for Schafer there is no significant difference between our verbally mediated knowledge of reality and our experience of it. They are the same, at least for the adult. Both, consciously or unconsciously, are apparent to us only through language. With *A New Language for Psychoanalysis*, Schafer (1976a) attempts both to modify the core metapsychological assumptions on which the practice of psychoanalysis has been traditionally based and to make the language of psychoanalysis a much more effective tool for doing what he contends it has always done. As he describes his new language: "it includes everything that psychoanalytic propositions have included from the beginning" (p. 10).[7] Schafer continues:

---

which the analysand defines and understands his or her history up to and including the present moment" (p. 16).

[7] A fuller discussion of the changes Schafer proposes is not relevant here. However, the fundamental rule Schafer (1976) offers is: "We shall regard each psychological process, event, experience, or behavior as some kind of activity, henceforth to be called action, and shall designate each action by an active verb stating its nature and by an adverb (or adverbial locution), when applicable, stating the mode of this action" (p. 9). With this change Schafer hopes to return a sense of agency and responsibility to the analysand and away from the various hypothetical mental structures whose actions classical psychoanalysis has often been occupied with identifying. The worthiness of this goal is not being disputed here (for that, see Stolorow and Atwood, 1992, p. 15), only the mechanism of achieving it.

Rather the difference lies in this, that in certain respects we shall speak about people more plainly, and, while continuing to emphasize action in the unconscious mode, we shall neither engage in speculation about what is ultimately unutterable in any form nor build elaborate theories on the basis of unfalsifiable propositions concerning mental activity at the very beginning of infancy [p. 10].

To put aside the question of whether the unconscious mode is actually utterable or falsifiable, as well as the categories of infantile experience Schafer later presents (Schafer, 1989, p. 7, quoted earlier), it is clear that in 1976 Schafer was seeking to discard the outdated and purify what he saw as the existing essence of psychoanalysis.

It may strike the reader as strange to consider Schafer's proposal for a new psychoanalytic language in connection with the question of his view of the experience of reality rather than with the question addressed in the next section concerning how that experience is communicated. The choice reflects what is perhaps most essential about Schafer's proposal. Schafer, in keeping with his view of the role of language as implementer of reality, ultimately and centrally seeks a psychoanalysis that will be able to influence, and even to control, not just communication, but actual experience. He argues that analysands will experience themselves, their world, and, most of all, their own behavior in a way psychoanalysis considers more helpful with the language changes he proposes (Schafer, 1989, p. 16). What seems most striking here is the reliance on sheer language modification to produce the kinds of pervasive and meaningful personal effects for whose production psychoanalysis has traditionally relied on alterations in the content of the unconscious. One can imagine that slightly more effective bridges between the conscious and the unconscious might be built with the issue of agency less cluttered by the psychoanalytic rhetoric of unconscious conflict. However, it is difficult to imagine the new language as radically changing an analysand's preexisting (and probably historically overdetermined) views of himself or his world. It is equally difficult to imagine large numbers of psychoanalysts intellectually imposing on their work a whole new language that did not evolve over time with their participation.

Because Schafer's views seem so intellectually derived, perhaps the key to understanding them lies in comparing two separate intellectual commitments he maintains as a practicing psychoanalyst. One commitment is to an understanding of psychoanalysis as one of many possible narratives, which, like all narratives, is only a version of reality and has no absolute foundation in the external world. This commitment seems to open the door to the merits of many narratives,

including those with which a given patient might be already conducting his life. The other commitment is to a specific and systematic
psychoanalytic narrative, which, if it is to be effective, he must pursue
with as close to an absolute allegiance as possible. This commitment
often appears to close that door. For Schafer (1976a), the latter
commitment to a particular psychoanalysis intrinsically includes the
precise language in which that narrative appears:

> It is only by means of sets of language rules that we are ever able to
> achieve a systematic approach to knowing anything. By adopting these
> rules, we establish what shall count as facts, factual coherence, and
> ascriptive limits; thereby we also establish the criteria of consistency
> and relevance in our psychological discussions [p. 4].

Even though Schafer has consistently made clear that his chosen
narrative is his only link to reality, the degree of closed and
unshakable commitment with which he proclaims his adherence to
classical psychoanalytic constructs is striking. Consider these further
comments on codifying the language of psychoanalysis:

> And we shall have to develop and apply this codification tirelessly
> and unflinchingly; for, if we do not obey the rules, we shall not really
> know or speak the language, and in the end we shall not have a single,
> coherent world to be psychoanalytic about. In the long run, it is one's
> fidelity to the rules that makes all the difference in systematic thinking.
> Here, one cannot be too faithful or fastidious [p. 6].

It is this fidelity, which cannot be too faithful or fastidious, that may
deserve consideration as an essential part of our context for understanding his conduct of psychoanalysis. It is only in the light of this
fidelity that the marked limitations of his particular use of the
hermeneutic circle can be understood. This concept of a circle is the
part of Schafer's (1989) psychoanalytic narrative that frames his
handling and shaping of all the material presented by the analysand:
"The life history, far from being linear or directional, is circular, for
psychoanalytic interpretation is circular. . . . It has no beginning and
no end" (p. 20). More specifically,

> [o]ne may say that the analyst uses the general past to constitute the
> individualized present that is to be explained while using that present
> as a basis for inquiry into the individualized past. Thus, while moving
> back and forth through time, the analyst bases interpretations on both
> present communication and a general knowledge of possible and
> probable pasts that have yet to be established and detailed in the
> specific case [pp. 19–20].

The tenacious fidelity of his commitment to his version of the psychoanalytic narrative that forms the ground of his work specifically limits the nature of any meaning discovered in this apparently open and constantly flexible process to that already specified within the preexisting binding narrative and therefore seems virtually to preempt the discovery of any new meaning. This commitment appears to operate as a substitute for and dedicated guardian against the full play of complex narratives otherwise characteristic of analysts and other humans. The search for coherence is revealed to be essentially a movement toward adherence.[8] Therefore, we must conclude that, for Schafer, the experience of reality is always the experience of a particular narrative, and, for Schafer qua psychoanalyst, the psychoanalytic narrative is not just a valuable means of grappling with the meaning of experience. Rather, reality is limited to the contents of psychoanalytic theory:

> [p]sychoanalysis consists of the construction of a present subjective world of a certain kind. Again, not *the* present world but *a* present world. Like the past, the psychoanalytic present is not more than one of a number of possible constructions. To be systematic, it must be realized through the persistent application of one set of categories. By this is meant the Freudian present achieved through the Freudian categories [p. 20].

The ability to apply that limited number of categories to all past and present experience is, for Schafer, the contribution of the psycho-analyst. He is typically the sole dispenser of his version of reality and the final authority over its meaning. When that contribution is effective, the analysand is similarly, and perhaps permanently, confined: "Under the influence of the psychoanalytic perspective, the analysand not only begins to live in another world, but learns how to go on constructing it" (p. 28). It would be more than unfair to portray Schafer's version of psychoanalysis, with its "multiple and transformable meanings" (p. 29) and active participation by the analysand, as a mere implanting of narrative or cloning of meaning. Nevertheless, the essential meaning of all facets of the analysand's life is forever changed, and that change, to the degree the analysis is deemed successful, occurs within the limits of the Freudian categories.

---

[8] Donnel Stern (1991) makes a similar observation about Schafer's "theoretical commitments, not personal prejudices developed in the interaction, as the primary imposition of order on the analytic material" and concludes that "Schafer misses the most important psychoanalytic application of hermeneutics" (p. 77).

3. What is the nature of the communication of the experience of reality as presented in the writing of Roy Schafer?

Only a few comments can be added here that have not already been suggested in response to the previous questions. The term communication, as it is commonly used in our culture, implies information transmitted from a sender to a receiver. In a system where "[t]he person, the reality, the analytic situation all are correlatives, and all are constantly in flux" (Schafer, 1989, p. 29), and even "[q]uestions and evidence are regarded as correlatives rather than, as Freud and most analysts have assumed, independent variables" (Schafer, 1994, p. 263), it is apparently a constant process proceeding in all directions. In such a process, the dispersal of information at all levels is less linear, like a telegraph, and more like the intermixing of a stew. In such a flux, Schafer's decision to cling faithfully to the Freudian narrative and to communicate that fidelity to his analysands is certainly understandable. However, the implementation of that decision is, by definition, also impossible; nothing, in such a system, is exempt from constant change, and no grip, no matter how practiced or how faithful, can maintain unchanged either "the person, the reality, or the analytic situation" and certainly not the psychoanalytic narrative. Thus, as in every aspect of Roy Schafer's formulation, we find a highly articulate rendition of a view of reality that he fails to incorporate completely into the deepest and most meaningful levels of his articulation of his practice. One is left with the real possibility that the psychoanalysis Schafer has ardently rescued from its vulnerable mechanisms and its underlying 19th-century logic ultimately may not settle in any more comfortably in the new neighborhood he has selected for it.

4. What kind of knowledge can reasonably be acquired on the basis of information about the past acquired in a psychoanalytic session as described by Roy Schafer?

Again, there are at least two answers. Speaking of certain unconscious behavior whose meaning (and relation to the past) may seem obvious to analysts, Schafer (1992) refers to,

> some versions of events that are so highly conventionalized or consensually validated that analysts routinely use them as criteria of what is "real" or "actual." In principle, relying on convention in this way is not a mistake. Consequently, there are times when analysts rightly speak of what is "actual" or "factual" in connection with

indications of unconsciously communicated messages and unconsciously performed reality testing. But, as I said, we should mean "actual" only in quotation marks, that is, within a commonsense or psychoanalytic convention of a binding sort [p. 216].

If this is the case, if common sense and psychoanalysis are to be regarded as equally "binding" conventions, then analysts may certainly be forgiven if they sometimes forget the quotation marks when they consider vivid narratives that coherently fit constructions of the patient's "real" past. Serious problems arise, however, if they attempt to extend that convention to any context outside psychoanalysis.

In accord with Schafer's (1980) espoused hermeneutics, no information acquired within the meaning system in which it is valid can then be transferred to a context outside of that system without losing that validity. "Validity, it seems, can only be achieved within a system"(p. 50). For example, the validity of a narrative about an analysand's having been sexually abused as a child which is constructed within a series of analytic hours is not necessarily valid at all within the context of a courtroom. Certainly no validity at all can be inferred sheerly from its emergence in another such epistemologically distinct context. On the other hand, it seems to be equally true, in Schafer's formulation, that such a narrative of abuse might achieve its own independent validity within a given system of legal jurisprudence with no handicap necessarily due to its original emergence in the course of psychoanalysis.

It is important to stress that the analyst's expertise regarding validity—that is, expertise concerning the "real" relation of a particular narrative to any other particular narrative—can never extend to other contexts. The analyst subscribing to Roy Schafer's hermeneutics can never ethically present himself as an expert regarding validity, or any other meaning, outside of the analytic session. His expertise, like his experience, is bounded by his narrative.

5. What kind of action can reasonably be taken on the basis of knowledge acquired in the psychoanalytic session as described in the perspective of Roy Schafer?

The answer to this question may be relatively complex epistemologically, but much simpler in practice. In practice, analysts and analysands must be guided by their own best judgment. Common sense, that is the conventionalized knowledge of one's time and region as embedded in the reigning cultural narrative of the world will play a major role in assigning information gained in psychoanalysis a role in outside behavior. The epistemological issue Schafer raises for the psychoanalyst is, however, potentially more interesting. At what point does psychoanalysis stop being merely an occupation and become a world view? For example, does the analyst continue to evaluate behavior outside the analytic session via psychoanalytic "categories"? How does the analyst hold those categories when, say, he attends his son's baseball game or goes dancing? At what point does the analyst supplement fidelity to the psychoanalytic perspective, or even temporarily abandon it? More pointedly, if the analysand is going to institute legal action resulting in financial ruin and prison for an outside party, in what capacity does the analyst testify? Having already theoretically given up any final foundation in the material reality on whose existence the legal system is based, the analyst whose commitment is with Schafer's espoused perspective would have little to offer the court. He or she could attempt to educate the court as to the nature of the psychoanalytic second reality and then speak about his or her analytic participation in constructing the narrative in question. To do this would probably be to endure the wringing of an alien reinterpretation of analytic material back into a legal version of the conventional first reality of our culture. Or the analyst could attempt to reverse his interpretations for the court and describe the patient's behavior through what might be called pre-analytic eyes. In so doing, however, the analyst would be totally giving up any claim to expertise. He would be abandoning the only context in which he was specially trained, and he would consequently have no basis on which to appear before the court as an expert witness.

Overall, Schafer's perspective on narrative in psychoanalysis introduces a degree of well-articulated intellectual refinement and, though his eminence in the field, an added degree of respectability to the psychoanalytic context of narrative. Although clearly no longer trying to straddle the metaphysical fence about the final discernability of reality, in the manner of Spence, Schafer, largely limiting his concept of narrative to the intellectual realm, thinks more often of intellectual systems than moment-by-moment "unwitting interpretations." Most of all, he resembles Spence in seeking to maintain traditional psychoanalysis. However, while Spence seeks to do this by consciously changing psychoanalytic practice, Schafer seeks to preserve it largely by modifying its underlying rationale without significantly disturbing actual psychoanalytic practice based on Freud's very different views. Ultimately, this attempt fails because the conflict between Freud's ideas and those more subjective, relative, and uncertain concepts inherent in the concept of narrative cannot be resolved by applying them only where they are complementary and by failing to apply them to actual clinical practices, where they may often be irreconcilable. A narrative metapsychology can theoretically justify a specific narrative, but to use it to justify one in which objectivity, certitude, and dominance of one narrative is the rule is not an exercise likely to end such an important controversy in psychoanalysis for long.

Robert Stolorow's Intersubjective Reality

Robert Stolorow's work is notable for the large following it has generated, as well as for the fact that, perhaps consistent with his ideas about the intersubjective generation of subjective reality, it has been developed and published in collaboration with colleagues George Atwood, Bernard Brandchaft, and, most recently, Donna Orange. Nevertheless, for convenience and because he has almost always been the lead author of the several books and articles he has contributed on intersubjectivity, we will refer to him alone in our phrasing of the questions we address to his approach and also from time to time in the text that follows.

1. What is the nature of reality as seen through the perspective of Robert Stolorow?

Stolorow envisions a psychoanalysis ultimately concerned with only one kind of reality. That reality is completely subjective. The objective reality that Spence calls historical reality is not denied, but it is simply not included in this approach (just how it enters tacitly is be discussed later). More precisely, the reality with which intersubjectivity is preoccupied is the reality of subjective experience, both felt and perceived, as it is mediated through interaction with others. This mediation through interaction with others is conceptualized as occurring in what Stolorow, Brandchaft, and Atwood (1987) refer to as the intersubjective field. While not a new idea in philosophy or even psychology, the concept of a socially derived intersubjective field is an important and innovative concept for a psychoanalysis founded on a view of separate individuals enmeshed with an objective reality.

Within the narrow range of reality intersubjective theory considers, the sole concept of external reality is the intersubjective field. No example of the narrowness of this focus is more striking than when trauma to a patient is explored. Sometimes no allowance appears to be made for the sheer independent impact of an externally imposed catastrophe. Instead, Stolorow and his colleagues (1987; Stolorow and Atwood, 1992) appear to locate the basis of traumatic stress exclusively in the lack of sympathetic and attuned social contact that accompany and precede it. For example, lack of preparation due to "early faulty affect attunement" is typically held to blame; that is, it is a failure of the early intersubjective field.

> Trauma is viewed here not as an event or series of events over-whelming an ill-equipped "psychic apparatus." Rather, the tendency for affective experiences to create a disorganized (i.e., traumatic) self state is seen to originate from early faulty affect attunement, with a lack of mutual sharing and acceptance of affect states, leading to impaired affect tolerance and inability to use affects as self-signals [Stolorow et al., 1987, p. 72].

Moreover, attunement at the time of the trauma is held to be equally vital: "It cannot be overemphasized that injurious childhood experiences: losses, for example—in and of themselves need not be traumatic (or at least not lastingly so) or pathogenic, provided that they occur within a responsive milieu (Shane and Shane, 1990). Pain is not pathology" (Stolorow and Atwood, 1992, p. 54).

This daring conceptual gambit, while seeming to amount to denial in extreme cases (severe mutilation, for example, cannot be that much less stressful in the company of friends), even if we concede that it has been overstated, deserves further exploration. At a minimum, it seems likely that trauma can cause lack of attunement as well as the reverse. Nonetheless, overall, the relation of trauma to attuned social contact, past and present, seems to be amenable to social research. It must be noted, of course, that since, almost by definition, much social trauma occurs in the presence of an unattuned perpetrator, the theoretical distinction intersubjectivity's view offers is not always a relevant or practical one in practice.

With respect to trauma, we must also note that, in practice, Stolorow obviously concerns himself with the historical reality of reports, if only in the context of pointing out the value of what the analyst discerns as a psychoanalytically proverbial "kernel of truth" in fantasy reported as history.

> It is common for experiences of abuse and seduction of a nonsexual or covertly sexual nature to be concretized and preserved in sexual symbolism. This insight into the kernel of truth encoded in a patient's fantasies opens up a whole new pathway for exploration, one that remains foreclosed when a patient's perceptions are dismissed as distortion [Stolorow and Atwood, 1992, p. 101].

To appreciate more fully the narrow focus with which intersubjectivity has attempted to approach the psychoanalytic arena, and some of what are seen here as its special difficulties, a few quotations and a historical comment may be in order. First, the historical comment: It is important to note that intersubjectivity in psychoanalysis is not an attempt, as are the perspectives of Spence and Schafer, to restructure the metapsychological foundations of classical psychoanalysis to fit the less certain and more fluid epistemological perspectives that continue to gain influence in modern psychoanalysis (as well as virtually every other intellectual field of endeavor). Rather, it has been, from the beginning, an attempt to further and consolidate what adherents may view as the advances of the self psychology of Heinz Kohut (1971, 1974, 1984) already made in that direction. What Stolorow states (with co-authors Brandchaft and Atwood, 1978) seems generally true: "we hope to highlight, broaden, and refine self psychology's essential contributions to psychoanalysis" (p. 15). Thus Stolorow and his colleagues begin with a focus already sharpened on the self and its experience and thereby leave behind the need to debate the role of objective external reality. Consequently, unlike Freud's, their view of the psychoanalytic domain begins far from a child's intermittent success and failure with a motor action that eventually helps him learn to achieve gratification in the "real" world.

> "Reality," as we use the term, refers to something subjective, something felt or sensed, rather than to an external realm of being existing independently of the human subject. In classical Freudian theory, reality is pictured in the latter way. . . . Our focus, by contrast, is on the child's establishing a *sense* that what he experiences is real, and on how this sense of the real develops within a facilitating intersubjective matrix [Stolorow and Atwood, 1992, p. 27].

A major problem that the constantly fluid intersubjective matrix appears to present to Stolorow and his coauthors may be related to the nature of theory building as we traditionally know it and as they attempt to employ it. Much theory requires something *else* that is not only distinct from itself, but also somewhat stable and repetitive, to construct a theory about. A theory that professes to be part of its subject must accept its lack of grounding in an independent perspective. A continually shifting and idiosyncratic intersubjective reality simply cannot provide the kind of solid ground for a theory of intersubjectivity that psychoanalysis has traditionally sought for itself (see Berger and Luckmann's, 1966, metaphor about trying to push a bus on which you are riding [p. 13]). This is not necessarily an insurmountable problem, only a limitation that must be recognized. It truly becomes a problem only when intersubjectivity, as a theoretical approach, seems reluctant to accept this limitation. In fact, intersubjectivity seems continually to operate with one foot planted outside its own premises.

Consider the following two quotes: "anything that is not *in principle* accessible to empathy and introspection does not fall within the bounds of psychoanalytic inquiry" (Stolorow et al., 1987, p. 5). With this statement Stolorow and colleagues seem to be saying something familiar about the experience of the self by both the self of the analyst and the self of the patient as the basis of psychoanalysis. This is clearly relevant to their clinical approach. Yet, how to reconcile this with a second statement, one that is arguably more consistent with Stolorow and his collaborators' mindset as traditional theory builders? In this second statement, they seem to suggest that psychological structure, as they envision it, has distinct properties that are a legitimate object of investigation while "the experiencing subject who initiates action" is not.

> We have found it important to distinguish sharply between the concept of the self as a psychological structure and the concept of the *person* as an experiencing subject and agent who initiates action. Whereas the self-as-structure falls squarely within the domain of psychoanalytic investigation, the ontology of the person-as-agent, in our view, lies beyond the scope of psychoanalytic inquiry [p. 18].

The second statement conflicts with the first because the self as structure (which is held to "fall squarely within the domain of psychoanalytic investigation") simply is not, and cannot be, accessible to empathy. It is only the person, as a unique "experiencing subject and agent," who can introspect or be empathized with, and who is, in contrast, only a "psychological structure," which can be said to possess the unique structure intersubjectivity posits for it. And, we might add, it is only the intersubjective analyst who can construct such distinctions.

Consider, for example, intersubjectivity's tripartite unconscious, which includes unique and abstract invariant principles. While without empathy and introspection there obviously could be no intersubjective approach, it may be these posited unconscious structures which constitute the main basis for intersubjectivity's claim to a place within psychoanalytic tradition. Without the hypothesized objective psychological structures so characteristic of psychoanalytic tradition, the intersubjective approach could conceivably be regarded more as an elaboration of such earlier empathic clinical technique as that of Carl Rogers (1955). One could say that the postulation of the structures that supplement the intersubjective focus on empathy and introspection may have been stimulated by the psychoanalytic intersubjective field. In any case, they are definitely not experienced through empathy, and their exclusively intellectual and inferential derivation makes the answers to the metapsychological aspects of the questions we choose to ask here considerably less consistent. All three of intersubjectivity's unconscious structures are *by definition* (see later) not subject to either empathy or introspection. They clearly cannot be known through psychoanalytic inquiry as defined by Stolorow and colleagues (although of course, like any other hypothetical constructs, they can be inferred). Nevertheless, Stolorow (1995) states clearly, "What an analyst investigates through empathy and introspection are the principles organizing the patient's experience (empathy), the principles organizing his own experience (introspection), and the psychological field formed by the interplay between the two" (p. 398). Overall, Stolorow seems to confuse two related, but very disparate processes: abstract cognitive inference of psychic structure, and the process of empathic resonance with affect.

A final observation can be made specifically about Stolorow's commitment to subjective reality. When it is operative it is virtually complete. At times he and his colleagues seem to view the very idea of external reality as a misconception. They associate the idea of an external reality with the historical misconception of "the isolated mind" (Stolorow and Atwood, p. 11), that is, a mind not correctly seen as developed and operating within its intrinsic intersubjective context, the necessary and purportedly sufficient social context on which Stolorow's perspective is based. "Invariably associated with the image of the mind is that of an external reality or world upon which the mind-entity is presumed to look out" (p. 11) they note. In fact, for the founders of the intersubjective approach:

The belief that one's personal reality is objective is an instance of the psychological process of concretization, the symbolic transformation of *configurations of subjective experience* into events and entities that are believed to be *objectively* perceived and known . . . attributions of objective reality, in other words, are concretizations of subjective truth. As we have observed this process in ourselves and others, we have become aware that it operates automatically and prereflectively [p. 92].

Vulnerable to logical attack as the belief in objective reality has become, it is unusual to see it diagnosed as a pathological condition (concretization), particularly in a theoretical approach emphasizing operating within the patient's perspective. Empathy stops here. One might assume that the analyst would introspectively decenter[1] in order to empathize with the patient who believes his or her perceptions are real. Particularly with psychotic patients, however, this is very clearly not always possible and often not done. For example, with a woman whose clearly articulated goal was to ascend to the holy trinity, the analyst's empathy was highly selective and possibly highly inferential:

Jane's analyst adopted a different strategy at their next meeting. Rather than allowing her to continue speaking of her religious plans and her goal of meeting with her old counselor, he stopped her from talking and insisted that for once she was to listen to what he had to say. He stated unequivocally that there was to be no meeting with her former counselor. He told her that he was bringing a new plan into operation, a plan in which she would become well again and return to live with the people who loved her. He added emphatically that he was himself the only person in this world she should be concerned about seeing, for it was in their work together that the goal of this new plan would be attained. In spite of Jane's initial resistance to these ideas, the analyst firmly insisted that she understand what he was communicating to her. She finally objected no more and began to cry. For about 20 minutes she sat quietly in tears and then thanked him and ended her appointment [Stolorow et al., 1987, pp. 153–154].

This selective empathy brought relief for this woman, but it required a waiting period for the anticipated consensual ratification of its attunement. It also required a degree of independent confidence in the analyst about his own perspective that seems to tilt the intersubjective field to a degree not different from that found in

---

[1] A simple term referring to what must be a complex and theoretically tenuous process: the analyst putting aside his personal perspective in favor of the patient's. (p. 3).

accounts of classical analysis. Apparently, empathic attunement sometimes moves toward empathic inference, and its final validation is a response that the analyst understands as indicative of validation. What this suggests, in addition to the previously noted lack of meta-psychological clarity at the foundation of intersubjectivity, is that in intersubjective clinical practice, as opposed to theory, the analyst's view of the patient's subjective state, even when the patient's state is not conscious, achieves the status of either the actual perception of reality or at least knowledge about it, even when the patient disagrees. Unfortunately, as with classical analytic interpretation, there is no opportunity to verify the hypothesized cause-and-effect relationship between the analyst's "correctness" and the patient's response. No way is apparent to eliminate the possibility that the analyst has simply filled a need, or otherwise provoked a new, more desirable response, not previously expressed at all by the patient. Consequently, it is one of the metapsychologically redeeming theoretical points of intersubjectivity that within its purview all that is usually held to be attainable or even desirable is that the patient should experience the analyst's interaction as attuned to his (primarily affective) experience.

A related metapsychological, and possibly ethical, problem again concerns the nature of agency in intersubjective theory. It is especially important to anyone seeking to place Stolorow's work within the psychoanalytic tradition of truth as the path to cure. It can be readily illustrated by contrasting Stolorow and Atwood's critical comment on Roy Schafer's concept of agency with an earlier statement of their own position. In the passages in question, a distinction is made involving the ontology of the self as agent, which is an area of dispute that the authors have with Schafer, and the self as structure, which is the focus of our discussion here. First the critical statement:

> More important, the continual embeddedness of the sense of agency, and of self-experience in general, in a nexus of intersubjective relatedness becomes, in Schafer's vision, obscured by the reified image of an omnipotent agent single-handedly creating his own experiences —another variant of the isolated mind in action [Stolorow and Atwood, 1992, p. 15].

On the other hand, Stolorow et al. (1987) had already written:

> From the standpoint of an outside observer, all our patients are continually performing actions. However, our concern, from an empathic-introspective vantage point, is whether or not they *experience* themselves as abiding centers of initiative. This experience of personal

agency, which is a basic constituent of a firmly consolidated self-organization, is a primary focus of psychoanalytic investigation for many patients. As analysts, we concern ourselves with the ontogenesis of the *sense* of personal agency, with early obstructions in this development, and with the reinstatement of the derailed structuralization processes in the transference configurations that become established [p. 19].

In other words, Stolorow and his colleagues deride the "reified image of an omnipotent agent single-handedly creating his own experiences" and yet revere the experience of it as "a basic constituent of a firmly constituted self organization." Given the analyst's reservations about agency, what is the nature of the validation that an analyst can provide who offers support for what he may see as his patient's illusion in this incredibly basic area?

Let us assume that this particular contradiction can be clarified and resolved in a satisfactory way. The more general issue remains of what the analyst does when a patient's reported experience is not consonant with one of intersubjectivity theory's tenets. For example, suppose a patient believes that when he faces the world alone he is at his best, and he seeks help to regain his ability to assume that posture. In such instances, is it better for the patient if the analyst keeps his supposedly superior intersubjectively informed position to himself? Then again, what kind of intersubjective field does an apparently empathic response based only on pragmatic or technical considerations create? It appears that attunement can occur authentically only with experience not incongruent with either intersubjective theory or the personal beliefs of the analyst. Actually, Stolorow and his colleagues do take a much more open stance concerning the possible variety of interactions between analyst and patient in a more recent book (Orange, Atwood, and Stolorow, 1997). However, this work is a primarily philosophical exploration in which many theoretical issues appear to fall by the wayside. In one of the few technical suggestions they offer, they note, "[I]nterpretations are suggestions, and it is critical to the analysis to investigate whether the patient believes he or she must adopt the analyst's viewpoint in order to maintain the therapeutic bond" (p. 39). One imagines here that they are referring to some specific interpretation and not to more basic belief held by the analyst. Also acknowledged, however, is that "all clinical work involves and takes place in the field formed by the interplay of two subjective worlds. . . . patient and analyst are similar, different, and complementary" (p. 17). What is not spelled out, or even seen as possible to spell out, is the central and intriguing question of how the interplay between those multiple aspects of the patient's and the analyst's worlds might optimally be conducted in accord with an intersubjective approach. Although the authors decline to make clear how they would arrive at such a decision, they do suggest that, given adequate information about the "particular meaning for this particular person," they would find an individual basis to arrive at an evaluation of a "particular interaction" (p. 32). Congruent with this stance, their examples, although interesting, are purposely more illustrative of the spirit (or "sensibility," p. 9) of intersubjectivity than definitive of intersubjective theory. They cannot be relied on for comparison with cases from which Stolorow's earlier observations were drawn in order to determine if that earlier data would actually elicit different conclusions today.

2. What is the nature of human experience of reality?

When we talk intersubjectively about the experience of reality we are talking about the experience of the intersubjective field and especially the experience of self through the medium of that field (Stolorow et al., 1987, p. 23). In short, there is no experience without the intersubjective field. In particular, "[W]e can work psychoanalytically and understand psychoanalytically only from within the intersubjective field" (Orange et al., 1997, p. 5). Obviously, it is the jointly or collectively created intersubjective field that serves as the theory's base in external reality.[2] While the intersubjective field is constantly being created in the present, individual invariant principles, in addition to the field itself, are held to shape each individual's contribution to the field. Invariant principles are held to be residues of earlier experience which relentlessly maintain their availability for activation in the present. Thus, the invariant principles that characteristically shape each individual's contribution to that field are typically born of interactions in the distant past. These "relentless," invariant principles of organization, once acquired, are virtually set in psychic stone in the unconscious.

Despite their psychological durability, however, Stolorow's commitment to a subjective present forces a conceptualization of these principles as pointedly having no psychic force or substance at all—conscious or unconscious. Their sole relation to overall psychic structure is held to be analagous to that of a blueprint for a

---

[2] One thing that the concept of the intersubjective field does is replace a Freudian, and hence Newtonian, mechanism for explaining interaction with one more congruent with contemporary field theory. The explanatory power of this term in psychoanalysis is less certain.

building (Stolorow and Atwood, 1992, p. 35). Stolorow's critical allegiance to subjective experience as the domain of his theory is strained with this late inclusion of a formative and not malleable personal history, and the concept of invariant principles may reflect that strain. The active selection of which principle is operating at any given moment is paradoxically left to an objectively real environment—real at least as far as the summoned invariant principle is concerned: "A person enters any situation with an established set of ordering principles (the subject's contribution to the intersubjective system), but it is the context that determines which among the array of these principles will be called on to organize the experience" (p. 24). Since the context cannot be held to perceive the principles, and the self is not conscious of the principles, and the principles, as blueprints, cannot perceive either, a mystery arises. What rules determine how a context is perceived? If invariant principles organize experience—including experience of the environment, that is, the subjective knowledge of the context to which intersubjectivity confines itself—then invariant principles might seem to be selected by other invariant principles. This mystery is never clarified, only deepened: "The organization of experience can therefore be seen as codetermined *both* by preexisting principles *and* by an ongoing context that favors one or another of them over the others" (p. 24). Here we have two inanimate and abstract things interacting to determine living (intersubjective) experience.

On the other hand, Stolorow et al. (1987) state: "In all cases the analytic stance toward the emergence of archaic modes of organization should be to promote their integration with other, more mature modes, thereby enriching psychological functioning, rather than to insist on their renunciation or elimination" (p. 32). It can arguably be concluded that these modes of organization can be integrated even though their invariant source cannot be changed. What can integration mean in this context? And what can the creation of new (more mature) invariant principles mean for the old ones? Are the new principles stronger because they are created through more attunement, or because they are newer? Stolorow and Atwood (1992) suggest that simply the fact that more of them are created "enlarges the patient's experiential repertoire." And, further, "It is the formation of new organizing principles within the intersubjective system that constitutes the essence of developmental change throughout the life cycle" (p. 25).

Overall, the creation of a powerfully controlling force from the past which never attains any substance in the psychological structure seems to reflect a strained attempt to maintain the limit of the self's theoretical domain to conscious and present experience of itself. Stolorow may be insisting on looking under a streetlight for what Freud has already found in the dark. It is difficult to imagine any way any psychoanalytic theory could more completely eviscerate either the unconscious or its roots in the past. This part of the unconscious (see Orange et al., 1992, p. 33 for intersubjective psychoanalysis's other two parts of the unconscious, both comprised of unarticulated experiences) is not only not seething (in the sense of Freud's comparably determinative area of the unconscious), it has absolutely no life at all. Yet, for Stolorow, invariant principles are paradoxically able to retain a theoretical role for the unconscious as the deepest source of patterns of experience and a basal psychic reality beyond empathy or introspection.

Intersubjectivity's key clinical process for identifying such internally determined patterns "accurately" (even where accurate is used to mean whatever it is with which the patient agrees) is equally perplexing. It may ultimately make sense and be able to validate itself only in a positivist context (such as that of classical psychoanalysis). Yet the intersubjective approach, like Donald Spence's search for historical truth or Roy Schafer's narrative approach, by its rejection of objectivity intrinsically and intentionally undercuts its own ability to know in such traditional ways. Like those approaches, intersubjectivity must attempt to provide a new basis for knowing to supplement what it has undermined. The intersubjective approach appears to attempt repair both by exaggerating its own commitment to the subjective and by hypothesizing unverifiable internal determinants it can then infer to both the analyst's and the patient's satisfaction. This repair is adequate if, as Schafer (1989) states, "Like the past, the psychoanalytic present is not more than one of a number of possible constructions" (p. 20), but Stolorow and his colleagues appear to be saying more. They appear to be asserting not only that subjectivity validates subjectivity, but also that intersubjective theory and technique provide the right (or at least the most pragmatic) lens through which subjective experience can be seen. Stolorow and his colleagues seem to saying that through that lens the patient's experience can be, if not glimpsed, at least inferred. They, wisely and consistently, do not attempt to establish any new metaphysical ground on which such diverse assertions can rest. Noting the knotty question, "How can an analyst be expected to reflect on the nature and impact of his own organizing principles, when his acts of self-reflection will be shaped by the very principles whose nature and impact he seeks to comprehend?" Stolorow and Atwood (1992) add: "It would be difficult for us, for example, to reflect fully on the particularizing impact of our principle of intersubjectivity, insofar as this is the central constituent of our analytic perspective. It must be left to others to integrate our contributions within a still more general and inclusive viewpoint" (p. 124). That basis must include, if not a clearer conceptualization of reality, at least a fuller discussion of psychoanalytic knowing.

In their most recent book (Orange et al., 1997) the authors do attempt to provide such a discussion. In this book, which is "devoted to broad-based philosophy of practice" (p. ix), the focus is clearly more philosophical than clinical. The result is "contextualism," as opposed to "antirelational, antihistorical, decontextualized conceptions of human nature" and which "means an ongoing sensitivity and relentless attention to context—developmental, relational, gender related, cultural, and so on" (p. 178). The authors, of course, are fully aware that such sensitivity and relentless attention can be applied only by another context-dependent sensitivity. Drawing on a wide range of philosophers from Aristotle to Gadamer, the authors appear to pull the postmodern mantle more tightly about intersubjectivity's shoulders and to withdraw from virtually any clinical certainty they may have seemed to display earlier. Whereas in *Psychoanalytic Treatment: An Intersubjective Approach,* Stolorow et al. (1987) begin by speaking of "[o]ur conception of psychoanalysis as a science of the intersubjective . . ." (p. ix), the more recent volume refers to intersubjectivity as a "metatheory of psychoanalysis" (Orange et al., 1997, p. 3) and as "from a clinical point of view" as "not so much a theory as it is a sensibility" (p. 9). Like Hoffman's (1983, 1991) social paradigm, this sensibility is held to be applicable to a full range of psychoanalytic settings (classical, interpersonal, and self-psychological). No conflicts are anticipated in such diverse settings because "[i]n our view, there is no distinct body of clinical theory or of 'technical' recommendations to be derived from intersubjectivity" (Orange et al., p. 9). In other words, intersubjectivity appears successfully to further distance itself from the objective view of reality and is thereby able to offer its subjective sensibility to other approaches that, at least to some extent, attempt to provide just such an objective foundation.

While it is clearly reasonable to interpret this new postmodern stance as evidence of an effort to make a laudable and timely movement beyond the demands for objective knowing of traditional psychoanalytic theory, for some it also may represent a premature attempt to rise above them. Intersubjectivity has previously provided a considerable body of specific clinical opinion that has been influential and even formative for many practitioners. Its own organizing principles, however, along with its underlying implications about cognitive structure, clearly remain; and the problems that arise in their application must, to the degree they are unresolved and are no longer even considered resolvable on a theoretical level, likewise remain to trouble the many clinicians who attempt to follow them. Whether the new understanding that posits that the struggle to resolve such clinical issues must be conducted independently in each individual instance with little guidance, but perhaps much inspiration, from intersubjectivity theory will prove clinically adequate for most of its practitioners remains to be seen. Perhaps reassurance may be found in the authors' statement that what they refer to as "[o]ur perspectival realism does not allow us the relativism implicit in more extreme postmodern views . . ." (Orange et al., 1997, p. 74). Consequently, from their subjective stance they do remain able to say that they "find certain psychoanalytic clinical theories, always embedded in frameworks of suppositions about human nature, more productive and intellectually coherent than others" (p. 74). Although this most recent effort does provide speculation about the uncertain nature of knowing in the intersubjective field (i.e., see their references to Gadamer, pp. 26–28, 72), it does not offer, and does not claim to offer, a view of the nature of experience which can provide additional clarity or specific direction when applied in the analytic hour.

3. What is the nature of human communication
    of the experience of reality?

Communication is to Stolorow's intersubjectivity almost as the flow of electrons is to electricity. It is the basic process by which the subjective becomes intersubjective and the same process (in reverse) by which validation occurs and the subjective survives. In the intersubjective view, communication is the essential process of humanness. It might be added that the process of communication is the basis of human (intersubjective) reality. Without communication humanity does not exist, and when communication declines below a certain level, humanity withers. Therefore to describe communication from within the perspective of the intersubjective approach is to touch on every aspect of that approach. Since much of the broad outline of this approach has been touched on earlier, I will make no attempt here to recapitulate its entirety. In the context of the question of the nature of the communication of reality, however, at least one major point should be underlined. In addition, certain basic questions about communication per se within the perspective of intersubjectivity merit consideration.

Stolorow and Atwood (1992) repeatedly emphasize that reality (the intersubjective field) is both constructed and maintained only through communication, and that "[i]f even the permanence and substantiality of the world are constituted and maintained by intersubjective fields, in a culture of pervasive psychological aloneness there is little to protect a person from feeling that the solidity of things is dissolving into thin air" (p. 11). It is also important to note that for them communication is, though largely transmitted verbally, at least very significantly affective and not just cognitive. Similarly: "'Reality,' as we use the term, refers to something subjective, something felt or sensed, rather than to an external realm of being existing independently of the human subject" (pp. 26–27). More explicitly:

> It is our view that the development of the child's sense of the real occurs not primarily as a result of frustration and disappointment, but rather through the validating attunement of the caregiving surround, an attunement provided across a whole spectrum of affectively intense, positive and negative experiences. Reality thus crystallizes at the interface of interacting, affectively attuned subjectivities [p. 27].

Thus, reality is a consensual process in which a child gains confidence in his ability to participate through supportive communication. Its crystalization "at the interface of interacting" has nothing directly to do with any objective reality the child might need to bump into several times in order to learn its location. It is apparently only when the child shares his or her affective experience of the bump through communication that the experience becomes real.

One problem with this perspective is that it suggests that, though lack of validation may lead to enduring damage, it cannot be experienced as real unless it is intersubjectively validated. This position does not appear to be clinically tenable. Loneliness, lack of love, and abandonment are among the most cited of formative experiences despite the fact that they are intrinsically not (in themselves) validating. Stolorow's view in this regard is, in fact, the opposite of what seems to be the case in both the clinical and theoretical literature of intersubjectivity as well as that of every other theoretical approach. Technically, of course, for Stolorow some such unvalidated experiences do not achieve reality, because their lack of validation, particularly during the earliest phases of development, tends to make them unconscious. Consequently they cannot technically participate in reality, which by intersubjective definition is subjective and conscious, but instead can only leave their pernicious mark as abstract and psychically insubstantial invariant principles, which cannot be directly communicated. Much trauma that occurs without any apparent accompanying attunement or later sharing (prior to analysis) can, however, obviously be both consciously recalled and formative in an experiencing person's view of his or her real world.

Stolorow and Atwood (1992) actively seek to rescue past experiences of unattunement (or giving up of subjective experience to maintain essential relationships or both) from the unconscious, but the authors seek less to make them conscious than to create the opportunity to communicate the missing curative attunement and thereby provide a new experience to form the basis for new operating principles. The means of retrieval is, like Freud's, to encourage verbal articulation. Although Stolorow clearly recognizes the importance of nonverbal communication, he seems primarily interested in it as preverbal rather than as a phenomenon concurrent with verbal communication. In fact, Stolorow and Atwood actually see repression as the prevention of the codification of experience in a form that would allow communication through articulation.

> In that realm of experience in which consciousness increasingly becomes articulated in symbols, unconscious become coextensive with unsymbolized. When the act of articulating an experience is perceived to threaten the indispensable tie, repression can now be achieved by preventing the continuation of the process of encoding that experience in symbols [p. 33].

Therefore subjective reality is simultaneously created in at least two disparate ways by any new verbal articulation of the past: first, by permitting traces of what was real in the past to attain present symbolic reality (and thereby also attain present affective resonance); and, second, by the new present reality the experience attains in the current intersubjective field (see the related discussion of Freud's *Nachtraglichkeit* in chapter 2).

A major question about communication in intersubjectivity theory concerns not the experience, but the reception, of communication— in particular, the burden of attunement on the analyst. When the analyst performs well, he observes:

> As the ossified . . . forms that have heretofore structured the patient's experiences are progressively . . . reorganized, a new and enriched personal reality opens up before him, made possible by the newly expanded and reflectively conscious structures of his subjective world.

Analysis thus introduces a new object into the patient's experience, an object unique in the capacity to invoke past images and yet also to demonstrate an essential difference from these early points of reference. . . . Every transference interpretation that successfully illuminates for the patient his unconscious past simultaneously crystallizes an illusive present—the novelty of the therapist as an understanding presence. Perceptions of self and other are perforce transformed and reshaped to allow for the new experience. Assimilation contributes the affective power inherent in the transference, while accommodation makes for change (Atwood and Stolorow, 1984, p. 60) [Stolorow et al., 1987, p. 103].

Keeping in mind the views of Spence and Schafer, both of whom share and amplify Stolorow's doubt about the nature of objectivity in psychoanalysis, how are we to understand the intersubjective analyst's astute performance? Stolorow et al.'s (1987) sophisticated extended comment about case study in general suggests only the beginnings of an answer.

The varied patterns of meaning that emerge in psychoanalytic research are brought to light within a specific psychological field located at the point of intersection of two subjectivities. Because the dimensions and boundries of this field are intersubjective in nature, the intersubjective conclusions of every case study must, in a very profound sense, be understood as *relative* to the intersubjective context of their origin. The intersubjective field of a case study is generated by the interplay between transference and countertransference; it is the environment or "analytic space" . . . in which the various hypotheses of the study crystallize, and it defines the horizons of meaning within which the truth-value of the final interpretation is determined. An appreciation of this dependence of psychoanalytic insight on a particular intersubjective interaction helps us to understand why the results of a case study may vary as a function of the person conducting it. Such variation, an anathema to the natural sciences, occurs because of the diverse perspectives of different investigators on material displaying an inherent plurality of meanings (Atwood and Stolorow, 1984, p. 6) [Stolorow et al., 1987, p. 7].

The authors supplement the purely subjective approach to evaluating psychoanalytic contributions to the intersubjective field with hermeneutic criteria. After mentioning subjective reality in the intersubjective field, they continue:

This avowedly subjectivist and relativist position should not, however, be taken to mean that we believe that any psychoanalytic interpretation or explanatory construct is as good as the next. In *Structures of*

Subjectivity (1984) we argued that psychoanalytic interpretations must be evaluated in light of distinctly *hermeneutic* criteria. These include:

> The logical coherence of the argument, the comprehensiveness of the explanation, the consistency of the interpretations with accepted psychological knowledge, and the aesthetic beauty of the analysis in disclosing previously hidden patterns of order in the material being investigated (pp. 5–6) [Stolorow et al., 1987, p. 8].

This is a tack similar to that suggested by Schafer.[3] In any case, as discussed earlier, the attempt to build an intellectual evaluative structure onto an avowedly empathetic process presents many intrinsic problems that are, to say the least, not easily solved. Intersubjectivity's response to its own narrow foundation has been an incongruent attempt to ground it more broadly without relinquishing the character of its more unique and parsimonious original structure. Consequently, it may be that the questions that intersubjectivity has had to face will prove more important to psychoanalysis than the specific resolutions that intersubjectivity has thus far offered.

4. What kind of knowledge can reasonably be acquired on the basis of information about the past acquired in a psychoanalytic session conducted according to intersubjective theory?

No knowledge acquired in the intersubjective framework can be understood within that framework without its specific intersubjective context. In fact, information about the past always has new meaning at the time it is expressed because the context in which it is reported must be different from that in which it was first initiated. In addition, the moment when it is first expressed—what Spence (1982) has called the "context of discovery" (p. 33)—differs significantly from the later time when its implications may be pondered (see Spence's "context of justification," p. 33). The relative fluidity of the intersubjective context means essentially that all knowledge is subjective and exists only at the moment it is experienced. Consequently, not only can

---

[3] Interestingly, it also sounds similar to the structure Stolorow proposes for the self: "The degree of severity of self disorder may be evaluated with reference to three essential features of the sense of self—its structural cohesion, temporal stability, and affective coloration (Stolorow and Lachmann, 1980)" (Stolorow et al., 1987, p. 116).

knowledge never reasonably be acquired about an objective past; but, because past intersubjective contexts cannot be resurrected, there is also no way of repeating a subjective past. Since even the present is specifically only subjective, there is no validation for any knowledge, ever, except self-validation and consensus with other subjective participants in the intersubjective field (via their own presumably disparate experiences of it, of course) at the moment of validation.

As suggested earlier, this is not to say that intersubjectivity does not make inferences and use them as though they were known. Such a process is the sole basis of all the generalizations that form intersubjective theory and many of their clinical interpretations. When such inferences are accepted as true by the participants in the discourse (i.e., the analyst and the analysand), however, they cease to be merely inferences and become more akin to Spence's "narrative truth." Thus, intersubjective theorists elevate their inferences by more or less pulling on their own subjective bootstraps and raising these inferences to the level of truth. For this process to work it does not matter which criteria are used as long as those criteria are agreed upon—although, of course, it matters completely for the kind of truth the process produces. Whatever that truth is, it then has acquired the subjective reality, simply through belief, which is the episte- mological pinnacle in intersubjectivity theory's own intersubjective field. Stolorow et al. (1987) refer to the process this way: "the only reality relevant and accessible to psychoanalytical inquiry is *subjective reality*—that of the patient, that of the analyst, and the psychological field created by the interplay between the two" (p. 4).

They then qualify this statement and add the critical and apparently (in their view) potentially objectively administered hermeneutic standards already quoted—coherence, comprehensive- ness, consistency and aesthetic beauty (p. 8). Once these underlying criteria are defined and accepted, the creation of reality can proceed in a more orderly fashion. This process is, of course, dependent on people with sufficiently reliable and acute (or at least homogeneous) subjectivities to perform it. This need for acute subjectivities raises the following, metaphysically central, question for both patients and analysts: Is what a severely disordered self experiences as true as what a more typical self (or an especially well-ordered self) experiences? The answer should theoretically be yes, but Stolorow and colleagues provide numerous examples in which the analyst's interpretations provide a particular "structure" to those experiences. Such interpretations ultimately determine the meaning of those

experiences, thereby underlining the conditional nature of intersubjectivity's commitment to the subjective.[4]

With a purely subjective stance we know only whatever we
experience ourselves as knowing. With its more intellectual and
theoretical posture, intersubjectivity reaches far beyond its subjective
roots and attempts to become another way of formulating the "truth"
about the human condition.

5. What kind of action can reasonably be taken on the
basis of knowledge acquired in a psychoanalytic session?

The answer to this question can only be as clear as our basis for
knowing reality compounded by the added uncertainty of the effects
of any particular action. Clearly, any analyst who believes he or she
knows what happened to a patient and that the result of a particular
action (say, testifying in court) would logically be helpful to that
patient is neither prevented nor supported by the intersubjective
approach. The fact that the analyst's experience is intersubjective
does not meaningfully differentiate him or her from a judge, jury, or
defendants, and he or she is free to participate on that basis. On the
other hand, the analyst has no basis on which to assert that whatever
information he or she brings to the nominally objective process of
the court is in any way superior.

It is worthwhile to point out that there does appear to be a nascent
morality emerging in the intersubjective discourse that distinguishes
it from typical discourse in many other places, but especially within
our legal system. There is an almost Rogerian suggestion persisting
intermittently throughout Stolorow's work that validation is the
essence of the optimal behavior people should perform toward
each other and that the failure to provide it is or can be "noxious"
(Stolorow and Atwood, 1992, p. 95). Children wither without validation and even adults, patients or no, require it as a steady diet. By
contrast, in this context, what would serious disagreement, let alone
vehement argument, entail for the people in its intersubjective radius
when "any threat to the validity of perceptual reality constitutes a

---

[4] See, for example, Stolorow et al. (1987, pp. 168–170) where a patient, perhaps
taking the intersubjective approach to heart, tells the analyst, "You *can* know my
whole life, can't you? Do it now! I know you can do it. Please right now. Okay, go!
Know my whole life!" (p. 168), which her analyst eventually reasonably translates as
based on the patient's belief that "if he could know her *whole* life, her life would then
become *whole* within his understanding" (p. 170).

deadly threat to the self and to the organization of experience itself"?
(p. 94). There does not seem to be much room for serious *and* healthy
opposition here. The lack of such room does not reflect the reality of
psychoanalysis, family life, or our society at large. Some heartfelt
conflict about how things are seen is part of the ebb and flow of
communication to be expected in virtually all intersubjective fields.
Unless we are to adhere to the position that all such spirited
differentiation of perspective is noxious and constitutes a deadly
threat to the self of others around us, there is a need to explore further
and understand this issue in the context of the intersubjective
approach. This issue bears sharply on the right of individuals
generally to validate their own experiences with both actions and
words even when others hold divergent views on matters they hold
in common.

6

Irwin Z. Hoffman's Uncertainty

*I*rwin Z. Hoffman's views are presented last because he has gone furthest among the theorists we have discussed in confronting the possibility of a psychoanalysis based solely in the context of subjectivity. His work is the source of much controversy within psychoanalysis and is particularly important to our discussion here. Many of the individual articles quoted here have also been included in only slightly revised form within Hoffman's (1998) most recent book. Consequently, for ease of reference, dual citations, separated by a slash, are provided when the published passages are identical.

1. What is the nature of reality as described in the writings of Irwin Z. Hoffman?

Hoffman, like the authors previously discussed, contends with an inability to know a world independent of his perceptions of it and finds a primary stimulus for his innovative thinking in the resulting ambiguity. At least within the analytic hour, however, Hoffman's approach (perhaps more in the tradition of Spence than of Schafer or Stolorow) compromises less in an attempt to stake out more solid epistemological ground. Rather, Hoffman stays near the nexus of his uncertain experience of the world and attempts to build a basis for a new perspective for psychoanalysis on that very point.

He bases his overall approach on a pervasive and undeniable uncertainty stemming from the inherent melding together of what has been described from other perspectives as psychic and external realities. He recognizes that forsaking the positivist assumption that all meaning has, or can have, a verifiable empirical basis (see Lacey, 1976, pp. 183–184) leads to a position with distinct, and very broad, implications for psychoanalysis which have not yet been fully confronted. He is careful to distinguish that position from the current movement within psychoanalysis to replace an understanding of human behavior as shaped primarily by biological drives with a view focusing on the formative power of relationships. He writes:

> Let me begin by immediately saying that the paradigm shift I have in mind is not the shift from the drive model to the relational model that Greenberg and Mitchell (1983) and Eagle (1984) have identified as central in the field. Put succinctly, the change that I regard as fundamental and still germinal in psychoanalytic theory and practice is from a positivist model for understanding the psychoanalytic situation to a constructivist model [1991, p. 76/1998, p. 135].

And what is the nonpositivist premise of such a constructivist model? Speaking of the underlying view of reality that his own and kindred radical critiques share, Hoffman states:

> This view is simply that reality is not a pre-established given or absolute. As Wachtel (1980) says, arguing from the perspective of Piaget's theory of cognitive development: "Neither as children or as adults do we respond directly to stimuli per se. We are always constructing reality every bit as much as we are perceiving it" (p. 62) [1983, p. 407/1998, p. 118].

The implications of this simple statement are the foundation of Hoffman's work. Focusing on certain key analytic interactions Hoffman states unequivocally that: "Both the process of explication and the moment of interpersonal influence entail creation of meaning, not merely its discovery" (1991, p. 91/1998, p. 150).

For Hoffman, however, the implications of his constructivism seem to apply significantly less to certain moments within the analytic hour and sometimes not at all later in the day when he may be assumed to construct or express his theoretical views. Consequently, one does not need to proceed far to encounter Hoffman's numerous refinements of Wachtel's (1980) generalization. These refinements appear to be part of a growing tendency within Hoffman's work to complement his continuing profound exploration of the implications of the process of mutual construction intrinsic to most interactions in the psychoanalytic hour with his growing elaboration of an objective context of "given realities" (Hoffman, 1998, p. xiv) on which to ground his constructivism. With the increasing elaboration of such an objective context, however, the integrity of Hoffman's constructivism is not supported but actually weakened. Since our interest here is on the contributions made by Hoffman's constructivism to psychoanalysis's understanding of the nature of reality, it is essential to point out these very different, and often recently articulated, threads in his work and their relation to his constructivism. The reader is thus forewarned that in this section we are commenting on a degree of ambiguity, a higher level logical ambiguity, lately inhabiting the thought of Hoffman, who might otherwise be thought of at a phenomenological level as the theorist of ambiguity par excellence. We focus our attention on his constructivism at that phenomenological level more fully in succeeding sections.

Some of Hoffman's more stark statements concerning an objective context for his constructivism may stem from a strong desire on his part to exorcise certain philosophical demons of radical relativism with which he has been associated (see Orange, 1992). Hoffman (1998) himself mentions the terms solipsism (p. 105) and moral relativism, in which "anything goes as to what can qualify as a good way to live" . . . (p. xix) as possible misunderstandings of his view. In the same volume he indicates a preference for the terms dialectical constructivism or critical constructivism over the term social constructivism because the latter term "leaves the door open to 'guilt by association' with radical relativism, with the impression that reality is merely a function of social consensus" (p. xix).[1] The concern about "guilt by association," admittedly a difficult, if not always a worthy, foe, may similarly be at play when he pointedly qualifies his earlier views by adding that "[a]mbiguity and uncertainty do not, however, connote the disappearance of objective reality and the rule of unqualified relativism" (p. xviii).

Hoffman does not present his more recent views simply as theoretical postulates. He advances a straightforward statement of belief "in an objective framework within which constructive activity takes place. That objective framework is made up, in part, of the characteristics of human action and experiences, which dialectical constructivism, itself, regards as universal" (p. xx). In particular, he holds that "it is *objectively* the case that experience is intrinsically ambiguous" (p. xx, emphasis added). Hoffman also claims a "kind of universal validity" (p. 58) for dialectical constructivism itself and

---

[1] Social-constructivism is the full term Hoffman (1991) formerly preferred. "The paradigm is called social-constructivism to capture both the idea of the analyst's participation and the idea of construction of meaning" (p. 74).

offers an elaboration of that universality a few pages later in an extensive footnote partially quoted in what follows. This elaboration includes the surprising implication that as a theorist he is able to see beyond the influence of culture and history and, in particular, that his ideas about human nature, on which he bases his views, are not themselves constructed. While these ideas are quite reasonable within a positivist framework, it is hard to find any foundation for them in a constructivism that has claimed to disdain any "preestablished given or absolute" (1983, p. 407/1998, p. 118).

> When I make assertions about the way experience works from a constructivist perspective I am claiming universal truth value for those assertions. For example, if I say that social realities are culturally relative in ways that are not fully knowable to the constructors of those realities, I do not mean to say that that assertion itself is culturally relative. The idea may emerge because of cultural-historical influences, but the truth value that is being claimed for it is transcultural and transhistorical. What may seem to be a resulting internal contradiction is more apparent than real and can be resolved with more precise use of language. Only *some* aspects of reality are socially constructed, in the sense they are manufactured by human beings. Among those that are excluded is the fact that humans, *by their nature*, are active agents in the social construction of their worlds [1998, pp. 76–77].

Within his objective framework he narrates a compelling existential view in which life exists against a background of death as the construction of meaning exists against a background of meaninglessness. This existential view then feeds back to his basic perspective: "What emerges as a kind of 'psychobiological bedrock,' as the immutable, transcultural, transhistorical truth, is that human beings create their worlds and their sense of meaning in the teeth of the constant threat of nonbeing and meaninglessness" (p. 16).

The first problem that arises between this admittedly profound existential view and Hoffman's own constructivism remains the enduring one. It lies in understanding how he, as a constructing subjectivity, particularly one who continues pointedly to emphasize the fallibility of the analyst as an authority on reality, attains such final knowledge. A more specific issue, but one of particular interest to our endeavor, is how that particular background of meaninglessness is to be known. If we unavoidably bring meaning as we perceive, it would seem to be a contradiction even to be able to construct or perceive such an ultimately virginal state. Insofar as this "bedrock" is psychobiological, Hoffman is arguably discussing not an external reality, but a genetically wired nightmare, actually full of meaning, which chases us toward the destinies it helps us shape just as fantasies of drive fulfillment may draw us forward. At times, however, Hoffman implies something much more concrete, something actual that can be and must be avoided. Quoting a statement by Ernest Becker, Hoffman (1998) states: "The construction of all reality requires blinders" (p. 16). Similarly he quotes Berger and Luckmann: "*All* societies are constructions in the face of chaos" (p. 17). These statements suggest a constructivism different from one that simply constructs an ambiguous reality. Here construction is construed as a choice one makes to avoid a reality somehow seen all too clearly.

Hoffman also espouses a certain notion of free will that suggests a major role for conscious choice in construction. He demarcates it as "'a space' between the source of influence and its impact, a gap in which I am present as an agent, as a choosing subject" (p. vii). Later, however, he adds a footnote that seems to reduce this potentially problematic "space" where the unconstructed might actually be momentarily contemplated to merely a tool of explication: "When referring to the more passive, unconscious process, the word choice is actually being used *metaphorically* to capture a dimension of experience that is neither simply a given that the person is not implicated in at all, nor an alternative that the person has actively decided upon" (pp. xiii–xiv, emphasis added).

Finally, Hoffman (1998) also offers the following conception of experience, which, while more modest in its claims, may indicate the basis of his certainty about some matters: "I believe experience can be thought of as composed, *first*, of symbolically well-developed, indisputable, relatively unambiguous features, *second*, of symbolically underdeveloped, ambiguous attitudes, feeling states, and frames of mind, and *third*, of totally untapped potentials" (p. 22).[2] What Hoffman appears to refer to when he speaks of "symbolically well-developed, indisputable, relatively unambiguous features" are certain agreed upon features of the analytic situation, such as the time and location of the appointment and the fee. He declares that "[t]hey exist no less 'objectively' for being functions of human construction and perception than do facts which exist independent of such activity, for example, that it is a daytime or nighttime hour" (p. 22). Here Hoffman is clearly shifting the meaning of the term

---

[2] This statement does not represent a new position but an elaboration. In a talk given in 1992 (and later published in 1996 and again in 1998), he described limitations on the infinite number of possible interpretations via the metaphor of the infinite possible numerical values between 5 and 6.

objective to one based on social consensus.[3] Whereas the positivist notion of objectivity, which Hoffman clearly eschews, specifies an independent external reality which can be observed objectively, Hoffman's constructivism substitutes a virtually independent social reality that can be observed without ambiguity. It is reasonable to assert that constructions seem truer with wider use. And certainly attitudes, feeling states, and frames of mind are much less subject to such consensual construction simply because prior to expression they are not subject to construction by others. Here though, Hoffman, in an attempt to ground his theoretical approach, appears to confuse consensual use with some inherent diminishment of the intrinsic ambiguity in the raw reality thus constructed. To be sure, there is nothing wrong with attempting to move to a social definition of reality in which reality is a social product of construction. But we cannot use such a definition to describe the process of construction itself without also admitting that we are constructing and not merely describing. To do so is to attempt (by ascending to a supposedly higher, poststructural perspective) to reclaim an objectivity very similar to that we have tried to leave behind.

Hoffman is not alone in his apparent yearning for some ground to replace the lost footing a positivist reality provides or to explain the increasing sense of confidence in such footing that years of experience are bound to bring. Even Spence (1982) has observed that "[o]nce a given contribution has acquired narrative truth, it becomes just as real as any other kind of truth . . ." (p. 31). Spence, however, by reason of his unwillingness to forsake an objective world, did not say that it becomes the same as any other kind of truth. Hoffman seeks to portray the world as offering both certainty and ambiguity, and he hopes to find both in one coherent, dialectical framework. If he finds human perception capable of both functions, depending on relative degrees of ambiguity located in the external world, he suggests a deterministic kind of constructivism in which reality is seen objectively when reality permits it. Often this view seems to be exactly what Hoffman means to suggest. If instead, he finds the degree of ambiguity located in human perception, he is led either to return to a view akin to Freud's most positivist views of a potentially objective perception sometimes clouded by unconscious interference or to rely on consensual use as the objective basis of reality. Although these views are not necessarily mutually exclusive, Hoffman offers no consistent amalgamation. It could be said that his vacillation along

---

[3] Although Hoffman uses the term objective with quotes here, that is not always the case (e.g., 1998, p. 16)

a gradient of ambiguity creates a metapsychological ambiguity that runs throughout Hoffman's work. Then again, some of his more clinically oriented discussions also suggest a more postmodern foundation that is less incongruent with his constructivism (e.g., Hoffman, 1998, p. 22, cited earlier).

Donnel Stern (1997), distinguishing not between "the objective" and "the constructed," but between "the given" and "the made," articulates the postmodern alternative particularly well:

> When we talk about the given and the made in psychoanalysis, then, we are referring not to the contrast between humanly constructed meaning and what came before it, but to what we find preconstructed and what we make of it. The events of the moment combine with the preconstructed past, and the world of others falls together with our preconstructed inner life [p. 6].

There is not likely, however, to be much solace for those who fear relativism in such a postmodern reality, insofar as "the givens" of Hoffman's "objective framework" are viewed there as merely yesterday's constructions.

More long-standing, but not unrelated to the foregoing discussion, and a controversial issue in its own right, is Hoffman's attempt to confine his theorizing to *social* reality. He believes he can clearly distinguish a realm that social reality occupies from that of physical reality. For example: "Moreover, the realm of interpersonal events is distinguished from that of physical events in that such events are highly ambiguous and consensus is much harder to obtain (Wachtel, 1980, p. 69)" (1983, p. 407/1998, p. 118). Almost 10 years after his first publication of these words, he elaborated on this same point, this time adding literature to physical events:

> I do not believe that constructivism in the context of studying human experience as such should carry the same meaning as constructivism in the physical sciences or in literary theory. Experience, taken as a whole, is partially constituted by what we make of it, retrospectively, in the context of interpretation, and prospectively in the context of experience shaping actions. . . . I do not believe that the same could be said reasonably of the motion of the planets or of the literal contents of a complete written text. The planets and the existing texts have a different sort of independence from the organizing activity of human subjects than does the flow those subjects experience during any given interval of time [1996, pp. 111–112/1998, p. 77].

Even if we accept, for purposes of argument, that physical reality is less ambiguous and less malleable to social construction, lack of specificity about the boundary between the physical and the social may make that distinction highly subject to exaggeration. The history of the physical sciences is more than adequate testimony to the malleability of man's perception of the physical world. More important, most of our "human experience" in the so-called social realm in which Hoffman sees greater latitude is also based on perception of physical reality. For example, in which category do we put a smile or a look of disapproval? The interpretation of facial expression and gestures is the basis of much of the formative experience of children as well as adults (see Scheflen, 1972, for a detailed discussion of this point). All behavior has a physical element that must be interpreted. As Schafer (1987) has noted: "[s]ome kissing may be retold as an attack that is close to hitting and some hitting may be retold as a sadistic form of loving that is close to kissing" (p. 331). Hoffman's inclusion in his statement of verbal communication put in written form is even more questionable. Not only lawyers and historians make their living arguing over written words.[4] And while Hoffman does concede that the interpretation of all kinds of phenomena is central to their experience, his attempt to separate the physical and the social may be unfortunate for the theoretical consistency of his views, and to this extent is important to note for anyone hoping to build upon his work. It is primarily of theoretical note, however, only since it does not actually surface in any of the numerous clinical examples he offers in his work.

On what basis *can* we ground a view in which reality is intrinsically ambiguous? This question has haunted philosophers and now may be destined to play a major role in 21st-century psychoanalysis. Neither Hoffman's nor anyone else's grappling with this issue can be expected to be conclusive.

It is also worth mentioning, even with an awareness that it is not likely to be persuasive to those for whom the avoidance of relativism takes priority in their pursuit of understanding, that the idea that construction is largely subjective need not lead logically or morally to chaos. If reality is, to a significant degree, socially constructed, people, to that degree, are circumscribed in the reality they can create independently. If, in addition, people are significantly circumscribed

---

[4] Roy Schafer also may have a bone to pick with Hoffman on this issue. Schafer (1992) states: "It would be arbitrary to insist that in consequence of interpretation only the reader has changed, for it can be argued that the poem changes with the reader as the reader becomes more expert. It is no longer the same poem. There is no determinate text of the poem. Markings on the page—the last resort of the *anticonstructivist*—are not the poem" (p. 184, emphasis added).

by the raw materials from which they construct, there would seem to be little chance that "anything goes." Thus may be derived the definite sense of the limits of possibility that circumscribes everything we do, this awareness of the historically meandering social channels within which we conduct our lives and that deepen and change with our passage, which may be central to our experience of reality. Hoffman does a great service by calling into question the exact nature of this experience. For insofar as his conceptions stimulate us to think more profoundly on how our understanding of current encounter is potentially anchored, not just epistemically, but also experientially, in terms of the course of our particular existence and the societies and historical circumstances in which our existence is carried out, Hoffman helps us direct our energy where it may be sorely needed— toward building a constructivist foundation for psychoanalysis.

2. What is the nature of human experience of reality as described in the writings of Hoffman?

Despite Hoffman's many qualifications, his constructivist model remains basically an attempt to ground psychoanalysis in the uncertainty inherent in continuous joint improvisation of reality. It is based on shared, necessarily speculative, interpretations of experience. This emphasis on the social nature of construction leads Hoffman (1998) to attempt to correct what he calls *"asocial conceptions of the patient's experience in psychotherapy"* (p. 99). He refers here to the classical perspective in which the analyst is the authority on reality for both the patient and himself (p. 110). If the analyst behaves with proper circumspection, the patient's flow of experience and associations is held to be independent of the analyst's personality (p. 99). Constructivism replaces this classical conception with a very different model. In the constructivist model, the analyst is as fallible as the patient whether he realizes it or not. In fact, the patient's transference is often very valuable corrective feedback concerning the analyst's unconscious behavior. Both the analyst's and the patient's experience is held to be deeply affected by their own participation and that of each other. Consequently, and most important, all psychoanalytic data are truly joint creations, "marked by a struggle with uncertainty," and never discoveries. For Hoffman (1987), the analyst ultimately finds his or her most solid ground specifically in uncertainty:

> The alternative that I am advocating is to have as a working assump-
> tion the idea that a patient's desires generally involve a complex,

shifting hierarchical arrangement of needs and wishes, and that it is virtually impossible to formulate an assessment of their relative weights and positions in that instant when the participating analyst is called upon to respond. After all, the analyst's actions (whether interpretations or other kinds of responses) are themselves embedded in and even partially constituting of this perpetually fluctuating arrangement of desires. Thinking it over is a response too, of course, which can be plausibly interpreted by the patient in various ways. The interaction within the session is continuous: there are no "time-outs" [p. 212].

It can be said of Hoffman that he looks much less for a solution to not knowing than he seeks a way of consciously conducting psychoanalysis within the context of uncertainty. Once the positive identification of an external reality is accepted as impossible, the separation of external reality from psychological factors that interact with it becomes almost moot.

To speak of "observable personality" in this climate and to organize an argument around the question of the relative weights of endogenous pressure and the influence of the external world without fully addressing the extent to which such terms and polarities are problematic are just too much fuel for the positivist fire, assuming, of course, that one has some interest in putting it out [1991, p. 87/1998, p. 146].

He adds in a footnote:

It should be noted that even "the most obvious, concrete observations that can made" are selectively lifted out of the "chaos" of "unfor-mulated experience" (Stern, 1983, 1989, cf. Gendlin, 1962, 1964). In another individual, in another culture, in another time, these "facts" might not matter in the same way or might not matter enough to be noticed at all [1991, p. 87/1998, p. 146].

In fact, it might be said that one cannot define an external reality at all without departing from a constructivist perspective. As suggested earlier, Hoffman's perspective is probably at its best not when it is attempting to answer the positivist question of what is "really out there," but when it adopts a positive stance toward not having an answer. Nevertheless, as indicated in the previous section, Hoffman cannot always resist speculating on what might be "really out there." This leads him to wrestle with the possibility that the experience of reality can somehow be distinguished from, or at least limited by, the order of things prior to a particular construction. Consider the following:

Neither the patient's experience nor the analyst's is some kind of silly putty that is amenable to any shape one might wish to impose on it, and, of course, even silly putty has properties that limit what can be done with it. Constructive activity goes on in relation to more or less ambiguous *givens* in the patient's and the analyst's experience. In fact some of those givens are virtually *indisputable* elements in the experiences of the participants and any plausible interpretation would have to take them into account or at least not contradict them. This goes for interpretations by each of the participants of experiences of the other as well as for interpretations that each directs toward himself or herself. Moreover, even the *ambiguous* aspects are not *amorphous*. They have properties that are amenable to a variety of interpretations, maybe even infinite interpretations, especially if we take into account all the nuances that language and tone make possible. But infinite does not mean unlimited in the sense that anything goes. There are infinite numerical values between the numbers 5 and 6. But that range excludes all other numerical values [1996, p. 111/1998, pp. 76–77].

When he uses the term givens for certain "virtually indisputable elements" that cannot be plausibly contradicted, Hoffman suggests that there is an objective reality even though the experience of it is ambiguous to various degrees. "More or less ambiguous" suggests the possibility of more or less not ambiguous; that is, more or less definite and, perhaps even more or less verifiable. Even with this view, Hoffman appears to drop the status of at least some of his interpretations from part of the creation of reality to that of reasonable estimates. His comments retain all the problems of positivism and add all the problems of relativism. In short, it is a positivism with very bad eyesight, and a relativism that keeps bumping into objectively hard things. Or at least lumpy things. Still, one has to respect the attempt, which is nothing less than an attempt to reconcile a putative abandonment of positivism with the common sense for which a kind of culturally accepted positivism has provided the common historical foundation. It is foreshadowed by, and is perhaps a variant of, Spence's (1982) simpler, but similarly insoluble dilemma: the dilemma of seeking to continue the search for a kind of truth intrinsic to psychoanalysis and finding that we ultimately cannot know it.

However, even ships that never touch the shore are dependent on their relation to it for their meaning. Freud built psychoanalysis on the shores of a positivist conception of history. No one can ignore that conception without losing a central source of the meaning of psychoanalysis. Hoffman plans to make the passage to a post-positivist port go as as smoothly as possible. He plans to use all the traditional language of psychoanalysis; only the meanings will be different. For example, commenting on a statement by Aron that "patient and analyst are both simultaneously subject and object," Hoffman adds:

> But that which is simultaneously both subject and object, is, in a certain sense, neither, because the meanings of those terms have been considered primarily in the context of their polarization. So we have to consider that we have moved into new territory where the boundaries among various categories have to be altered. In effect, we have new terms of discourse even if we continue to use old ones. As noted earlier, in connection with the polarity of endogenous pressures and perception, if it would not make our writing and speaking ridiculously cumbersome, we would and should be saying or writing "quote, unquote" all the time, for example, in conjunction with the terms *transference, countertransference, reality, fantasy, intrapsychic, interpersonal, subject, object, individual, and social* [1991, p. 98/1998, pp. 157–158].

What would these potentially cumbersome quotation marks signify? The marks seem to suggest that we are now able to see those processes in a more sophisticated, that is, constructivist, way. Beyond that, they simply define the original context out of existence. Although they will continue to refer to the same processes, they will be understood very differently. In effect, the terms will no longer carry their traditional meanings. Their traditional foundation will be deleted. There may be an assumption here that one can modify all the parts and the whole of psychoanalytic theory will still cohere and remain standing in the same or analogous ways. Yet that assumption is not supported in Hoffman's writings and is probably not justified. Hoffman does not really replace the foundation he removes. Where psychoanalysis once stood, Hoffman leaves only mystery. This may actually be a reasonable assessment of psychoanalysis's current state, but no overall structure can be maintained by a perspective that stops there.

One might also question whether any language can be commandeered in this way (see Schafer, 1976a, for discussion of a different approach). A more fundamental question, however, is whether Hoffman actually has a vested interest in keeping both the old language and its old foundation accessible. Certainly, he retains a need for some basis for making clinical decisons and assessments. Indeed, a consistent feature of his work is his attempt to provide the constructivist analyst with coping tools for dealing with the uncertainty of the clinical hour. At times, however, in the very act of delineating such tools he seems forced to call on old language and old terms. Consider the following clinical discussion:

In saying that I was disidentifying with the father's persecutory superego there is another imprecision that amounts to a kind of shorthand. I could only identify with the father to begin with to the extent that he had qualities akin to some objects of identification in my own life. Similarly, of course, the disidentification could only occur in my own experience relative to those internalized objects. No externalization (Sandler et al., 1969) of internal object relations in the patient can occur unless it finds a "mate" in the internal object relations of the analyst [1994, pp. 204–205/1998, p. 207].

This description contains as a vital component the perspicacity of unconscious processes, which Hoffman views as a central element in his constructivism. The component is troublesome in itself because it seems to suggest an unconscious objectivity. However, the passage also utilizes other concepts, which even quotation marks do not seem to bring within Hoffman's framework. What do the fairly precise mechanics of "disidentification," or even "internalized objects," mean in a context of not knowing? What is the basis for a rule that identification with a stranger requires identification with akin objects, when the one who reports such dynamics lacks "privileged access to [his] own motives . . ." (1994, p. 215/1998, p. 216) or anyone else's? Surely, uncertainty can not simply be disregarded as a consideration once it is acknowledged. And yet how else is Hoffman to proceed if he wants to communicate his constructivist insights to his fellow analysts?

Particularly noteworthy in terms of assessing his position vis-à-vis traditional psychoanalytic concepts are Hoffman's efforts toward new and supplementary ways of knowing. One important source of information for Hoffman is the patient's transference. Since this is, again, something that cannot be known directly because both its observation and its creation are changed by the analyst's participation, it is intriguing to observe that Hoffman believes that transference "acts as a kind of geiger counter which picks up aspects of the analyst's personal response in the analytic situation which might otherwise remain hidden" (1983, p. 408/1998, p. 119). Hoffman continues: "What the patient's transference accounts for is not a distortion of reality but a selective attention to and sensitivity to certain facets of the analyst's highly ambiguous response to the patient in the analysis. What one patient notices about the analyst another ignores" (1983, p. 409/1998, p. 119). Here we seem to be talking about a relationship between perception (transferential) and reality (the analyst's response to the patient) in which that perception is very acute, but very limited in breadth. This acute perception sees only a certain very few aspects of the analyst's complex and presumably varied behavior during the course of the many hours of the analysis, but it is not a distortion. Perhaps it is like a flashlight attempting to illuminate a whole landscape on a moonless night, but revealing only one small area vividly. However, this formulation, acute though it may be, comes with a price tag in terms of the consistency of the overall theory; for saying reality is seen selectively is quite different from saying it is inherently ambiguous or uncertain.

Another specific tool put forth to clarify clinical interactions is retrospective exploration, a psychoanalytic tool with its own considerable history. Hoffman, citing a communication from Gillet, sees that "[e]xperience, taken as a whole, is partially constituted by what we make of it, retrospectively, in the context of interpretation, and perspectively, in the context of experience shaping actions. Thus the term 'constitute' has different meanings in the retrospective and perspective contexts" (1996, pp. 111–112n/1998, p. 77n]. In other words, retrospective exploration is not only an activity focused in the past, but a chooseable, "experience shaping" present action that may actually be done with a focus on the future. Here Hoffman offers a specific contribution to a shift away from a psychoanalysis based on history.

At other moments, using the term critical reflection, he seems to focus on the past as the past and even to view the process of reviewing it as quite objective. Indeed, there are certain times when it would not be excessive to view his arguments as a slightly higher constructivist tower for a positivist perspective. Yet, at the same time, he suggests a focus on the process of construction itself which is extremely valuable.

> Psychoanalysis can be viewed as a psychologically complex kind of relearning in which a major objective is to promote critical reflection on the way the patient's reality has been constructed in the past and is being constructed interactively right now, with whatever amalgams of repetition and new experience the new construction entails [1991, p. 97/1998, p. 156].

Moreover, whatever towers Hoffman may be tempted to erect, he is at his most forceful in discouraging any confidence in just such hubris. Here he uses ridicule to make a point about clinical objectivity.

> I think we've clung to the idea that with continual hard work, analysis of transference and countertransference, and critical reflection, we can *neutralize* our personal and theoretical prejudices so that their effects will be negligible. Continual doing and undoing, that's the new solution. Our hands are *not* clean; we all know that now. But we figure that if we keep washing them maybe we still can get rid of most of the

dirt (or the blood), or at least enough so that what remains will not be detectable even by ourselves [1996, p. 109/1998, p. 75].

Other attempts by Hoffman to find clearer vision (or less dirty hands) within a constructivist vision also fail to provide much abiding relief for the self-consciously uncertain analyst. Such attempts include "objectivity" (in quotes), which Hoffman defines in this instance as "not an objectivity that enables the analyst to demonstrate how his ideas and expectations distort reality," but, interestingly, as "the tendency which is inclined toward understanding more than enacting" (1983, p. 413/1998, p.124). This tendency is not likely to become very dominant, however, because, as Hoffman notes (quoting Mitchell, 1988) the analyst must be "charmed," "shaped," "antagonized," and "frustrated" for the treatment to be "fully engaged" (1992, pp. 9–10/1998, pp. 187–188). Hoffman has also made the point that "at any given moment" the analyst can't tell to what extent he is resisting "the pull of the neurotic transference and countertransference" (1983, p. 413/1998, p. 124). He does recommend reliance on consensus, particularly (and essentially) with the patient, and, most important, valuing uncertainty itself (Hoffman, 1987, p. 211). Lest his readers work too diligently to counteract uncertainty, he wisely adds the injunction to avoid too much analyzing because "you are bound to suck the life out of the experience" (1996, p. 128/1998, p. 91). He also recommends avoiding a reliance on theory or research data in specific situations except to "sensitize the analyst to certain possibilities" (Hoffman, 1987, p. 208) and not to rely on "theoretically based convictions as to technical correctness" because "a strong sense of conviction of this sort is usually unwarranted and unfortunate for the process" (1996, p. 128/ 1998, p. 91).

It is consistent with Hoffman's approach that what may be his most significant guidelines for knowing involve minimal recourse to an external standard. He proposes a distinction between experience dominated by transference and experience that is not, the distinction being based on the patient's experience of patterns in his or her own behavior. Preceding his comments with the proviso that no aspect of the patient's experience of the analyst's inner motives can be "unequivocally designated" (1983, pp. 393–394/1998, p. 103) as distorting or faithful to reality, Hoffman goes on to state:

> In rejecting the proposition that transference dominated experience
> and non-transference dominated experience can be differentiated on
> the grounds that the former is represented by fantasy which is not

divorced from reality whereas the latter is reality based, the radical critic does not imply that the two types of experience cannot be distinguished. Indeed, having rejected the criterion of distorted versus realistic perception, he (the radical critic) is obliged to offer other criteria according to which this distinction can be made. For such critics the distinguishing features of the neurotic transference have to do with the fact that the patient is selectively attentive to certain facets of the analyst's behavior and personality; that he or she is compelled to choose one set of interpretations rather than others; that his or her emotional life and adaptations are unconsciously governed by the particular viewpoint he or she has adopted; and, perhaps most importantly, that the patient has behaved in such a way as to actually elicit overt and covert responses that are consistent with his or her viewpoint and expectations [1983, p. 394; 1998, pp. 103–104].

One aspect of these proposed differentiations worth highlighting is that they verge on suggesting a possible focus on interacting experiences of *patterns of constructing experience* rather than on observable individual behaviors or even observable patterns of external behaviors. This is an important idea not merely because it is potentially clinically useful, but because it suggests a method of clinical appraisal that is congruent with a constructivist view. (We build on this important idea in the final chapter.)

A characteristic of some of Hoffman's later additions to the constructivist analyst's set of coping tools is that they do not simplify and clarify his perspective. Instead they add almost infinitely complex dimensions to his perspective. We refer here to his concept of figure and ground as well as his conception of dialectical relations. It is important to note that neither of these concepts is offered as a model of reality, but only as a way of seeing it. With regard to figure and ground:

> The notion of figure–ground relationships is central to the transition to the social-constructivist paradigm. Often the change in the way things are viewed has the general form that what had been polarized between analyst and patient is now understood in terms of multiple, fluctuating, complementary figure–ground relationships within each of the participants. For example, when we reverse figure and ground, the patient's associations become interpretations, and the analyst's interpretations become personally expressive associations. Searles (1975) reverses figure and ground when he writes about the patient as therapist to the analyst. "We name our professional conferences as gatherings of psychoanalytic therapists and psychoanalysts. That aspect is in the foreground. But in the background, the fact is that there are few, if any, places where one could find a greater concentration of psychoanalytic patients." In general, it is a good idea to call

things by whatever aspects are usually in the foreground, with the understanding that the resulting terms often connote complementary aspects that are in the background [1991, pp. 100–101/1998, p. 160].

Ostensibly even more complicated than "multiple, fluctuating, complementary, figure–ground relationships," although obviously overlapping in many important instances, are dialectical relationships. It is impossible to overstate the growing importance of dialectics for Hoffman. As he noted recently, "Whereas I used to think of the great divide in psychoanalysis as that between objectivist and constructivist thinking, I now believe it is more to the point to say that it is between dichotomous and dialectical thinking" (Hoffman, 1998, p. 26). For his purposes, Hoffman has written, "[T]he following definition by Ogden (1986) has been useful: 'A dialectic is a process in which each of the two opposing concepts creates, informs, preserves, and negates the other, each standing in a dynamic (ever changing) relationship with the other' (p. 208)" [1994, p. 195/1998, p. 200).

In many instances Hoffman uses these two terms, figure–ground and dialectical, almost interchangeably. For example:

The relation between repetition of pathological aspects of the past and relatively new experience is usually highly complex and paradoxical. In fact, it is generally useful to view their relationship as dialectical, that is, each not only serves as ground for the other but is actually on the brink of evolving into the other (Ghent, 1992) [1996, p. 126/1998, p. 89].

This apparent interchange is accented by the peculiarly static and unlifelike image of two mirrors that Hoffman uses to provide a visual metaphor for his concept of dialectics. It is a metaphor that does not permit us to imagine a synthesis.

But when we think about the poles within each pairing in dialectical terms, we are challenged not only to recognize their obviously contrasting features, but also to find the effects of each pole upon the other, and even aspects of each pole represented within the other. One might think in terms of two mirrors positioned opposite each other so that we can see the endless series of reflections of the two within each. The relationship between psychoanalytic discipline and expressive participation is dialectical in that sense [1994, p. 195/1998, p. 200].

Hoffman uses these two tools repeatedly and often with extremely edifying results. For example, his discussions about breaking rules as opposed to maintaining analytic discipline (Hoffman, 1998, pp. 90–91), his ideas about self-expression for the analyst as opposed to a continual focus on the patient (p. 148), and, most important, his notions about the dialectic between the world seen as given and the world as constructed (p. 155) are important and fruitful. For Hoffman, every dimension of the psychoanalytic experience—and of human experience generally—is subject to being viewed in connection with its opposite. One could easily fill a page with mention of such pairs and their page citations.

The following quotation, which, again, draws on Berger and Luckmann (1966), summarizes Hoffman's world view and the heavy investment in dialectical reality he has built into his theoretical perspective. He has constructed a psychoanalysis in which "exposing" dialectics occupies a central place. And what he says in this context can also be taken as a summary comment on human experience generally:

> We all live in innumerable, concentric worlds within worlds. At the outer limits there is the sense of our mortality in the context of infinite time and space. Moving rapidly inward, we find human history, the cultures and subcultures to which we belong, and then our family and individual histories. The psychoanalytic situation can be thought of as a special kind of interaction designed to expose the dialectic between the activity of patients in constructing certain problematic aspects of their lives, past and present, and the pre-established givens with which they have had to live and with which they have to live now in the immediacy of the relationship with the analyst [1991, p. 95/1998, p. 155].

One particularly incisive and sophisticated distinction Hoffman also makes is between such dialectical relations and similar, but critically different experiential variants of the same relation:

> [T]he most useful and powerful differentiations that can be promoted in any psychoanalytic therapy are not between pathogenic types of interactions and their literal opposites but between such interactions and healthy variants of them. The believable and generalizable differentiations are not between an intrusive parent and an analyst who never impinges on the patient at all, but between one kind and degree of intrusion and another; not between a pathologically narcissistic parent and a totally selfless analyst but between such a parent and an analyst with narcissistic qualities that seem be to integrated with sincere interest in the patient's growth; not between a sexually abusive parent and an analyst who shows no evidence of sexuality, but between that parent and an analyst who, for example, compliments a patient

on his or her appearance in a way that could be construed as flirtatious, but who seems to be consistently respectful of the patient, attentive to his or her other qualities, and invested in the patient's development [1992, pp. 8–9/1998, pp. 186–187].

That paragraph suggests an ability to make small, but clinically crucial distinctions (and undoubtedly crucial too for the patient to continue to be able to make them in other relationships) that can be made only in the context of a fine grasp of a subtle and consistent social reality. Such sensitivity is part of the appeal of Hoffman's work, notwithstanding that it is otherwise at odds with his portrayal of the analytic hour as essentially ambiguous and uncertain.

Thus Hoffman engages in the paradox of developing an epistemology of not knowing and finds himself simultaneously moving toward offering an increasingly refined and complex awareness— an asymptotic approach to psychoanalytic knowing that seems likely to have an enduring impact on the future of psychoanalysis.

3. What is the nature of the communication of the human experience of reality as described in the writings of Irwin Z. Hoffman?

Hoffman's constructivism typically treats the distinction between reality and the experience of reality as moot and the communication of the experience of reality as a major mechanism in that reality's creation. Within the psychoanalytic hour the issues of reality, its experience, and its communication are inseparable. Our previous discussion has already touched on many of the points relevant here. Perhaps the major point to be added is that, in Hoffman's view, communication of experience, particularly verbal communication of experience, is subsumed under a broader category, that of participation. That is, Hoffman is concerned with all participation in interaction—not just that usually labeled as communication—which he sees as having a profound and formative effect on the experience of both participants in that interaction. Speaking of psychoanalysis undertaken within his "social paradigm," Hoffman states that "the personal participation of the analyst in the process is considered to have a continuous effect on what he or she understands about himself or herself and about the patient in the interaction" (1991, p. 77/1998, p. 136). He adds: "Not only is the patient's life story a matter of historical reconstruction, but also a piece of new history is being constructed right now in the immediate interaction" (1991, p. 78/ 1998, p. 137). Later, in the same article, he concludes more pointedly:

"Both the process of explication and the moment of interpersonal influence entail creation of meaning, not merely its discovery" (1991, p. 91/1998, p.150).

Given those statements, it seems reasonable to say that Hoffman has an almost semiotic understanding of communication. All experience signifies something to the person experiencing it. All experience is constructed as meaning. Everything that is experienced is understood as a communication regardless of how it may or may not be verbally acknowledged. In this sense, it may be said that Hoffman's view of communication is actually broader and more comprehensive than that of any of the theorists previously considered.

It is also significant that Hoffman acknowledges an important level of experience that is "relatively individual" and not primarily identified with an intersubjective field. For Hoffman, the relation between the social and the individual is both central and complex. Referring to this relationship, he says:

> The constructivist paradigm actually demands taking account of both relatively social aspects of experience and relatively individual aspects. Berger and Luckmann (1967) take pains to emphasize that "subjective biography is not fully social" and they discuss the dialectic between the individual and the social. Whichever aspect is in the foreground can be understood only in the context of its complement in the background [1991, p. 102/1998, p. 161].

Nevertheless, all reality is held to be ultimately rooted in its social context, and "[a]ppreciation of the value of uncertainty in practice goes hand in hand with appreciation of the intersubjective nature of the psychoanalytic process" (Hoffman, 1987, p. 214). Consequently, and most important, all psychoanalytic data are truly joint creations, "marked by a struggle with uncertainty" (1994, pp. 200–201/1998, p. 204).

4. What kind of knowledge can be reasonably acquired on the basis of information about the past acquired in a psychoanalytic session?

No knowledge can ever simply be "acquired" in a dialectical-constructivist framework. Even when Hoffman considers experience as relatively indisputable, its predetermination is never absolute. For one to respond meaningfully to this question, the word constructed must, to some degree, be substituted for "acquired." Even then, as extensively discussed earlier, the answer arrived at must remain, characteristically, uncertain. It is worth emphasizing, however, that the word uncertain is probably a very conservative term for describing the analytic hour, which is often portrayed in this perspective as considerably more dynamic and ambiguous than the word uncertain might suggest. Actually, to the degree that meaning is continually created as we go, then the knowing of meaning (uncertain or not) is not a goal but a process. Not only is this process not a thing that can be acquired, it is actually probably inappropriate to refer to it as ever "constructed," at least in any sense of the word that suggests the possibility of arriving at a final state. The process is not only uncertain, it is probably more precisely conceptualized as an aspect of the continuous and often erratic flow of life, a direct result of the flow of the meaning making of living persons. At any given moment, the word impression seems a better description of the results of that process than the word knowledge. Therefore, in Hoffman's dialectical-constructivism, it is plausible to suggest that knowledge is actually replaced by impressions, which are understood as constructions, although for practical purposes (perhaps even for such purposes as theory building) they must be treated as knowledge.

This perspective seems particularly relevant to the true-or-false concept of knowing embedded in the "false memory" controversy. Hoffman acknowledges this when he notes: "The swing of the pendulum in Freud's thought from literal seduction in childhood to drive-determined fantasy (complemented by phylogenetic memory) in the etiology of neurosis seems like a thesis and antithesis that are just begging for the synthesis that constructivism could offer" (1991, p. 86/1998, p. 145). This notable quote suggests a resolution to the "false memory" brouhaha in which both sides lose equally. If all perception (and its later recall) is construction, then obviously no independently "true copy" of the past is ever possible and even the implantation of memories is unlikely to be reliable. The question remains, however, particularly for those persistent researchers, lawyers, and aggrieved persons who remain on the trail of a reality where guilt and innocence can be found and punishment conducted: Where (and when) were the preponderance of materials used in the contested construction obtained? Hoffman, of course, provides no answer to this problem, which might please such tenacious searchers; and there can be no satisfying answer to such questions within the dialectical-constructivist perspective. There is no point outside of the inherently and pervasively ambiguous process of human perception from which a clear and objective view of a patient's disclosures can be reported. That does not mean that Hoffman himself does not make critical evaluations and decisions based on them. It means only that, within his perspective, he cannot provide the assertion of certainty about recollection that many members of a culture imbued with certainty about an objective external world have come to expect. To the contrary, his purpose, at least within psychoanalysis, is precisely to undermine such assertions.

Hoffman articulated some of the fine points of his position when he spoke about patients' misconceptions about their own history in 1983:

> [w]hat is corrected is not a simple distortion of reality but the investment that the patient has in shaping and perceiving his interpersonal experience in particular ways. Moreover, the past is not explored in a spirit of either finding out what really happened (as in trauma theory) or in the spirit of finding out what the patient, for internal reasons only, imagined happened (the past understood as fantasy). The patient as a credible (not accurate necessarily, but credible) interpreter of the therapist's experience has as its precursor the child as a credible interpreter of his parent's experience and especially his parent's attitudes toward himself (see Hartmann and Kris, 1945, pp. 21–22; Schimek, 1975, p. 180; Levenson, 1981). The dichotomy of environmentally induced childhood trauma and internally motivated childhood fantasy in etiologic theories has its exact parallel in the false dichotomy in the psychoanalytic situation between reactions to actual countertransference errors on the analyst's part and the unfolding of pure transference which has no basis or only a trivial basis in reality [1983, pp. 419–420/1998, p. 131].

The denial of the possibility that any observer can reliably make, or monitor in anyone else, a shift between objectivity and subjectivity, between external reality and psychic reality, is key to Hoffman's work. Hoffman's psychoanalysis is conducted in the shadow of the Pandora's box Spence reluctantly opened. Once Hoffman's premises are accepted, the designation of any thought or observation as fact becomes untenable. The ramifications of basic and intrinsic uncertainty may not yet have been fully explored by Hoffman or anyone else in psychoanalysis. There may be no technique, no form of "critical reflection," no wholesale redefining of basic terms, no simple acceptance of uncertainty that can mitigate that fact sufficiently to prevent the general undermining of the basic structure of psychoanalysis as it has existed heretofore, even in constructivist circles.

5. What kind of action can reasonably be taken on the basis of such knowledge acquired in the psychoanalytic session?

Hoffman, although accepting of the need to act and, when possible, act wisely, provides precious little in the way of concrete guidance about the analytic hour, and absolutely none regarding situations arising outside it. He does offer many general principles for within the hour which, although simple in expression (often to the point of verging on being social-constructivist homilies), often turn out to be extremely complex, dialectical, and, of course, uncertain in application.

> [W]hile general principles may provide a model or framework within which the analyst can comfortably work, they cannot dictate what the analyst should do at any given moment. So, for example, the analyst may operate with the general principle in mind that he is always a participant in the process, or that there is always more going on in the interaction than what is manifest or conscious in either the patient or himself, or that his overall posture should be consistent with the idea that the relationship is a means to an end, not an end in itself, but these and other principles leave much latitude for how the analyst might act in a particular instance [Hoffman, 1987, p. 207].

Hoffman contends that there is no definitive external basis for action outside the immediate (analytic) situation in which it occurs. Even the hard research much sought in the field generally is specifically discounted as a source of such guidance.

> My own position is that evidence that is accumulated either in case studies, even of the kind Edelson (1986) has called for, or in systematic empirical research does not justify anything more than tenable hypotheses that may or may not apply to any particular case. Even the most carefully designed hypothesis testing research that is addressed to specific psychoanalytic propositions, however valuable in terms of buttressing or shaping theory, in most instances should only be hypothesis-generating from the point of view of the particular analyst. In this respect, the results of such research are not unlike what one learns from a case study in that they sensitize the analyst to certain possibilities that may apply to a particular patient at a particular moment [p. 208].

Theory is similarly discounted. Multiple theories are particularly valued for their ability to free the analyst from the influence of any one theory.

Familiarity with various theories can widen the range of possibilities that we can consider in our work. Multiple perspectives interrelate in ways that are often reciprocally corrective and implicitly dereifying of each other. But no theory should be the basis for rationalizing a sense of anxiety-reducing certainty in practice where a good dose of psychoanalytic skepticism and uncertainty may be, ironically, just what the doctor ordered [p. 214].

One issue that seems almost paradoxical in relation to Hoffman's overall view arises from the fact that he often seems to suggest a very individual basis for the analyst's actions. Is Hoffman saying that meaning is determined socially, but action is an individual matter and you are on your own? Clearly, actions are the essence of the participation that creates social meaning and are neither isolated nor independent: "Both the process of explication and the moment of interpersonal influence entail creation of meaning, not merely its discovery" (1991, p. 91/1998, p. 150). Perhaps Hoffman (1998) is simply anticipating his conception of free will (p. vii). This indirectly raises another major area of concern about Hoffman's perspective. Put simply, Hoffman's perspective can be used to justify an infinite number of contradictory statements and actions. As noted earlier, there are outer limits, as there are when one is asked to select any number between two other numbers, but within the range of things from which a therapist is generally held to be able to choose many opposites remain.[5]

Lastly, let us consider a particularly controversial action—the analyst's sharing some of his or her feelings with the patient. Hoffman (1991, 1998) states clearly that "there are times when it makes sense for analysts to reveal some aspects of their experience to patients, including, when it seems pertinent, references to their reservations about doing so" (1991, p. 89/1998, p. 148). What are those times?

I believe that what the therapist does at such moments, although it may reflect a great deal of clinical and theoretical sophistication, is also invariably personally expressive and cannot be understood merely as the application of a principle of technique in any simple sense. Moreover, the full nature of what is expressed by the action is

---

[5] Putting aside any weighing of the potential value of contributions by this perspective to psychoanalysis, one must sympathize with the individual analyst methodically attempting to learn social-constructivism. A stronger word, such as pity, may be more appropriate for the new psychoanalytic student seeking to ground himself in Hoffman's perspective.

not transparent to the therapist, the patient, or anyone else. In the first place, behavior and the experience it reflects are intrinsically ambiguous and subject to a myriad of compelling explications and interpretations. In the second place, as a participant in an interaction, the analyst's ways of construing his or her own behavior and experience are bound to be influenced to some degree by unconscious factors. Such factors and their effects certainly cannot be prescribed. So what is not possible is that the therapist at such a moment will simply treat the patient with an appropriate intervention of some sort on the basis of a correct diagnostic assessment of the patient's general condition or even of his or her state of mind [1992, pp. 2–3/1998, pp. 180–181].

The concern that has historically fettered analysts in this regard is, of course, that the analyst's participation will befog and befoul the "blank screen" his or her visage is held to present, and thus the pure flow of intrapsychic material otherwise tapped by the patient's projections on that screen will dry up. The undercutting of this concern is one of Hoffman's major goals.

> The traditional idea that it is always better to explore the patient's wishes in this regard under conditions of abstinence and deprivation is another reflection of positivist thinking. The implication is that the "true" nature of the wish or need will be exposed if the analyst does not "contaminate" the field by yielding to the patient's pressures. In the constructivist model, whatever way the analyst responds is likely to affect what is then "found out" about the intensity and quality of the patient's desire [1991, p. 89n/1998, p. 149n].

However, the removal of the need to attempt to present a blank screen still tells us little or nothing about how or when to proceed. Elsewhere, Hoffman does have the largesse to admonish the analyst to subject his or her actions to "analytic scrutiny." He then adds that "[w]e also have to try to *act wisely* even while recognizing that whatever wisdom we have is always highly personal and subjective" (1996, p. 109/1998, p. 74).

Hoffman is notably astringent in his tone toward those who (like Stolorow and his colleagues) suggest that striving for perfect rapport with the patient's inner state might provide the best guide for the analyst's actions.

> I am anticipating that some might argue that perfect empathy and attunement, like perfect objectivity, are merely ideals to strive for with the understanding that we are always falling short of them despite our best efforts. My reply is that I do not think it is good to set up intrinsically irrational ideals that do violence to human nature.

Aspiring to walk on water and striving to be able to do that are bound
to *interfere* with learning to swim [1996, p. 22/1998, p. 86].

He adds that it is important to appreciate that

the analyst is always in a position of some uncertainty as to the nature
of what has emerged in the patient and in himself or herself as
wellsprings for action.
    Ultimately there is no escape from the responsibility that falls to
the analyst to act with as much wisdom as possible even while
recognizing the action's subjective foundation [1996, p. 127/1998,
p. 90].

Perhaps among the actions Hoffman recommends so imprecisely,
none come closer to the heart of the constructivist approach than
soul searching, negotiating, and changing: "The work requires an
underlying tolerance of uncertainty and with it a radical, yet critical
kind of openness that is conveyed over time in various ways,
including a readiness to soul-search, to negotiate, and to change"
(1994, p. 215/1998, pp. 216–217). It is the readiness for these three
actions, with their implied humility for the analyst, that may provide
Hoffman's greatest impact on how psychoanalysis is done. In general,
Hoffman makes us face that: "[W]hatever we can become aware of
regarding the cultural, theoretical, and personal-countertrans-
ferential contexts of our actions, some things are always left in the
dark. One might say that one of the contexts of our actions is always
the context of ignorance of contexts. And yet, act we must" (1996,
p. 110/1998, p. 76).

    Hoffman's perspective intentionally deepens the dilemmas it
explores far more than it guides.

    Overall, Hoffman's views are courageous in their acceptance of
the limitations inherent in the incorporation of a subjectivist view
into a psychoanalysis built on one's relation with an objective reality.
Like Spence, Hoffman confronts the limitations of modern psychoanalysis from deep within its structure. From that position, the
present situation may be clear, but the next step, understandably,
may be nowhere in sight. Given that, acceptance with integrity is his
wisest recourse, and he does that more fully than any major theorist
in psychoanalysis has thus far been willing to do. Although he too
may struggle against it, his greater acceptance of what Spence saw
with so much foreboding—the far reaches of a psychoanalysis with
no solid touchstones and no hope of arriving at one—has the potential
to help focus our view of both psychoanalysis and the world in which
it takes place.

Common Threads

$\mathcal{W}$hile my presentation has tended to highlight the differences in order to distinguish the perspective of each writer, there are many common threads in the ideas of Donald Spence, Roy Schafer, Robert Stolorow, and Irwin Z. Hoffman. This chapter is a very brief discussion of some of those common threads. The discussion is again organized on the basis of the five questions that served as the basis of our discussion of each author individually.

1. What is the nature of reality?

Each of these writer's diverse speculations about various issues related to the ultimate nature of reality lend themselves to at least a slightly different interpretation, but some generalizations can still be made. In particular, reality is always seen as having a significant degree of ambiguity, and that ambiguity is held to derive in large part from within the perceiver. Spence tends to blame that ambiguity largely, but not exclusively, on the limitations of human beings to perceive and communicate this reality. His view of the problem might be said to be like that of an early sailor who, although he suspects his compass never reads true north, still blames his compass and hopes for a way to improve it. Moreover, Spence seems to see, but never quite seems to accept, that the reality he perceives is potentially always intrinsically polarized by meanings that come from him and those around him. For Schafer, reality cannot ever be demonstrated.

Only versions are available, so the nature of reality is largely a moot point he does not trouble to ponder. Perhaps he can be likened to someone who, on discovering that there is no precious metal underlying the world's currency, feels quite comfortable designing and printing his own. Stolorow avoids the problem of external reality by limiting his stated interest to the subjective and its reifications. Perhaps a little like a person who begins by saying, "I don't know about art, but I know what I like," Stolorow ignores the external and pursues the truth through the eyes of individual experience, though he soon seeks to construct a highly sophisticated theory with which to generalize about that very endeavor. Hoffman vacillates about the nature of an underlying reality but ascribes an ultimate meaninglessness to reality per se and varying degrees of ambiguity to reality as we know it. By attempting to operate continually at the nexus of what he sees as two gradients of ambiguity, reality and its experience, Hoffman builds a structure of little solidity, but perhaps much wisdom. Like a psychoanalytic Talmud,[1] his works can profitably be perused for that wisdom by an individual practitioner, but one practitioner's conclusions regarding any specific clinical problem are likely to differ from those of another practitioner whose search is prompted by a similar concern. Because, in practice, Hoffman's approach builds such a highly sophisticated flexible structure on a quicksand of ambiguity, it is hard to say if his approach is destined to be widely accepted in years to come. It cannot, however, fail to contribute to the growing recognition of the problem of not knowing that is currently at the fore of psychoanalytic thought.

2. What is the nature of the human experience of reality?

The experience of reality is always, to a significant degree, an interpretation. In various ways and to various degrees, all the theorists whose work is discussed here make that assertion an important part of their perspectives. As the preceding pages have, we hope, made clear, this assertion is very different from almost all the positions Freud took regarding both an objectively knowable present and an objectively knowable past.

It is also important to note that each of these perspectives focuses on the products of subjective perception, that is, narrative or

---

[1] Hoffman (1998) has noted that the analyst "acts as a kind of secular clergy" (p. 14), and he considers it important to acknowledge and explore the moral authority inherent in this dimension of the analyst's role (pp. 5–10).

construction, without attempting to establish a foundation in a particular subjectivist understanding of subjectivity itself. That is, there is no consistent notion of how subjectivity works that differentiates itself from classical structural conceptions. These latter conceptions emphasize an ego that largely can and does observe an external reality—save for the subjective distortion and interference imposed on it by the unconscious. To be sure, a psychoanalysis that hails subjectivity as central and intrinsic to all perception is probably not best built on an understanding of subjectivity as interference. We suggest later, in the final chapter, the possibility of constructing a theory of subjectivity based primarily on conscious subjective experience, a theory that understands such experience as a creative process situated in subjective time and grounded in the accumulated subjectivity of the society in which it occurs.

In each of the men considered here there is a tendency to assert that knowing is more possible if one tries harder. By either retrospective introspection, decentering, or some similar process, one is able to reduce uncertainty and, perhaps, bring reality more into focus. The implication of that tendency is probably not best read as: through will power, we can sharpen our senses. Again, the traditional psychoanalytic view suggests that we can, by conscious editing, minimize such distortion as arises owing to the derivation of more meaning from the unconscious than is useful. In a framework where all meaning is subjective, the creation of a boundary between useful meaning and meaning that contaminates or is contaminated suggests incredibly discerning mental processes. Where all is subjective, the issue is no longer simply to cleave as closely as possible to what is really there. The perceiver must be able to discern not only the accepted reality, but the difference between a refinement enriched with meaning and an idiosyncratic embellishment beyond social utility. The possibility of such processes suggests a more complex conception of the reality principle and raises potentially stunning heuristic questions about just how such processes could be conducted structurally. If there is no objective reality to orient the process, what is the process organized around? How can we discriminate the imbuing of reality by the ego from wishful processes of the id? Can we discriminate healthy functioning from pathology? Such questions are inevitable when the underlying principle of the theoretical system subtending processes of perception and discernment is reversed. These questions merit further psychoanalytic consideration, and we speculate about them in the following chapter.

Time, a dimension of the experience of reality not heavily discussed by any of these writers but mentioned by all, is not an arena of significant conflict among them. For all of them, narrative or construction (or both) take place in the present, but only in the sense that all psychoanalysis takes place in the present. In an important sense, narrative here can be distinguished from construction in that narrative is timeless. It is timeless in the sense that we lose our present awareness of time when the focus of a narrative becomes our focus. It seamlessly transports us away from the time in which it occurs to the time it is about, which then virtually becomes the present. Narrative is timeless in exactly the same way that the unconscious is held to be timeless, and it is also bound by external time in exactly the same sense. For example, a given narrative can hypothetically be expressed and received virtually anytime, but its meaning is heavily influenced by the exact temporal context in which its contents are apprehended.[2] This emphasis significantly differs from that of Freud, for whom the context of both the present and the future was always primarily the past. Since time can be seen as a subjective experience underlying all other experience, any understanding of subjectivity should include some specific role for subjective time. Yet no such conception has been advanced by the writers we have considered, perhaps because they all derive their ideas in a psychoanalytic context, where time is external reality.

3. What is the nature of the communication of reality?

Looking for consensus on this question among the theorists we have considered, we can say that, for each of them, to a greater or lesser extent, communication always involves creation and not merely transmission of something preexisting and external to the communicator. It tends to be seen as a process specific to the moment and context in which it occurs and is not easily subject to generalization. Although the limitations of communication are variously acknowledged with regret, resignation, or appreciation in the authors' approaches, its essence remains uncertain, ubiquitous, and absolutely

---

[2] This simple formulation is, of course, different from a basic hermeneutic approach, which sometimes involves seeking to interpret a text purely in its own terms—a perspective Stolorow (and, even more, self psychology) approaches by way of the continual, uncritical validation of patients' subjectivities in their own terms. Girard (1986) provides a discussion of the limitations of this approach with texts that concern human affairs. He argues that the truth of a particular ancient text, which describes the causes of the plague in Europe as due to the poisoning of the water by the Jews, can never adequately be evaluated without additional modern knowledge of how diseases are spread and how anti-Semitism functions. This argument is equally valid for contemporary narratives of abuse.

central to the human condition. For each of the four contemporary writers we consider, communication is largely language arranged in the form of narrative.[3] While there are many critical and complex issues relating to narrative's inner workings, they yield priority here to broader concerns about the overall conceptions of reality and subjectivity that underlie our very idea of narrative. These very basic concerns include whether, in the absence of any pretense that our experience includes such a thing as an objective world, we can assume an ability to narrate anything about any*thing*. In an essential way, we are talking about a world without "things." Consequently, we are talking about a conception of language not as an approximation of things, but as a system for which we acknowledge that no definite referents exist.

How are we to evaluate narrative's significance if it has no definite referents? What does the very word communication convey to us? Obviously it means *something*. But so does any sound, say a sound the wind makes. As with the wind, one part of the answer seems to lie in that sound's meaning to us as cocreating listeners. To go further, however, perhaps it would be useful to conceive of language not as a reflection or sharing of our established knowledge, but rather as a reflection of our never knowing for certain. Perhaps, in this connection, we can say that words, even such words as communication, represent not simply an attempt to relate what we believe we know, but also an exquisitely refined attempt to complete, and even actually to share, something specific and personal that must remain forever incomplete. I refer here not to the gap between people but to something more individual. This gap is the personal one that lies between the experience we can never fully communicate and the world we can never fully know. It may be that the attempt to fill this gap is part of the essence of humanness. In this scenario, the sometimes maddening inexactitude of language can be seen as one of its greatest advantages and, paradoxically, its most accurate feature. In the next chapter we focus on our view of how of this gap affects us and how we may strive to fill it both individually and consensually by means of narrative. We use the term construction to describe our overview of this process.

---

[3] Whether that means it is limited to language is another question. This question involves further questions, such as, How much of experience or even communication do we refer to when we say "language"? If we encode all experience as symbols, at what level does the experience on which the encoding is based occur? What is the discriminatory power of a generalization about language if it applies to all experience? If experience is much more than symbols, how shall we understand that part which is much more?

4. What kind of knowledge can be gained on the basis
   of information gathered in a psychoanalytic session?

These writers hold in common that knowledge is always at least
somewhat uncertain and not reliably generalized to any other context. Among the important potential additional contributions of what
are grouped here as narrative approaches is the sheer humility they
imply as appropriate for psychoanalysts in their day-to-day work.
Nothing in any of these theorists' writing suggests that there is any
way for an analyst reliably to discriminate true and false memories.
Indeed, there is no way for the analyst reliably to discern an objective
reality in the past. And there is no sure yardstick for the analyst to
measure current distortions and thus to make universally valid
inferences about the structure of the mind that might themselves
serve as a basis of such measurements. Not only do these four
theorists as a group fail to offer a resolution of the false memory
debate, they approach the point where we could consider theirs to
be a joint declaration to the effect that psychoanalysis has nothing to
say on this question. It is true that Spence never surrenders his fight
to bring psychoanalysis within range of objective truth, and Schafer
never yields to any devaluation of his psychoanalysis simply because
it remains just one of many possible narratives. Neither does Stolorow
seem willing to part with intersubjectivity's access to the psyche's
internal structure and his ability to make inferences based on that
access. Hoffman too, at times, cannot resist the claim to know. And
yet all of them, especially Hoffman, have so undercut the ground on
which they might stand in any concrete instance of these issues that
whatever position they might ultimately choose to take retains almost
no authority to convince. Basically, we are left with a psychoanalysis
that, by virtue of an inability to detect a real past, also has no way of
even deciding what is unconscious distortion and what is not. Ego
and id can no longer be distinguished as a practical matter. Only
one kind of psychoanalytic knowledge remains—the knowledge of
a particular person at a particular time in interaction with another
person. All actions based on such knowledge must acknowledge its
humble origins, and, we might add, all actions should be judged
accordingly.

5. What kind of action can be taken on the basis of knowledge
   about the past gained in a psychoanalytic session?

The answer is fairly clear and contradictory: nothing is certain and
action must be taken, even if the action taken is no action. One action

that all these writers have undertaken on the basis of knowledge they have gained in psychoanalytic sessions is to construct theoretical perspectives. All these writers appear to seek to maintain a somewhat contradictory context for their narrative which not only includes a real world as we know it, but a real psychoanalysis as we know it. In a basic way, they seek to build on and be validated by subscribers to the psychoanalytic foundation their work is designed to undermine and replace. What they may be said to be seeking is a new psychoanalytic narrative that can reasonably be validated in the context of the traditional one (see Spence, 1982, 1987, for his suggestions in this regard). There also appears to be a largely unverbalized, self-justifying narrative in use by the writers discussed here which may bear more examination. That narrative seems to suggest, in each case, that their perspectives are actually a closer approximation of the "real" process of psychoanalysis than was the classical perspective. Yet subjectivity cannot logically be used as a foundation for statements about what is real. Just as it is a contradiction for proponents of physics' uncertainty theory to declare that their view is based on objective observation ("look! *nature* tells us that the world is not determined" [Schwartz, 1995, pp. 46–48]), saying that psychoanalysis is *objectively* uncertain involves a similar mistake.

In trying to assess and accept such contradictory positions, readers may be tempted to draw on conceptions of paradox or dialectics. Both of these terms describe a relation between two things which only apparently cannot be simultaneously true. Without pausing here to distinguish these two potentially powerful explanatory terms, we can say that their usage may mask certain contradictions that are neither dialectical nor paradoxical. It is true that the observation that a person can experience himself or herself as subjective and objective at the same time, or that people can create their social world and yet also be created by it, may be explained with narratives involving concepts of paradox or dialectics. These are complex, many-faceted relationships, about which either approach might have much to offer. Neither of the two terms, however, can justify two contradictory positions existing in exactly the same sense at exactly the same time. If one accepts that they can, one is abandoning much more than an objective reality. One is abandoning a basic feature of logic and, with it, a preponderance of the value of conscious discourse as we know it, including psychoanalysis. It is not reasonable to assert that we cannot know objective reality and also that this not knowing is the most realistic basis for a new psychoanalysis. Likewise, it is also not reasonable to assert that only by seeing through the lens of the subjective will we understand the *real* human condition. And it seems equally questionable to say that all reality is a construction, but ours actually works better. The best the proponents of any perspective discussed thus far may logically proclaim within the limitations of their perspective is that "it seems to explain things better to me." It is my position that such contradictions in the work of the theorists we have discussed are due to the fact that their work arises in the context of a discipline whose positivist underpinning permeates every aspect of its character.

This is especially true with regard to the data they consider. Although at key times the authors may struggle effectively against such underpinnings and have thereby achieved extremely worthwhile and original insights, their conclusions cannot totally escape the impact of the fact that the essential nature of the data with which each of them concerns himself remains largely the same as that of classical psychoanalysis. Spence, in particular, never forsakes such data, but largely directs his efforts to regain the secure grip on them which psychoanalysis once believed it had. Schafer simply retains his classical facts in narrative clothing. Stolorow posits an intersubjective field but typically focuses on individual psychic states and their invariant principles; and Hoffman brings his bold recognition of uncertainty largely to the same clinical questions that psychoanalysis has always addressed. Consequently, they do not offer significant areas of new data. This is not to say that they do not have imaginative ways of approaching old data. Rather, a new approach, based on new assumptions, should generate new data. Just as portrait artists add something that is not in photographs and the use of the special theory of relativity to plot a rocket's course adds data not even considered in charting the flight of airplanes, a constructivist approach should involve data of its own, data with which it is consonant in terms of logical self-consistency and also is uniquely qualified to describe. The data to be discovered here, I contend, concern the role of subjectivity in construction. While these theorists attempt to shift their focus from the objective to the subjective, they have little new and systematic to offer about subjectivity itself other than some degree of acceptance of its limitations. At present, a constructivist narrative that would point the way to such new data remains to be articulated. In the course of our discussion in the final chapter we attempt to lay some groundwork for just such a narrative. We approach subjectivity differently by making it the center of our concern. As part of this attempt, we view subjectivity as a process with characteristics that are themselves open to subjective interpretation and all data as primarily data about subjectivity itself. We hope thereby to begin the task of suggesting not only a slightly different perspective, but also some different "things" to explain.

In Search of a Constructivist
Metapsychology

$\mathcal{E}$ach of the perspectives explored in this book represents an effort to find a new ground for psychoanalysis. In each case that new ground does not include the assumption that there is an objective external reality that can be known and on which theories of individual development and psychoanalysis in general could be based. As we have seen, however, each of the writers considered, Donald Spence, Robert Stolorow, Roy Schafer, and Irwin Z. Hoffman, stops short in practice of the very abandonment of such an external reality that he proclaims, in varying degrees, in his boldest statements.

One possible reason for this stands out. As Gergen (1985) has pointed out, there is no other solid ground for psychoanalysis or any social science to stand on. There simply has not evolved, either from a narrative perspective or in the growing sophistication of social constructivism, a broadly endorsed alternative means of establishing agreement about what is true.

How can psychoanalysis proceed as a discipline, let alone a "science," without such a basis?[1] Obviously one possible answer lies

---

[1] Merton Gill (1994) described what may currently be a common adaptation to this situation: "A pragmatic view in which one's theory is constructivist but in which one works as though correspondence is possible may seem to be fudging principles, but it is the necessary stance of the clinician" (p. 155).

in a collective agreement not about reality per se, but about a process of investigation and a point of view from which psychoanalysis will proceed. On what grounds, though, could such an agreement or such a point of view be evaluated and chosen? In the absence of such an agreement, it is more than understandable why each of the writers considered here maintains some degree of rapprochement with classical psychoanalysis's roots in the claimed objectivity of early 20th-century science.[2] However, this lack of an agreement should not prevent us from exploring the implications of their work even beyond the point of no return.

In going beyond the point of no return, I have elected to speak of the search for a new metapsychology. Obviously, the term metapsychology already has a meaning in psychoanalysis. It refers specifically to the combination of the dynamic, economic, and topographic points of view. Here, however, I am using the term metapsychology in the more general sense of an overarching theoretical framework rather than referring to the specific application of the term established by Freud. The search is for a different theoretical structure with which to reorient psychoanalysis in keeping with recent constructivist and narrative contributions.

In the process of searching for a constructivist metapsychology for psychoanalysis, issues must be touched on that have, in other contexts at other times, concerned many, if not most, philosophers. It is important to stress that what is sought here is primarily a new *psychoanalytic* underpinning. The major burden of our discussion concerns a particular set of assumptions found in the constructivist writings considered earlier, assumptions quite distinct from those that have traditionally underlain psychoanalysis. The explorations conducted here do include some philosophic contributions (specifically Alfred Schutz's use of the concept of bracketing), but the explorations are geared more to present debate within psychoanalysis than to elaboration of philosophic antecedents; and they are more oriented toward creating a sketch of a metapsychological whole than to indulging in the many metaphysical debates that might be enjoyed about its parts.[3]

---

[2] It can be argued that Freud, in order to create the unconscious, which by its nature could never be empirically proven, was himself forced to begin to cut at those roots. Regarding such theory building, Freud (1915b) stated: "A gain in meaning is a perfectly justifiable ground for going beyond the limits of direct experience" (p. 167). His justification suggests a willingness to construct, long before he justified it in connection with clinical interpretations (Freud, 1937).

[3] Spezzano (1993) comments: "Philosophers are welcome to participate in the psychoanalytic or historical or literary conversation, but the point in our field, as in any field, is that they are in the conversation and not transcendent to it" (p. 15).

Obviously, an alternative metapsychological foundation must, to the degree it is utilized, profoundly effect the nature of any concepts that are erected on or within it. Consequently, we touch on the possible impact of the ideas offered here on clinical conceptions currently in use. In addition, we are interested in using the results of these explorations to begin to address the questions about memory and abuse which were raised at the very beginning of this book. To repeat, however, the explorations conducted here are done primarily with a view to suggesting innovation at the metapsychological level of psychoanalytic theory designed to be consistent with a variety of current narrative and constructivist positions.[4]

More is required of a metapsychology for a constructivist psychoanalysis than merely to assert that subjectivity be its exclusive focus. What is required is a theoretical perspective on subjectivity on which a constructivist psychoanalysis can be based. Such an understanding obviously can no longer ground itself on an objective external reality, nor, on the other hand, can it totally ignore that which subjectivity is subjective about. It also cannot simply leave subjectivity floating with no theoretical frame of reference in terms of which it might be understood. Finally, such an understanding, though even consistent, parsimonious, and focused clearly on the metapsychological dimensions under discussion, must itself be seen as subjective and not as an attempt to stake out a claim to a closer approximation to any external truth.

In this connection it is important to note that it is completely usual in our culture to use the words *a reason* to refer to something factual in an objective world which somehow accounts for our "reasonable" behavior. What is the nature of a reason for which no such referent—there can be none in a constructivist view—can ever be claimed? Such a reason must be based on "facts," which are always, to some unknowable degree, the creation of the reasoner. To make a necessarily very tentative approach toward a psychoanalysis based on a reason of this latter sort, it is essential to include the ideas of several writers not previously discussed here and to speculate in ways that may not typically be found in the psychoanalytic literature. Among

---

[4] Charles Hanly (1995) has suggested the broader category of "critical idealism," which clearly would include the approaches we have described as narrative. Hanly notes: "Analysts who propose idealism as an epistemology for psychoanalysis place themselves philosophically in the tradition of Plato, Descartes, Kant, Hegel and, in modern times, Husserl, Merlau-Ponty, Sartre, Feyerabend and the later Putnam." Hanly also notes that the use of hermeneutics does not distinguish critical idealists from what he calls "critical realists" though each makes quite different use of it (p. 903).

the writers to be included are Christopher Bollas (1992), Arnold Modell (1990), and especially D. W. Winnicott (1971).

Overview

The perspective offered here does not seek legitimacy by claiming for itself a "higher" objectivity. It simply claims to offer a perspective on the experience of knowing and, even more to the point, not knowing. It asserts that *all* knowing is a process that partakes only in some unknown measure of an uncertain reality and that, in the process of partaking in that uncertain reality—and only in that process—experience is created. Paradoxically, although based on ultimate ambiguity, this perspective unbendingly admits of no other way of knowing than the construction it posits, only other ways of construing knowing. This does not mean there cannot be fantasies (experienced qua fantasies) or theories (experienced qua theories) about what has not been experienced. It is to say that approaches to knowing human experience, such as psychoanalysis, may find more satisfaction by asking questions oriented to human experience and by accepting their own fallible experience of the answers they find.

At the bottom of every theoretical system may be found some basic ways of seeing the world that are shared by all the proponents of that theory. These ways of seeing include assumptions about what kinds of experience are most and least worthwhile. Such assumptions cannot be avoided. Truth, virtue, and objectivity, as well as their opposites, falsehood, sin, and distortion, are examples of how such experiences are labeled in other perspectives. The idealized experience that replaces truth or virtue in the perspective tentatively offered here is *optimal participation in construction*. This is, however, at best a term literally under construction. Part of the aim of this chapter is to contribute to the development of a meaning for this term.

The general characteristics of experience, as suggested by the previously discussed approaches, can largely be summed up in the following statement: Experience is always constructed rather than simply encountered, interactive as well as individual, unique rather than verifiable through repetition, a constantly subjective process rather than a series of discrete objectifiable episodes, and characterized by a constant flow of reciprocal modification in relation to other experience. The ideas presented in the following pages represent a nascent attempt to begin an integration and reformulation of these characteristics of experience. Although we consider a range of potential clinical understandings, particular weight is assigned to the relevance of the views put forth here in relation to trauma. Trauma presents a special theoretical and clinical challenge to any constructivist perspective because of the strong demand trauma can create in many patients and involved parties to know what "really" happened.

Premises

The view presented here involves some very basic premises. To outline them, it is necessary to introduce a few concepts and terms to refer to them. First, perhaps the easiest to communicate, is that everything we discuss is conceived as part of an overarching unitary process that ultimately can be understood only as a whole. In a sense, this has always been characteristic of psychoanalysis's understanding of the entire psyche. Here, however, the discussion of each aspect of our conception of the process of subjectivity is intended *primarily* to contribute to an overall view of a process of subjective experience.

Second, the overarching unitary process of subjective experience is seen as a cyclical one. This cycle possesses both a general human configuration and, in individual instances, characteristic elements of style and content. These characteristic elements of individual process are a major focus of our approach. That is, constructions about how a given person creates (or constructs) his or her reality is seen as more important than any particular experiential example of that process. Third, this cyclic process is considered as occurring in a sequence of time, which is itself subjective. That is, we are concerned with the experience of sequence. The general configuration of this subjective process can be traced through three postulated stages of experience within the larger cycle indexed temporally as "moments." These stages refer to a view of the moment prior to experience, the moment of experience, and the moment after. Since our focus is on the subjective experience, which is often described as constituting a personal "reality," we use the term reality in that subjective sense in reference to each "moment." The term experiential reality refers to the moment of experience itself; the term potential reality, to the moment prior to experience; and constructed reality, to the moment after. Each of these "moments" has elements in common with the others as well as unique characteristics; an example of an element common to each moment is memory. Memory is previously constructed experience, can be experienced itself directly (as memory), and has the potential to be experienced in the future (in recall). The description of each "moment" includes both the unique and the shared aspects of that period.

These three moments are themselves an arbitrary construction. We might have offered a variety of other ways of emphasizing the constant and endless intake and recycling of experience that consciousness performs. We have chosen the three moments described hence because they allow us to present some of the complexity of that intake and recycling process in an organized sequence. No separate clinical relevance can be attached to any of these moments. Considerable clinical relevance is intended for the process as a whole.

Experiential Reality

Any focus on conscious experience tends to order the process in a certain way. Since our overall conception is that of a cycle, our description can begin equally well with any part or "moment" within that cycle. Experiential reality is considered first because it is our major focus in the process being depicted. Neither the concept of potential reality nor that of constructed reality can be understood in our framework without it. We reserve the term experiential reality for that moment when conscious experience occurs—it is that moment which we experience as the present. It is the ongoing instant when construction is experienced as complete. That is, what is seen is held to be what exists exactly then. This act of experiencing typically involves components that spring from two sources: (1) an uncertain external world and (2) an equally uncertain subjectivity of the experiencing person. Unfortunately, there is no pot in which to boil down this moment of experience and identify its exact components or their proportions. Stephen Mitchell (1992) appears to recognize a similar state of affairs when he states that "human experience is fundamentally ambiguous" (p. 280).

Because of its fundamental ambiguity, this conception of experience must remain both basic and general. If, however, instead of focusing on the sources of the experience we focus directly on our view of experience itself, some apparently slight, but actually very important, changes in the terms of our discourse become possible. If, instead of speaking of sources of the process of experience, we speak of specific elements within that process, it can then be reasonably asserted that two specific basic elements are needed for experiential reality to take place. One is consciousness; the other is that of which consciousness is conscious. Obviously these two concepts are embedded in each other. One cannot exist without the other. Interaction between them, when considered from a subjective level, is organized as unitary, meaningful experience. Such interaction, when considered from a theoretical level, can be called construction. It is a basic and essential assumption of this perspective that some degree of construction occurs constantly when consciousness is present. Construction can almost be said to have a place in this perspective analogous to that of friction in the basic mechanics of physics. No interaction between consciousness and that of which it is conscious occurs without it.[5] Consequently, on the subjective level, there can be no such thing as experience without construction. Consciousness is always construction. This says nothing about how optimal the construction process may be, or how consensual, or useful, or gratifying the results may be deemed in any individual instance. These are obviously important questions, questions that are the legitimate province of psychoanalytic treatment. More speculation about them is presented later.

One basic principle of construction may be that it represents an attempt by consciousness to create experience capable of being organized into an integrated whole in accord with standards that are themselves socially constructed. That is, no matter whether the analyst posits a need for organic homeostasis, a self with selfobject needs, or a general need for relationship with significant others, experiences must be integrated in order to proceed. Without a significant degree of such integration, we cannot proceed as a unit in any direction and the structure of our lives will truly resemble that of our dreams. The psychologist William James once elaborated this idea in a currently relevant and still provocative way: "ideas . . . become true just in so far as they help us get into satisfactory relations with other parts of our experience" (quoted in Rorty, 1996, p. 7).

For now, it is sufficient to establish that, in this discussion, consciousness is also always construction and that the construction of reality is the only experience of reality. This conception appears to be similar to what Loewald (1960), speaking through and perhaps beyond his distinctly classical background, has expressed so succinctly: "there is neither such a thing as reality nor a real relationship without transference" (p. 254).

---

[5]Analogues with the physical have been a dangerous tradition in psychoanalysis because they have opened the door to reification and levels of literal elaboration that arguably have been deadening to the development of psychoanalytic understanding (for a classical discussion of such comparisons in relation to the notion of internalization, see Schafer, 1972). Because such metaphors can also have incredible power as narrative short cuts, however, they are occasionally employed here. Obviously, no literal relation of any kind to any physical process is intended.

Constructed Reality

Constructed reality simply refers to constructions whose basic character endures and remains available to consciousness after the first time in which they were constructed. Such constructions are, however, inevitably, at least to some degree, constructed afresh each time they return to the focus of experience. They are, to quote Donnel Stern (1997), "what we *can* make *now* out of what we *have* made *then* . . ." (p. 4). For this process to achieve coherence, it is critical that its cyclic nature be underlined. In this process, when the external world is subjectively encountered, it becomes an experienced reality. Experienced reality endures as constructed reality, which, once it slips from consciousness, reemerges only as a kind of potential reality, to be reinterpreted to some degree once more as current experience. For example, with regard to constructed reality, the act of reading a favorite (already constructed) poem may be experienced very differently when the reader is alone and it is raining outside than at a later date when other activities and people compete with the same poem for the reader's attention. More important, a childhood remembered alone may be experienced very differently than when it is recalled within the context of a session with an analyst (see Modell's, 1990, discussion of Freud's concept of *Nachtraglichkeit*, especially pp. 15–19). Often, however, the additional construction added to constructed reality is probably slight. A sink or a sidewalk may be constructed very similarly every morning. Usually, a cigar is just a cigar. Consequently, we must say that the term constructed reality can be used to refer to any constructed experience regardless of how much modification it may undergo in future (re)constructions. It can be used to refer to constructions currently existing between an earlier construction and possible reconstruction in current experience. It can also refer to the large body of constructions whose basic subjective character is closely approximated again and again in slightly different circumstances and by different people. It is in this latter sense that we can say that "reality in the world, like realism in a picture, is largely a matter of habit" (Goodman, 1978, p. 20). Another way to refer to this kind of "habitual" reality is as consensual reality. Obviously, there is no way any individual can directly experience the consensual aspect of a reality because experience, while always socially constructed, is always experienced individually. Nevertheless, the concept is an important part of our experience as well as of our perspective here. Consequently, we offer a brief working definition specifically of the constructed reality we refer to as consensual reality. That definition is restrictive in that it limits consensual reality in three ways: 1) its construction can be experienced as habitual and reflexive; 2) its construction requires no present interaction with particular others; and 3) part of its construction involves an assumption and an intermittently recurring experience of social validation that it is shared.

Potential Reality

Potential reality, the third "moment" considered here, is proposed as a concept to resolve a critical metapsychological question. The question is about how we regard the nature of the world external to consciousness. It is the question raised, but left unanswered, by the basic shift in focus proposed in different ways by each of the writers we considered earlier. The shift in focus referred to is the by now familiar one away from the evaluation of subjective experience of an objective reality and toward the acceptance of subjective experience as the sole experience of reality to which psychoanalysis has access. Once this shift is accepted, it remains necessary to select from a variety of ways to regard the existence of an external world. Without this selection, no shared theoretical frame of reference for a constructivist psychoanalysis is possible. Construction must be of something, else there is no contextual framework for subjectivity. But all frameworks, even when shared, are not equally useful. Psychoanalysts surely cannot maximally help patients cope with their day-to-day lives by taking a purely solipsistic position that no world exists except in our minds. It is similarly doubtful that they can simply say, as Stolorow sometimes has seemed to suggest, that the external world per se should not concern us at all and that, in fact, thinking of the world as independent of our experience at all is a form of reification of our experience (for example, see Stolorow and Atwood, 1992, p. 92). We could, with Spence (1982, p. 54), think of the external world as something to be increasing approximated.[6] This option, however, merely seems to wed the uncertainty of constructivism to all the limitations of the traditional objectivist view of reality.

The issue of external reality from a subjective point of view has been much pondered in philosophy, especially in the branch of

---

[6] The psychologist George Kelley (1955) has expressed a similar idea most interestingly in the context of his individually and exclusively cognitively oriented discussion of constructs. After affirming the conventional reality of the world and of the reality of ideas he adds: "though the correspondence between what people really think exists and what really does exist is a continually changing one" (p. 6).

philosophy called phenomenology. Edmund Husserl, and, in particular, his student Alfred Schutz, dealt with it in the manner least likely to impart unintentionally additional connotations. They used the methodological device of "bracketing" (see 1970). "Bracketing" in this instance refers to a deliberate setting aside of all ontological questions about the essence or nature of "things" so that the mental process of experience remains the central concern. Our approach is similar in many ways, but we remain concerned with the nature of things insofar as they enter into our understanding of the nature of experience. The possibility suggested here is that the world external to subjectivity be framed as potential experience, that is, not as things in themselves, but only as one constant source of one component of subjective reality. This idea does not involve the elimination of external reality from our formulations but emphasizes its constant inclusion as essential to subjectivity: subjectivity is always subjective about something. In fact, although ambiguous, the existence of an often undeniably present world demands that its constant impact be recognized. Construction cannot occur without it.

The concept of potential reality is construed here as everything existing in time prior to the moment of experience and viewed from the perspective of its potential impact on experience. Seen in this way, potential reality refers to much more than external reality; that it includes, without exception, everything that is not (yet) the focus of consciousness. By allowing our discourse to include previously unknown elements of the external world which continually affect us, we open the door to consideration of all the critical aspects of human existence of which we are not conscious. It is not logically possible to posit the influence of an external world that exists prior to becoming part of our reality without including in it the equally credible concept of unknown aspects of ourselves with the same potential. Such aspects obviously must play a major role in any psychoanalysis and consequently play an equally great role here in our discussion. More specifically, the processes described in the psychoanalytic concept of the unconscious must be included in the category of potential reality.

To take this point one step further, we can say that not only are potential reality and experiential reality intrinsically related, but neither can even be conceptualized without the other. Ogden (1986) clearly sees consciousness and unconsciousness in this way. He refers to them as dialectically related: "In psychoanalysis, the central dialectic is that of Freud's conception of the relationship between the conscious and the unconscious mind. There can be no conscious mind without an unconscious mind and vice versa; each creates the other and exists only as a hypothetical possibility without the other"

(p. 208). This is a view with which a constructivist metapsychology must agree. We would add, though, that this dialectical relation extends to all of potential reality and not just those aspects of it that are internal.

Just as there is in the traditional psychoanalytic view never a way to know the unconscious directly, there is no way of directly knowing what is included in our more general concept of potential reality.[7] In psychoanalysis there has been an unfortunate tendency to assert a direct knowledge of the unconscious, a tendency not only to talk of travel on the royal road toward the unconscious, but to speak as though analysis regularly visits there. Transparently, dreams, parapraxes, fantasies, and free associations are, to the degree that we become conscious of them, no longer part of the unconscious. Although they are undoubtedly indicative of the contents of the unconscious, we have no way of knowing to what degree. Like all potential reality, they undergo construction as they are experienced. From this perspective, it is reasonable also to consider them as examples of the nature of construction. We can hope that speculations based on such data might tell us something about how we consciously construct new material; perhaps they might even give us clues to the source of that material.[8] Of course, if this is true, we should be able to see some similarity between how we treat our dreams, for example, and how we consciously treat new material coming from a variety of other sources. This similarity might be accentuated when, in both cases, the material is too complex or accumulates too rapidly to process instantaneously. To examine this possibility, we need to ask: does the structure of our experience in all situations we initially see as confusing or chaotic have common elements? I suggest that such common elements exist and that they must be considered intrinsic to the transition from potential to experiential reality. Further, as I propose later, individuals make this transition in characteristic ways.

Memory

All constructions, to some degree, function as context for every subsequent construction. In fact, in the exact sense that each con-

---

[7] Speaking of the unconscious, Freud (1915b) said: "It is of course only as something conscious that we know it, after I has undergone transformation into something conscious" (p. 166).

[8] Matte-Blanco (1988) makes a related point when he notes that the asymmetrical logic of the deepest levels of the mind are only known to us through the logic of the more conscious mode. He suggests the possibility of a logic that could include both (p. 92).

struction changes the total consensual context in which it occurs, each construction changes the totality of the individual's constructs. Constructions do not disappear into separate files in the unconscious or just become buried under new archeological deposits. It may be reasonably asserted that though previous constructions no longer occupy the focus of awareness, they are never totally beyond the reach of consciousness. In fact, the flow of conscious experience out of present awareness is probably best seen not merely as into storage away from consciousness, but equally well as more like the wake of a boat, which shifts from its moment in foreground to a lifetime of receding and changing shape. To encounter what remains of any section again requires only turning consciousness' attention back and plowing through it again. This metaphor, while extremely limited, underlines one point: Memory can be conceptualized as a constant part of the process of constructing reality and as never completely severed from consciousness. Thus, consciously integrated contributions of conscious experience may endure in consciousness as receding background until present consciousness returns them to the fore.

Something similar to what can be said about remembering can also be said about forgetting. For example, Jacob Arlow (1995) has suggested that forgetting itself is an active and informative process. As he made clear, memories that hide by substitution or distortion also continue to index that which they seek to hide. With such apparently contradictory, but succinct statements as, "Every bit of forgetting is a form of remembering," "We cannot forget what we are unable to recall," and "It seems that we remember in order to forget and that we succeed at neither," Arlow points directly at the paradoxical nature of memory when it is studied from the perspective of conscious representation of the past. Things forgotten may still be experienced as very important and as a source of great frustration (e.g., the location of plane tickets) or as events too terrible to remember, in which case their inaccessibility may be a relief. On this basis, even forgetting must be seen as a construction. Consequently, in the perspective offered here both memory and forgetting are seen as contributing to future construction and as constructions in themselves.

The Social Context of Construction

A psychoanalyst's interest in the sharing of constructed reality tends to be focused on the smallest social units, that is, primarily formative dyads as well as the psychoanalytic couple. It includes shared realities in infancy and in fantasy, as well as those such as a patient's often remarkably similar experiences with mother, lover, and analyst. We cannot, however, adequately represent the notion of constructed reality without alluding to the very broadest social implications. As Jerome Bruner (1990) has said, "To treat the world as an indifferent flow of information to be processed by individuals each on his or her own terms is to lose sight of how individuals are formed and how they function" (p. 12). It is necessary, for even the briefest explication of the concept of constructed reality, to expand our discussion beyond individual, or even small group, experience. Historically, the achievement of broad consensus has been offered as a final proof of the objective nature of reality. In this view, consensus is no longer evidence of "objective" reality but is itself a central form of construction.[9] For example, in infamous colonial Salem, many people experienced "witches," to whom they might have assigned quite different identities only a few decades earlier or a few hundred miles away.

To explain adequately the social significance of constructed reality, even for our limited purposes, requires a brief return to the concept of narrative. The terms narrative and construction (or social construction; see Hoffman, 1991, p. 74) are related subjective processes that were defined earlier.[10] In the context of the process we are presenting here, the term constructivism directs our attention specifically to the complex moments in the process when the experience of reality is created; and narrative refers specifically to its most overt, verbal, and often social expression. Narrative creates an experiential reality for the listener, but, for the narrator, much of what is presented is obviously already constructed.

Consequently the term narrative applies most fully when we consider the social elements of what we have labeled constructed reality. In addition, the term brings our attention directly to the subjective dimensions that such terms as communication tend to frame

---

[9] Schlesinger (1995) has noted, in an observation relevant to the reliance on consensual standards of reality, that there are more people who have reported sightings of UFOs than there are psychoanalysts.

[10] Gill (1994) has provided an additional general working definition of constructivism: "Constructivism is the proposition that all human perception and thinking is a construction rather than a direct reflection of external reality as such" (p. 1). For an definition of narrative see Polkinghorne (1988, p. 11). This excellent definition was cited earlier and again in this chapter.

as error.[11] Polkinghorne's (1988) definition of narrative (previously quoted, but worth repeating) is particularly rich in this regard:

> a scheme by means of which human beings give meaning to their experience of temporality and personal actions. Narrative meaning functions to give form to the understanding of a purpose to life and to join everyday actions and events into episodic units. It provides a framework for understanding the past events of one's life and for planning future actions. It is the primary scheme by means of which human existence is rendered meaningful [p.11].

To this we might add that narrative provides a means for sharing the meaningfulness of human existence, a possibility without which human existence not only would not be truly human, but would not psychologically, or ultimately even physically, survive.

Narrative is an essential part of the cyclical nature of the process of construction. Part of narration is itself cyclical because the narration a person experiences is an essential part of what he expresses toward others, which is, in turn, part of the narration he receives. The popular saying, "What goes around comes around" is both a summary and an example of that process. Berger and Luckmann (1966) express similar ideas more sociologically. With regard to the social transmission of knowledge, they state, "An important principle for our general considerations is that the relationship between knowledge and its social base is a dialectical one, that is, knowledge is a social product *and* knowledge is a factor in social change" (p. 87). Commenting even more basically in regard to human nature, they say, "While it is possible to say that man has a nature, it is more significant to say that man constructs his own nature, or more simply, that man produces himself" (p. 49).[12]

---

[11] A typical definition of the term communication includes: "The exchange of thoughts, messages, or information, as by speech, signals, writing, or behavior" (*American Heritage Dictionary*, 1991). The implication is that the communication is of some objective *thing* separate from the communicator or even the manner of communication, which, in the absence of error, is to be sent and received uniformly. We use the term communication only as a convenient way to refer to both the expression *and* reception of a narrative as a single interactional exchange.

[12] Gadamer (1960) (discussing Husserl's approach) offers a similar idea with a different emphasis. Coming from a particular place in what we have called the cycle of construction, he notes that an individual's experiences are derived from their relation to the total experience of humanity. "The flow of experience has the character of a universal horizon consciousness, and only from it is the discrete experience given as an experience at all" (p. 245).

Narration involves much more than just the receiver and sender, and much more than a single isolated instance of communication. Because in every social group (community, family, dyad) narration is recycled again and again, and because older narrations serve as context for newer ones, we are really talking about a continual flow of social construction with no definite boundaries.[13] In this perspective not only all narration but, through the process of communication, all experience, ultimately serves as context for every subsequent experience within any community. Through narration, all experience is partially woven both by and from the community in which it occurs. In fact, one definition of community might be the degree to which that process occurs. Since our focus is not sociological, we will not attempt to explore the degree to which any particular group, or the entire population of the world, is effectively a community by this standard. We can, though, posit that in the same sense that a fly landing on a skyscraper moves it slightly, or that the famous Chinese butterfly of chaos theory might eventually transform storm systems in New York (Gleick, 1987, pp. 8, 20–23), any communication anywhere in the world is part of the total (ongoing) construction of the world and contributes to context everywhere. Because of the limitations of space and language, we cannot maintain a focus here on the full breadth and complexity of this process. Insofar as our interest is chiefly psychoanalytic, our sharpest focus here is not on society as a whole, but merely on each experiencing member of the analytic pair. This perspective, however, is partially defined by, and ultimately cannot cohere logically without, its larger social context.

Paradoxically, the continual flow of narration can also be experienced by a participating individual as a dilution or loss of personal meaning. At the simplest level, a secret repeatedly shared typically loses its charge. Winnicott (1971) described just such a

---

[13] Levenson (1991), in his exploration of the utility of general systems theory systems for psychoanalysis describes an open system as "one which is in continuous exchange with its environment. . . . able to import energy from the outside and maintain itself in equilibrium. Depending on the level of openness, it can either maintain its level of organization (homeostasis) or it can actually increase in complexity" (p. 50). Citing Von Bertalanffy, Levenson quotes: "Man is not a passive receiver of stimuli coming from an external world, but in a very concrete sense creates his own universe" (p. 50). The significance of general systems theory here is that it constitutes a distinct body of theory about process in which, at the highest level of open-system complexity, many of the characteristics attributed to the psychological process described here are anticipated.

process. He accounted for this experience purely subjectively. That is, it occurs not because of any postulated objective spread of narration, but because it is perceived that way by the initiator. For Winnicott, the dilution occurs "because the transitional phenomena have become diffused, have become spread out over the whole intermediate territory between 'inner psychic reality' and 'the external world as perceived by two persons in common', that is to say, over the whole cultural field" (p. 5). This dynamic can be said to be at the nub of a paradox that has particular meaning for psychoanalysis. Meaning may be individually lost as it is socially constructed. This paradox may lie near the core of Freud's "talking cure" (in many cases, a particular loss of meaning may well be what is sought). It also may lie near the core of what may be a virtually universal need for fresh experience.

Discussion

Psychoanalytic Antecedents

Insofar as the metapsychological viewpoint we are attempting to sketch here has arisen largely through the contemplation of the efforts of contemporary theorists working within psychoanalysis, it is to be expected that much can be found within the psychoanalytic tradition which in one way or another anticipates what we have to say here. Put another way, as we search for a kind of data that a self-consistent constructivist metapsychology is particularly qualified to describe and interpret, we do well to consider that some of that data may already be in evidence, though currently described in a different, possibly less consistent, and perhaps more metaphorical fashion. With this in mind, let us briefly examine some of the thinking of Winnicott, Bollas, and Levenson.

If we look for related formulations in the annals of psychoanalysis to inform the cyclic process of reality we have sketched here as part of a basis for constructivism, there are many possibilities. Certainly Freud's structural construction of the id, ego, and superego have relevance. Placed in a temporal framework, the id clearly initiates purely subjective impulses, the ego mediates the ever-present interface of those impulses with the external, and the superego is the repository of influential prior constructions handed down from generation to generation. This congruence is, however, quite limited, and the element of process, particularly cyclic process is, in Freud's work, largely implicit.

Parallels can be more easily found in the formulations of Winnicott (1971) regarding intermediate space and the experiences of internal and external reality within which it occurs (particularly as elaborated by Modell, 1990). To make even the most basic comparisons with Winnicott's work, however, it is necessary to redefine the basic context of his concepts in keeping with a social-constructivist perspective. Winnicott's term designates a space that is intermediate between an objective external reality and a psychic reality operating in relation to that objective external context. Here that space is seen as intermediate between two aspects of a subjective reality, that is, between what the individual is currently experiencing to some extent uniquely and that which society has, in large part, previously collectively constructed. Similarly, Winnicott's spatial metaphors must be assumed to correspond significantly to the sequential framework implied here. However, with such audacious leaps, Winnicott's three spaces—internal, transitional, and external—may be stretched to bear a suggestive relation to what have been referred to here as three moments in the cyclic process of construction. More specifically, Winnicott's concept of internal space may be related to some of the unique internal facets of experiential reality, transitional space may be seen as the setting where reconstruction takes place, and external reality can be viewed as constructed (consensual) reality, which typically appears as established in external space. Notwithstanding the perils of translation, Winnicott's views about each person's experience of transitional space can inform our conception of that initial vulnerable instant in each construction during which integration into a unique meaning begins. Consider his statements that "the third part of the human being, a part which we cannot ignore, is an intermediate area of *experiencing*, to which both inner reality and external life both contribute," and that "it shall exist as a resting place for the individual engaged in the perpetual human task of keeping inner and outer reality separate yet interrelated" (p. 2).

Winnicott's overview of the dynamics of this process notes its role as a refuge from stress: "It is assumed here that the task of reality-acceptance is never completed, that no human being is free from the strain of relating inner and outer reality, and that relief from this strain is provided by an intermediate area of experience which is not challenged (arts, religion, etc.)" (p. 13). Part of what may be garnered here that is equally valid for our perspective is that, when experience is not pushed out of balance toward conformity to consensual reality or toward accommodation to shrill psychic demands, the dynamic of the process of "relating inner and outer reality" can be an experience that may be considered integrative. The concepts of a balanced process and of a goal of maintaining a constant level of integration are a nascent formulation of a clinical standard for evaluating construction. Clearly, the development of such evaluative standards is essential for a perspective that focuses on the process of construction.

In general, the three kinds of personal spaces suggested by Winnicott can perhaps be most meaningfully seen as ways of conceptualizing parts of consciousness' overall experience of itself during each of the phases of the process we have sketched here. That is, the human process of creation of meaning may intrinsically involve some personally idiosyncratic things whose character and acceptability, especially to the person from whom they spring, is very much uncertain, some things experienced as indisputably and consensually certain and, some things offered up for transition from one to the other—thereby creating unique experience and eventually changing what is regarded as certain. It is important to add that, in this reformulation of Winnicott's work, all construction—that is, all experience—starts, ends, and to *some* degree exists only as transitional phenomena (i.e., construction subject to continual possibilities for reconstruction). Consequently, all experience also is to some degree, first possession; that is, even the most repetitive experience is constructed each time, to some degree, in a new way and is, to that degree, a fresh experience. Both transitional phenomena and first possession are seen here as intrinsic parts of the process we describe as a continual and intrinsic aspect of consciousness—the creation of reality. Like Winnicott (1971), we are "concerned with [the experience of] the first possession, and with the intermediate area between the subjective and that which is [experienced as] objectively perceived" (p. 3). Such constructions in transition clearly lie at the heart of most psychoanalytic sessions. They may also lie at the heart of experience in general.

Some interesting extrapolations of the basic ideas expressed here can be found in the recent work of Christopher Bollas (1992), provided we continue to allow ourselves the freedom to translate into our own frame of reference. Bollas's highly sophisticated and often literary style is, though rich in layers of meaning, often difficult to pin down. Rather than limit himself to a positivist or a constructivist discourse, he simply uses his verbal skills to span them. Thus, Bollas (1987) speaks as though he were an objective observer of others' behaviors. He also refers to "a necessary illusion that the world we discuss is there to be experienced" (p. 30). That said, much of what Bollas writes is not only compatible with a constructivist perspective, it is also a source of what may be exactly the kind of new data we seek. Thus, speaking of dreams, he says:

When we attend to the ego's transformation of dream theme into dramatic fiction, we are indeed acknowledging a creative function in the dream process, and we are wiser, I believe, if we note that the dream does not simply bring us into communication with instinctual or memorial experiences; it brings us into contact with our own internal and highly idiomatic aesthetic: that aesthetic reflected by the ego style typical of each of us [pp. 80–81].

This statement not only suggests a psychological unity embracing the entire personality but also implies that it is consciousness which is the transformer of the unconscious's gifts. It reminds us that each of us has a unique aesthetic style that pervades our conscious experience derived from that creative function. For our purposes here, just such a creative function is considered as the epitome of what we perhaps more mundanely term construction.

Finally, it is important to devote some brief attention here to a theorist who appears to recognize fully the ambiguity of experience, yet who does so on the basis of ambiguity inherent not in reality, or the ability to perceive, but only in language or semiotics. The psychoanalytic ideas of Edgar Levenson, in particular as he presented them in *The Ambiguity of Change* (1983), are of major interest here because his views at that time approximated those offered here in many respects. Levenson draws on the work of Gregory Bateson and Harry Stack Sullivan (who apparently drew at least as heavily on information theory, as it was available to him at the time, as on Freud [Levenson, 1983, p. 124]). Levenson supports the perspective offered here when he views Freud as so distracted by the contents of his patient's revelations that he became preoccupied with classifying those revelations into either historical truth, drive-induced psychic reality, or some mixture of the two, when he could have much more fruitfully concentrated on the process by which the content was presented. Speaking generically of "a patient," Levenson sounds a constructivist note when he states: "in his discourse with the world he shapes and perpetuates it." He introduces a different focus of uncertainty, however, when he adds, "It is through symbols that one not merely knows but constitutes the world" (p. 51).

The basic idea that there is an objective reality that comprises the basis of our experience, and that unfortunately is always wrapped to some degree in the vagaries of linguistic and semiotic communication, contains within it the idea that such defining communication is somehow a qualitatively different and less exact process than all the others of which the world is composed. The problem becomes less inherent in the dialectics of experience and more due to the fact that human language and communication cannot hold up their end. Since Levenson's semiotics seems to include all observation and expression implicated in communication, it is as though nothing escapes its distorting lens. And since nothing escapes this lens we simply have to take his word for it that there is clear and objective reality outside our imperfectly symbolized experience of it. It is not always clear how important such an objective reality is to Levenson. He acknowledges that no final knowing is attainable; but, he also suggests that the analyst can teach the patient skills that will "make it possible to distinguish the nuances of interaction" (p. 12) (i.e., correctly) and that his approach may be "close to the way the brain/ mind really works" (p. 103). Levenson's semiotics seem to provide a limited, but instructive example of a near-constructivist perspective rigorously applied, but in the narrowest possible way. It also may provide a possible source of metapsychological damage control for positivists of various disciplines trying to adapt to a new paradigm.[14] Though such a focus on communication can bring psychoanalysis closer to a constructivist position, its likely result is a focus on barriers to deciphering an objective external world and, in particular, a shift away from shared experience and toward the goal of an objective study of communication. The process of construction of experience described here suggests something quite different.

Constructing Physical Reality

A separate theoretical issue that merits some discussion is the applicability of constructivist views to the so-called physical world. While this may seem a small point, it is a vital one for the integrity of the constructivist perspective and even more important for psychoanalysts dealing with possible physical as well as psychic trauma. It appears much simpler for some theorists to accept a role for construction in events seen as in the social realm than for those accepted as in the physical world. Hoffman (1998), for example, has stated clearly that "the realm of interpersonal events is distinguished from that of physical events" (p. 118).

---

[14] This discussion is limited to a few particular positions advanced by Levenson. It cannot begin to indicate the sweep of Levenson's insights and intellectual explorations. In his more recent book, Levenson (1991) offers a series of essays that explore a wide variety of intriguing ideas.

A distinction between the experience of the physical and the experience of the social may be proposed on many grounds. For example: the potentially "concrete" experience of the physical versus a social experience essentially limited to inferential data about others; the possibly unique role of language in social experience; even the idea that there is a special tendency to compromise objectivity in social investigations and not in physical investigations because the objects being studied in the social investigations occupy the same "domain" as the inquiring subject. Habermas (1972) has noted that interpretations derived from social investigations are typically held to be further defined by the context in which they are applied whereas theoretical propositions about physical reality are basically held to be beyond such contingencies (p. 273). These distinctions provide a basis from which to construe physical and social reality differently. They are examples of effective ways of construing experience into categories. Experience can be (and has been) considered real or contrived at a host of various points. Different ways of categorizing experience do not in themselves, however, seem to provide a strong argument that construal itself is not a central and essential process within all or, in this case, both categories. The issue, then, is: What is the most effective way for a constructivist psychoanalysis to construe the physical world?[15]

It may seem that not to posit a firm distinction between the experience of social reality and that of physical reality is to challenge the physical sciences.[16] However, there is nothing in psychoanalysis's consideration of a perspective of all perceived reality as constructed which challenges any other discipline's particular construction. In any case, every discipline is, to some degree, already currently dealing with such challenges within its own field. Psychoanalysis is obviously just one of many in this regard. If any segment of the psychoanalytic community is, however, to find a solid theoretical foundation for a constructivist perspective of experience it cannot logically exclude certain (i.e., physical) categories of that experience. The reason that such exclusion is illogical is not only that powerful

---

[15] For in-depth discussion of distinctive and conflicting views of reality emerging from various disparate social arenas, see Latour (1993).

[16] Gill (1994) began his final book with a statement of the view that the natural sciences are themselves constructivist (though less obviously so than the human sciences) simply by virtue of being developed by human beings. "As such, they are determined in part by the nature of the perceiving or thinking human beings. They are constructed from the human perspective. They are relative to that perspective" (pp. 1–2).

social determinants reside in physical categories of experience.[17] It is illogical because to eliminate or even deemphasize the consideration of the physical in a constructivist perspective is basically to make an argument based on the assumption that we can objectively evaluate when there is or is not ambiguity. This assumption entails several dubious postulates: a) that ambiguity is itself an external characteristic we can perceive objectively; b) that the physical is obviously not ambiguous and the social obviously is; and c) that when ambiguity is present we perceive it and then choose to supply our construction. The acceptance of any of these assertions would seem to invalidate totally the logic of the constructivist position.

Conscious and Unconscious

Another theoretical issue of considerable significance for psychoanalysis which has been touched on, but not sufficiently, is how to construe unconscious processes within the context of constructivism. Specifically, if unconsciousness is seen as a source of potential reality, what additional implications for the nature of consciousness and the unconscious does that have? Because of Freud's allegiance to an independent and objectifiable framework, the goal of consciousness was, first and last, to function according to the reality principle. For example, in the structural model, consciousness in the form of the ego first evolved from the id in relation to the demands of the real, external world. The ultimate function of the reality principle was to serve unconscious (instinctual) forces by making their gratification in the external world more likely. Even though, when necessary, smaller aspects of reality were sacrificed by the defenses in the process of maintaining a larger overall orientation to reality, it was always that overall objective relation to reality which remained the conscious psyche's central task throughout. The constructivist position simply does not permit that perspective.

In addition, the dual conceptualization of a highly influential and very conscious (of both itself and the external world) *un*conscious and of a consciousness which is never directly conscious of the *un*conscious, but which nevertheless perceives external reality with

---

[17] For example, the experience of climate, wealth, and infectious disease, or such individual physical considerations as facial expressions, gestures, personal appearance, and ever-popular sex and violence, form an intrinsic part of the basis of social reality. To this list many may wish to add the instincts.

photographic fidelity, only to lose its crystal clarity at critical moments as it succumbs to the primal undertow of the unconscious, may not be the most parsimonious foundation for positing a process of construction. It is particularly difficult, for our purposes, to endorse the concept of an unconscious that is more conscious than consciousness. It is not that these ostensibly conflicting functions cannot be, or have not in fact been, resolved in coherent theoretical constructions (e.g., Freud, 1915b; Roiphe, 1995, pp. 1186–1187). It is just that they become almost overwhelmingly complex and tenuous in a constructivist framework. In any case, the basic idea of even separate but equal active roles in construction for conscious and unconscious processes tends to lead to the idea that there is a part of the mind which perceives an objective reality, and another part that subjectively shapes it (see Freud, 1915b, p. 171). It is almost as though, with the proper kind of psychosurgery, the subjective portions could be blocked and we would really see. Because such conceptions are exactly what a constructivist perspective seeks to avoid, the simpler alternative that the more definitive role in the construction of experience be allocated to consciousness itself must at least be considered.

This is not to underestimate the complexity and ability of what is not conscious to compel physical and mental behavior. Just as a malfunction of the pancreas can send a person scrambling for sugar and verbalizing all manner of accompanying rationalizations, the unconscious clearly can dominate consciousness. All felt need and all emotion can be construed to originate in this basically autonomic way. Indeed, it is chiefly in regard to this immense, ongoing realm of behavior that is initiated outside of consciousness that an analyst may offer a view of the source of a person's motivation that is as authoritative as the person in question (for a related discussion see Spezzano, 1993, pp. 39–40).

Similarly, the unconscious may still be seen as containing, and in some ways organizing, all the results of experience. Essentially there is no contradiction between viewing construction as a conscious function and assigning all the complex functions that the autonomic nervous system (or a computer) could do to the unconscious. It is easy to imagine either one's autonomic nervous system (or a computer) recording vast amounts of material and organizing it according to the logic Freud found in dreams. Things or events could be categorized with any part of themselves, with other things that share the same property or are similar in any part, or with their opposites, or with events that occurred at the same time. None of this implies construction. Consequently, it seems reasonable to suggest that the unconscious does not construct (except in the sense that all living tissue does so simply by reacting selectively). The unconscious is seen here as a constant source of psychological input on which consciousness is often forced, and sometimes may choose to draw. It shares this part of its status with purely physiological forces or unsought stimulation from the external environment. The idea advanced here that construction is primarily a conscious process is not necessarily intended to imply an enhanced view of the possibilities for conscious control of that process. What is enlarged in such a perspective is only the possibility of conscious awareness. One of the most paradoxical and important features of consciousness may be that it is never fully in control of itself. It is not only in dreams that consciousness can be a refreshing ride or a white knuckle nightmare. This perspective attributes that fact partly to an ultimately irrepressible unconscious and partly to an external world that also continues to defy our attempts to dominate it. However, it is to the intrinsic nature of the process of consciousness itself—the process whereby we construct—that we look to here as a center of that experience of unpredictability.

Consciousness constructs, but can never fully determine, that of which it is conscious. Humans control what they contribute to their own consciousness largely by what they do in response to what they have constructed. It is an element of faith within this perspective that for most observers the realization that whatever is observed is also constructed will result in some added degree of empowerment. That is, perhaps construction can be more easily reacted to in a way that modifies future construction when it is recognized as constructed.

Basically, a constructivist framework broadens the focus from the intrapsychic realm to every source of input to consciousness and locates the very center of action in consciousness. Many things may be responded to differentially—in the limited ways that all living tissue makes distinctions—but all psychological knowing is finally constructed by consciousness. Love relations, strange lands, and poetry have their impact directly on consciousness as well as through their placement in the unconscious, just as the contributions of the unconscious have their impact directly and not just indirectly through love relations, strange lands, and poetry. Despite their great impact, these aspects of the unconscious are all, and must remain, potential reality, and they can neither exist for us nor have any significance until the moment, and to the degree, they are constructed by us.

Clinical Considerations

Constructions of Mental Health

Freud's understanding of dream symbols as refugees from the unconscious slipping through defenses under the cover of night to subvert a consciousness otherwise locked on reality (together with his similar understanding of slips of the tongue, and other forms of parapraxis) forms the historical core of much of clinical psychoanalysis. Clearly, if the constructivist path is chosen, many parts of this clinical core of classical analysis are thrown into question. To begin with, a consensual standard of mental health that is based on conscious clarity about objective reality must be replaced. Newer standards must ultimately be based not on estimates of an ability to perceive an objective reality without an unacceptable level of unconscious interference, but perhaps on a fairly explicit, but as yet undeveloped, notion of an optimal process of construction. Though several such notions could probably be derived from the existing literature (Hoffman, 1991, p. 97, has offered several relevant comments) and a few more are suggested here, no articulated and consensually agreed on standard exists within the current framework of constructivist psychoanalysis. The development of such a standard remains an essential task for the future.

The clinical applications of such a standard must take into account not only the patient's conscious and unconscious process as constructed with the analyst (and including the analyst's construction of his or her own processes), but the relation of the analyst's and the patient's joint construction to the consensually constructed reality of the community in which the patient lives. Obviously psychoanalytic technique adapted to this newer understanding is also required. Such a technique would involve facilitating the joint construction of reality (and probably a new understanding of how reality was constructed in the past) rather than correcting a deficient process of adherence to an objective reality, just as the analyst's participation in such joint construction involves a great concurrence of personal and professional involvement.

The perspective articulated here views the varied meaning of experience, both concrete and abstract, as human essence rather than an objectifiable degree of error or distortion. In fact, in this perspective the traditional epistemological concepts of truth and error can be considered to be in some ways analogous to the theological concepts of sin and virtue.[18] Both sets of concepts have long and useful histories as reified and absolute realities, but their inherently judgmental impact can have severely limiting effects on the practice and theory of psychoanalysis. The focus suggested here is not on correcting individual constructions, but on understanding through participation, and thereby modifying, the process of construction.

Another issue is that traditional psychoanalysis has always emphasized conflictual relations among parts of an inferred unconscious psychic structure. It has done this as a means of understanding the pathology supposedly resulting from those conflictual relations, from which pathology the unconscious structure was inferred in the first place. For our purposes a different tack must be taken. Internal conflict can be considered as a product of a deficiency in the process of construction. For instance, internal conflicts may be seen as produced by a process of construction that is not adequately integrative. Hoffman has noted some possible examples of a deficient constructive process. One is the repetitive creation of very few and not particularly diverse constructs, particularly those associated with relationships, and particularly those entering repetitively into the relationship with the analyst (Hoffman, 1983, p. 419). Another is the related failure to employ subtle distinctions in constructions (Hoffman, 1992, pp. 8–9). Such narrowed processes of construction may produce internal conflict when they fail to assimilate adequately a more diverse potential reality. Further, the accumulation of peripheral experience not accounted for in initial constructions may result in additional constructions that may appear idiosyncratic when viewed alone. For example, a patient who sees a parent (or the analyst or both) as uniformly loving may need to construct in an increasingly idiosyncratic manner to maintain that initial construction. Such a positive view of a parent may even result in unduly negative constructions by the patient about herself. Such additional constructions can then even come into conflict with the idea that the patient was actually loved by the parent seen as uniformly loving.

Another obvious candidate for less than optimal construction is an extensive participation in fantasy. Fantasy may often function as an adaptation to a world seen as impervious to additional construction. A fantasy world where only personally screened external

---

[18] This connection is apparently not new. Speaking of John Dewey, Rorty (1996) notes that "[h]e agreed with Nietzsche that the traditional notion of truth, as correspondence to the intrinsic nature of reality, was a remnant of the idea of submission to the will of God. When Sin goes, so should the duty to seek for such correspondence" (p. 7).

contributions are admitted may compensate for unpleasant daily existence in a reality experienced as imposed. The complete commitment to subjectivity, of selecting fantasy as the major basis for day-to-day construction, can be the all too familiar one of psychosis. Winnicott (1971) clearly distinguished the disconnected quality of fantasy as compared with dreaming or daily living.[19] He noted that, "[b]y contrast, however, fantasying remains an isolated phenomenon, absorbing energy but not contributing-in [sic] either to dreaming or to living" (p. 26). He said of a patient that "while she was playing the other people's games she was *all the time engaged in fantasying*" (p. 29). A little later Winnicott summarized his position by stating, "It will be observed that creative playing is allied to dreaming and to living but essentially does *not* belong to fantasying" (p. 31). Fantasy may be an attempt to minimize construction of the external world in order to minimize further integration of what has already been generally constructed as undesirable.

In this connection we might consider Bollas's (1987) description of a condition in which the opposite reaction occurs. Bollas describes a "normotic" condition (pp. 135–156) in which there is minimal fantasy, indeed, little apparent subjectivity of any kind. Though the world is seen as comprising already given objects and events, the individual suffering this malady does not retreat to a world in which his construction is definitive. Instead he remains in a world in which he too is almost exclusively constructed by others. Such an individual has chosen to identify his experience solely with what he experiences as consensual reality. His own constructive participation is not even an issue. Even when he was a child, it was never honored: "Instead of being mirrored by the parent, the child is deflected" (p. 151). The result is a person who does not consciously construct the world so much as he sees himself being repetitively constructed by it. Such people may display all the concrete signs of enjoying the social and economic success they are sometimes able to achieve in dealing with the reality to whose perceived lack of malleability they have adapted. Such a process of construction as theirs obviously has minimal room for all the perceptions and internal experiences not provided for in the social milieu. Consequently, even the smallest emergence of such experience can cause conflict.

The concept of the "normotic" personality is particularly noteworthy here because such persons strive to live with a minimum of

---

[19] The complete commitment to subjectivity, that of selecting fantasy as the major basis for construction, is the familiar one leading to psychosis.

that creative element in their personal experience which we have held to be essential to experience. Drawing on Winnicott (1971), Arnold Modell (1990), and Johan Huizinga (1950), we can refer to that essential element as play. The term play comes close to conveying the experiential essence of the personal process we have referred to here as experiential reality. As Modell (1990) points out, both "Huizinga and Winnicott understood that playing is a *shared* construction of reality which takes place within a level of reality that is different from that of ordinary life" (p. 29). It is impossible to overstate the centrality of this concept for either man, especially Winnicott (1971) in his understanding of psychoanalysis. For him, "The natural thing is playing, and the highly sophisticated twentieth-century phenomenon is psychoanalysis. It must be of value to the analyst to be constantly reminded not only of what is owed to Freud but also of what we owe to the natural and universal thing called playing" (p. 41). Speaking of psychotherapy in general, he observed that "[t]he general principle seems to me to be valid that *psychotherapy is done in the overlap of the two play areas, that of the patient and that of the therapist*" (p. 51).

It is important to remember that, though the remarkably similar concepts of play developed by Huizinga and Winnicott are useful here, each of these men framed his concept of play in a context of belief in an objective external reality, for which we have substituted a particular concept of consensual reality. It is reasonable to suspect that it was this maintaining a belief in a positivist external reality which forced Winnicott to posit a more flexible metaphorical space called "potential space," which he envisioned first between the mother and the child, and later between the individual and the environment. Obviously a reality that is constant and objective is not suitable for such a space. It was only in this not already determined space that the often transformative and creative process of play could be conceived as occurring. As Huizinga (1980) so compellingly notes:

> [I]n acknowledging play you acknowledge mind, for whatever else play is, it is not matter. Even in the animal world it bursts the bonds of the physically existent. From the point of view of a world wholly determined by the operation of blind forces, play would be altogether superfluous. Play only becomes possible, thinkable and understandable when the influx of *mind* breaks down the absolute determinism of the cosmos. The very existence of play confirms the supra-logical nature of the human situation [pp. 3–4].

There is nothing in this view with which constructivism cannot agree.

It is necessary, however, to stipulate that lack of flexibility of constructs should not uniformly be regarded as a form of pathology. For example, it is also possible to view such inflexibility as conviction. The presence of some convictions that are inflexible is consensually held to be a positive characteristic in our society. True, such "strong" convictions may occur because of a history of construction in a social context that necessitated great rigidity for one to continue to participate and survive. They also may occur because of a high level of personal integration. A particular construction may so integrate and support so many previously constructed views and understandings that the individual's failure to endorse such construction would constitute an experience of self-nullification.

The Genesis of Constructive Capacity

To fully develop a psychoanalytic understanding of mental illness in a constructivist framework also requires a more genetic understanding of the development of each individual's particular capacity to construct. Though Freud (1941) envisioned a relation between mother and child that was the model of every later love relation (p. 188), he saw the sense of reality as more broadly derived from experiences of instinctual frustration and gratification of all sorts. More congenial to our approach are Winnicott's and Bollas's views of the mother–child relation. Winnicott (1971) too saw some frustration as part of a healthy development, but he notes that:

> Nevertheless, *at the start* adaptation needs to be almost exact, and unless this is so it is not possible for the infant to begin to develop a capacity to experience a relationship to external reality, or even to form a conception of external reality. . . . The mother, at the beginning, by almost 100 per cent adaptation affords the infant the opportunity for the *illusion* that her breast is part of the infant. . . . Psychologically the infant takes from a breast that is part of the infant, and the mother gives milk to an infant that is part of herself. In psychology, the idea of interchange is based on an illusion in the psychologist [pp. 11–12].

With exactly which reality are we to contrast these illusions? In the end, we are left to ask if, in the initial stages of this critical transformation, there even can be such a thing as an illusion, and, if there is, in whose experience it may be found? Here it might be worth noting in passing that, according to Huizinga (1950), the word illusion is "a pregnant word which means literally 'in-play' (from *ilusio, illudere or inludere)*" (p. 11). Obviously, as in a constructivist framework, Winnicott's use of the term illusion is a relative one, meaningful only in relation to an alternative construction. In Winnicott's formulation, however, timely participant support from the mother for such basic and "illusory" individual constructions later becomes the foundation of a generalized capacity to experience reality. It is important to note that for Winnicott (1971) the acknowledgment of subjectivity of our basic beliefs remains an essential prerequisite for socialization throughout adult life:

> Should an adult make claims on us for our acceptance of the objectivity of his subjective phenomena we discern or diagnose madness. If, however, the adult can manage to enjoy the personal intermediate area without making claims, then we can acknowledge our own corresponding intermediate areas, and are pleased to find a degree of overlapping, that is to say common experience between members of a group in art or religion or philosophy [p. 14].

Consider Bollas's (1987) elaboration on transformational objects. Here the idea of illusion has fallen away and been replaced by "a recurrent experience of being."

> A transformational object is experientially identified by the infant with processes that alter self experience. It is an identification that emerges from symbiotic relating, where the first object is "known" not so much by putting it into an object representation, but as a recurrent experience of being—a more existential as opposed to representational knowing. As the mother helps to integrate the infant's being (instinctual, affective, environmental) the rhythms of this process—from unintegration(s) to integration(s)—inform the nature of this "object" relation rather than the qualities of the object as object [p. 14].

What Bollas is essentially describing here is a mother–child relation in which not only could the self and its integration be seen as constructed, but the very process of bringing into consciousness is itself constructed. The mother's body is the child's first experience, and, though both mother and child may initially construct it as continuous with the child, that construction must soon give way to a series of other constructions that never end during the lifetime of the child. It is pointless to identify any of them as illusion. The child's need to share a common sense of reality, and to contribute to it in a way that is personally meaningful, remains intrinsic to the construction process throughout life. And the manner in which that sharing is done, and the quality of personal contribution accepted, also becomes a constructed reality that resonates throughout all future personal constructions. It is on the basis of our attention to such resonance that constructivism may be recognized as a relational approach and the quality of intimacy experienced in the process of construction understood as a major clinical consideration.

The Role of the Analyst

In the constructivist perspective the world exists as an opportunity for experience. Already full of things constructed and constantly being constructed again, the world presents itself as more the literal embodiment of our dreams and less as their antagonist. True, we are guided in our constructions by the larger society, whose construal of its collective experience we may, to a high degree, actively share. We may even actually be constrained to share this collective construction under threat of severe social penalties. We can, however, in every single case, also regard ourselves as participating to a significant degree in creating every thing we know. It is obvious that there is an infinite variety of collective and individual ways and styles of creating reality, but from this perspective, experience and some level of existential responsibility are inevitably intertwined. Nowhere is this more true than in the analyst's office.

What is the basis of the analyst's expertise, and consequently, responsibility? How can the analyst defend, or be criticized for, any action? As seen here, the constructivist analyst's main claim to authority as an analyst lies in his or her openness to sharing in constructing the reality that the analyst and the patient inhabit together. The analyst also typically possesses an extensive array of highly evolved (extensively modified over time) constructs to abet openness. Nonetheless, the major significance of the array of evolved constructs is not that of sharpened intellectual tools at the ready. From our perspective, that significance, like the significance of whatever articles or books the analyst may have written about those constructs, is probably more akin to that of mounted animal heads in the home of a hunter. These constructs, to the extent that they capture the analyst's creative clinical processes, merely suggest that the analyst is experienced and has demonstrated skill at coconstructing. The analyst, it is hoped, remains exemplary in the prowess to construct anew and provides a model and an experience of that process often not available elsewhere in the patient's life.

Since the analyst holds authority only as an expert participant, and not as a judge or clinical standard bearer, all experience is, within the constraints of his subjectivity, accepted by him as equally worthy of attention. This idea contrasts with Latour's (1993) observation that not only Freudians, but social science in general has always been more interested in deviation than concurrence with what was seen as "objective." Analogously, the analyst gains authority not mainly from his offering his relatively unique perspective on the patient, but chiefly from his openness and sensitivity in enacting his understanding of sharing and thereby jointly constructing a new perspective.

A second source of the analyst's authority is that he was not present at the time that many of the patient's earliest constructions were constructed. Consequently, the analyst deals with them as verbal representations, which do not disrupt him to the same degree as if they were personal experiences constructed as having occurred in the context of his own private history. As a result, the analyst introduces less of his own urgency into the considerations and thereby requires less flexibility from the patient in the process of jointly constructing the patient's life. Further, the fact that the analyst often learns of these original constructions through reconstructions occurring much later not only in the patient's life, but also in the analyst's, and even society's, life may augment that effect. To take an extreme case, it is easier, say, to evaluate a patient's attempt to bomb a building in the 1960s, than to ponder associations if the rubble is on the evening news. The availability of an intervening, fuller social context thus plays a role in analysis similar to what Warnke (1987) has described as the progressively increasing ability of historians to understand history in general (p. 19). This is not to say that the personal relationship between the patient and the analyst is necessarily, in the immediacy of any given moment, less vulnerable for the analyst than for the patient. It is to say that there are several factors supporting the cohesiveness of the analyst's ability to construct, and thereby his authority, factors that do not similarly affect the patient.

A final source of the analyst's authority may be described as a major goal of the analysis to dispel. While not appropriate to pursue extensively here, it must be included in any discussion of psychoanalysis. Patients bring important aspects of the analyst's authority with them. A new analysand often comes to the first session already having constructed the analyst as having an authority superior to the patient's with regard to the ability to understand the patient's life. Additionally, a sophisticated analysand may come to treatment having selected the analyst as superior to others who might have been engaged. In unfortunate cases, this may be the patient and the analyst's first shared construction. This source of the analyst's authority can never correctly be viewed as simply a resource in the hunt for less than optimal ways of constructing. This source of the analyst's authority is the tail of the tiger itself. Its shared reconstruction, as it plays out in all the fullness of its rich and multivalent transferential and countertransferential ramifications, forms a central task in treatment.

Constructivist Psychoanalysis

Throughout this chapter we have explored different issues relating to the possibility of a constructivist psychoanalysis. The following discussion cannot hope to summarize all these issues, but it can serve to underline a few major points and add a few more that have thus far been overlooked. Because the practice of psychoanalysis is so complex in all its forms and the latitude of individual behavior by both analysts and patients is so broad, any brief discussion of the potential contributions by constructivist analysis to the practice of analysts of any other orientation could easily prove as provocative as it is helpful. It is probable that there are few beneficial aspects of any form of psychoanalysis which do not appear to some degree in the work of analysts of most other theoretical orientations. Certainly the writers discussed here are not the only analysts currently using similar approaches in their work, and, to a lesser degree, constructivist thinking also enters into the work of many relationally oriented analysts. What is missing is a constructivist foundation and an overall perspective that is congruent with that foundation. It is the search for that foundation and perspective that we have attempted to join here.

In this section we attempt to make a few very general distinctions regarding the overview we have offered. To simplify the discussion we once more call on Freud. It is relatively easy to differentiate between Freud's techniques and those of virtually any modern psychoanalysts and this is equally true of the work of a hypothetical exemplary constructivist analyst. We can easily contrast Freud's (1937) eagerness to have his patients accept his interpretations (because he usually believed such acceptance meant the interpretations were right) with the stance of a constructivist analyst who never seeks, and in fact tends to avoid, a process in which the analyst's view is simply accepted. The constructivist analyst participates in such a way as to contribute to the development of a process. He hopes the treatment will enable the patient to perform that process later with others. The immediate goal is never simply to supply a particular meaning, but continually to offer meaning by way of contributing to the process of continually changing meaning arrived at jointly. This goal is not usually verbalized by analysts of other theoretical orientations, but it has recently been closely approached by Fonagy and Target (1998). While stopping short of specifically envisioning coconstruction, they clearly emphasize the aim of stimulating the patient's portion of the process: "It is our premise that a crucial therapeutic aspect of psychoanalysis, for both children and adults, lies in its capacity to activate people's ability to find meaning in their own and other people's behavior" (p. 104).

A related issue pertains to the use of theory in general. For our example we refer to object relations, but what is said here about the risks of an object-relational approach also potentially applies to other theoretical positions, such as an approach grounded in structural theory. Consider introjected objects. An additional layer of relational complexity arises when they are added to our mental picture. Speaking of the British analyst Paula Heimann, Bollas (1987) notes that she "knew that at any moment in a session a patient could be speaking with the voice of the mother, or the mood of the father, or some fragmented voice of a child self either lived or withheld from life." There is no reason to doubt that the "shadow of the object" (the graceful metaphor by Freud for internalization of a significant other which happens to imply minimal intrapsychic corporeal presence) "leaves some trace of its existence in the adult" (p. 3). It is not clear, though, that in a process geared to optimal shared construction it is clinically helpful to the patient or helpful to the analyst to imagine such traces as introjects of sovereign identity which independently assert their own constructions from time to time. While there is no doubt that every object relations approach ultimately seeks the integration and unification of personality, both the goal and the path chosen may be different than is optimal for a constructivist. A central facet of a constructivist approach must be its focus on the full breadth and depth of consciousness as a continual process of construction and not on other processes of which the patient is held to be unaware and whose sources may be designated by the analyst. Generally, in the view outlined here, a constructivist approach attempts to approach the patient's consciousness as an integrated whole that functions in a unified way in interaction with the analyst's whole consciousness throughout treatment.

In addition, unless such a multifaceted conceptualization of internal object relations is seamlessly internalized by the analyst, mastery of it can become as esoteric and formidable as grasping the patient's own deepest meanings. While virtually all analysts allow theory to slide into the background during their deepest work, analysts obviously do draw heavily on their theories to guide and enhance their practice. And any analyst may be tempted to stop exploration at the point where observed behavior seems explained—

when the analyst has offered to the patient an interpretation with which both express satisfaction. By perhaps unconsciously presenting it as the conclusion the analyst experiences it to be, however, the analyst has *to some degree* created and participated in a construction that has the potential to preempt other, unspecified meaningful aspects of both the patient's and the analyst's individual subjectivity. It is exactly such small, but sometimes precious, possibilities of which a constructivist approach is constantly driven to remain aware. That is, constructivism focuses its attention on all forms of participation in the creation of meaning, especially those preempted or otherwise diverted by the participants as they work together.[20] To be noted, it is the exemplary process of discussion of such small possibilities and not primarily the increased awareness of the forms of diversion or the potential interactions diverted that lies nearest the heart of the approach put forward here.

It is consistent with the foregoing statements to state specifically that the psychoanalytic art of participating in the constructions of others is probably best practiced with a minimum of inference and a maximum of direct experience. This point has an even more obvious, but clinically important, corollary. That is, only what is manifest is available for direct experience. Without specifically noting that such observable behavior is more available to experience than are the inferred psychic depths, Levenson (1991) offers the following: "I would like to suggest that the art of psychoanalysis, the aesthetics of psychoanalysis, is the pursuit and elaboration of the highly personal, idiosyncratic patterning of the much maligned and disregarded manifest content, the surface" (p. 84). Among the approaches most outstanding in this regard is that of David Shapiro (1965). Shapiro's work can be seen not only as a focus on the surface that is subject to direct experience, but as a focus specifically on the style of that surface. From his observations of style he moves directly to infer "modes of experiencing," which are potentially very relevant here. For example: "We may assume, in other words, that the compulsive person behaves in the manner that he does, under the impact of a given impulse or external provocation, not only because of modes of response or activity, but also because of *certain modes of experiencing or perceiving* that impulse or stimulus. These are the matters to which a clinical study of neurotic styles must address itself" (p. 17, italics added). Some conceptualization of characteristic processes of

---

[20] A thorough and rewarding exploration of the process of creating meaning in psychoanalysis from a more hermeneutic perspective can be found in Donnel Stern's (1997) *Unformulated Experience.*

construction must be a basic and necessary part of any psychoanalytic constructivist approach. We have already referred to some such processes, particularly in our discussion of "Constructions of Mental Health"; it seems clear, too, that Shapiro's perspective might contribute greatly to further clinical applications of a such an approach.

Finally, however constructivist understanding may evolve in the future, constructivist analysts will continue to have to come to terms with a need to evaluate the narratives their patient presents in the context of prevailing narrative standards in the communities in which they are presented.[21] Psychoanalysts must relate, to some degree, to all the standards commonly in use in the communities to which they and their patients belong. Despite the view that there is never any possibility of either objective observation of the source of original experience, or of a pure repetition of the experience on which current narratives are based, constructivist analysts are often forced to participate in procedures and processes based on different assumptions. For example, in a legal system that makes binding life and death decisions based on determinations of the past, participating psychoanalysts must search for their own role and, ultimately, their own constructs. This is exactly the kind of conscious process constructivist analysts may share with their patients. It is also the process that both patient and analyst may often choose to employ, though to a less stressful degree, throughout life.

Trauma

Trauma represents the most severe test for a constructivist psychoanalysis. With recollection of specific trauma, the patient's primary focus does not appear to lie with any aspect of his or her subjectivity. The patient's focus tends to be drawn to what is seen as a very specific and concrete experience that was almost totally externally determined. In fact, the removal of any doubt on the part of the patient that she is even partly responsible for the event she recalls is often part of the treatment. Here the uncertainty intrinsic to the constructivist analyst's theory and the patient's sense of reality meet in full dress. Constructivism must survive this encounter to be viable as a

---

[21] Obviously such standards are also constructed differently not only by analysts and analysands, but by all different observers, including social scientists and jurors. However, there is, also obviously, a degree of commonality of construction in each community (which may be useful as a definition of the degree to which community exists).

clinical approach. The following discussion is intended as a contribution to that encounter.

When we talk about memories of trauma we are still talking about new constructions of previously constructed reality, which was originally based on some particular direct experience (even if that direct experience was only of someone else's narrative). When some semblance of that original experience reappears as memory, it has, in each case, followed a unique path. That path includes an original experience of a combination of external and subjective influences, and possibly many reconstructions, in varied contexts prior to the present. Those who would retrace such steps must add their own constructions in the process.

In attempting to retrace those steps, at least four issues must be faced. One is the topical problem of how to attempt to distinguish between the various experiences on which narratives founded only on memory may be based. These various experiences may include, but are not limited to, direct experiences, narratives provided by others, fantasy, similar but distinct events, and even a wish to deceive by lying. Second is the question of how close the original construction of an experience was to constructions that might reasonably be expected from someone constructing largely in the context provided by the more or less accepted consensual constructions of the society at large. That is, to what degree was the initial construction idiosyncratic? Third is the problem of how to appraise the extent and kind of additional construction that has occurred since the original experience. Fourth is the problem of how to appraise the extent and kind of construction that has been added by the person exploring these issues with the patient/victim. Given such considerations, it is impressive how realistic a sense of the past people seem able to communicate. But this degree of realism might be a gift horse that would not bear too deep an examination (e.g., see Loftus, 1993) and certainly not one on which to place the main weight of psychoanalysis. This is never more true than when trauma is involved.

Different psychoanalytic authors contributing to our overall knowledge of trauma have conceived of the nature and effects of trauma very differently. For example, some studies have focused on concentration camp victims (e.g., Auerhahn, Laub, and Peskin, 1993). Others, more theoretically oriented, have stressed violations of the stimulus barrier (Freud, 1920; Krystal, 1968). Stolorow et al. (1987) have based their understanding of the effects of trauma on "impaired affect tolerance and inability to use affects as self signals" (p. 72). Kinston and Cohen (1986), on the other hand, see trauma more generally in terms of "[t]he failure to meet ego needs" (p. 337). Finally, sexual abuse of children by adults is the subject of a voluminous and swelling body of literature and various theoretical interpretations (for example Davis & Frawley, 1994, Renvoize, 1993). What is being offered here is a general formulation of trauma that includes only physical and emotional trauma that is both extreme and incontestable in all frameworks.

Trauma can be seen not so much as constructed as an over-whelming, externally initiated interaction conducted largely *despite* existing psychological constructs. That which might otherwise be constructed overwhelms the construction process and therefore the constructor. We know this has occurred when only others are able to supply a narrative. The traumatized person lacks the ability, the opportunity, or both to initiate, create, or integrate this interaction. Potential reality overflows the capacity to construct it, and the result is not a reality created by one's experience, but a loss of one's capacity to participate in it at all.

With such trauma, the process of construction can be said to roll in reverse. The external world dis-integrates the process of construction. Even reality that has repeatedly been constructed in the past may suddenly lose its currency. When this reality is crushed, the trusted may be no longer to be trusted, that which was okay may no longer be okay, and what was good may now be very bad indeed. Nothing more clearly demonstrates the constructedness of reality than severe trauma. Suddenly massive new constructions are required to replace the old. At the same moment, the capacity to construct is at least partially crippled: "Living in all its continuity, creativity, and connectedness stops at such moments" (Auerhahn et al., 1993, p. 434). In particular, the flexibility and openness necessary for shared construction is lost. The result may include constructions that are repeats of previous constructions, or adoption of construc-tions that are offered by others (possibly even persons initiating the trauma). It also can result in idiosyncratic or limited constructs that are especially questionable in the larger, consensually constructed reality of society.

In extreme instances, trauma can result in no construction at all, that is, a blank space corresponding to what has been referred to as primal repression (Kinston and Cohen, 1986). Kinston and Cohen focus on the process of repair of such blank spaces. They con-ceptualize such repair as involving "having certain experiences *for the first time*" (p. 347). At such a point, "[t]he analysand is now ready to develop a deep understanding of the events which have affected him, of the historical continuity of his life, of his basic needs as a human being, and of the constraints and possibilities for him and the future" (p. 347). In short, the patient is ready to construct (and reconstruct) all the basic narratives about his life. Kinston and Cohen suggest the possibility of a psychoanalytic role for narrative constructions as a means of direct repair of what they conceive of as specific injuries. Such construction, designed for reparation, is clearly distinct from, and in this instance held to be more desirable than, an interpretation designed to introduce an aspect of consensual reality to a consciousness conceived of as misled.

Though the implications of these findings remain to be explored, they raise the possibility that there are two distinct kinds of psychoanalytic interpretations and that a balanced use of both might be essential to achieve a basis for maximal effective participation in the social construction of reality. In its most basic formulation, what is being suggested is that consciousness relies heavily on both 1) its own central sense of shared reality, referred to here as consensual reality and 2) the meaningful linking of the personal and the social in constructed experiences from their inception at the periphery of consciousness.[22] Interpretations linking previous individual constructions with consensual reality may aid in their integration, while the evolution of new narrative may be critical with newly encountered material. Neither assertion can be adequately supported here, though it is easy to summon up the history of philosophy and science in support of consciousness' probably survival-driven need to find and share a consensual reality; and the history of art and literature in support of the need for personal meaning regardless of what may be seen as real. Coconstruction of the latter sort may be an essential aspect of any traumatized person's recovery: "It is only when survivors remember *with* someone, when a narrative is created *in the presence of a passionate listener*, that the connection between an 'I' and a 'you' is remade"(Kinston and Cohen, 1986, pp. 436–437).

Recovery from trauma apparently requires an experience probably not dissimilar from that originally shared with the parent in whose arms shared constructions were first initiated. A key question in the process of recovery is the nature of the relationship between analyst and patient. Rapport is the word frequently used by clinicians to describe the key correspondence of belief and emotions between the

---

[22] Gadamer (1960) has used the term "the fusion of horizons" in a related, but more comprehensive way to describe a similar personal/social linking. Stressing a self-awareness of both aspects of consciousness as part of his proposed hermeneutics, he notes for example that "[p]art of real understanding, however, is that we regain the concepts of a historical past in such a way that they also include our own comprehension of them" (p. 374).

analyst and patient. In a purely constructivist framework, though, rapport cannot include a shared belief in anything external to the present. In a constructivist framework, rapport is deeply shared experience in the present. Verbal construction may or may not be a part of rapport. The infant in the mother's arms cannot ask if the mother believes her; it is the mootest of points. Correspondingly, for the severely traumatized person, the issue is not whether rape occurred or whether Auschwitz existed. There is no clinical point in invoking theory to qualify such powerful and painfully established realities. The point is that such experience be shared, constructed, and reconstructed, in a manner that mobilizes and repairs the construction process itself until a narrative that integrates the traumatic experience in the deepest and most unifying way is established.

The request by a patient for evidence of identical beliefs about an external event is much more than a demand for rapport or validation. It may provide important diagnostic information about that patient's ability to construct, and it may suggest a serious lack of optimal experience with joint construction in the past. In such a case the therapist may experience a need continually to convey to the patient that she has complete faith that the patient is sharing the truth of his or her experience and that such sharing is what is most important for the success of their work together. In return, the analyst commits to an equal standard for participation. In a constructivist framework, there is never any reassurance that can be offered beyond that.[23]

The judicial standards for evaluation of a narrative constructed by a victim of trauma obviously involve quite different dimensions. Basically, the construction created must be seen as having maximal potential correspondence with consensual reality of the society at large. In other words, if other persons in the society had been present at the original trauma, they would have constructed a similar narrative. This narrative typically has as its central theme the allocation of blame. This concern is obviously very different from the clinical concern. Clinically the focus is not the relation of current constructs to past events, but the need to reestablish what might be described as the forward motion involved in the traumatized

---

[23] The truthful sharing of experience, particularly current experience, is arguably the essence of free association. Freud had the wisdom, when he specified free association for the patient and evenly hovering attention for the analyst, not to specify, that is, not to preconstruct in any way, the nature of the interface between the two. Thus, unimpeded experience and its optimally shared construction became a possibility, and its obstacles a possible focus of psychoanalysis.

individual's resuming the fullest possible active participation in the social construction of meaning.

The legal system can be said to be designed to achieve a broader social resolution than the return of individual integration typically sought clinically. The clinician can participate with awareness only that his or her participation will be seen from that perspective. The focus from this perspective is clearly not whether what really happened in a particular instance can be ascertained; the issue is whether optimally functioning consciousness is involved in its construction.

Summary

We have seen how Freud came to rely on a fantasy of objective reality located in the past and how more recent constructivist psychoanalysts have increasingly sought reality in subjective experience of the present. To move toward a formulation of a theoretical underpinning that might support these constructivist writers, a specific metapsychological formulation has been sketched. This formulation has focused not on how humans negotiate the separation between a discrete world and their needs based on their history, but on the more basic, inescapable, and constant integration of human awareness with all that is external to it within the flow of experience. To construct this formulation we have elaborated a set of suppositions about experience in not only a subjective but a temporal framework. This framework attempts a very basic distinction between the moment before, the moment of, and the moment after experience. Certain characteristics and qualities have been assigned to each of these moments. The moment before construction includes everything that has the potential to be experienced. This is referred to as potential reality. It includes everything not currently being experienced, including internal sources of experience traditionally assigned to the unconscious. The second moment includes everything currently part of experience. It is the subjective experience of reality on which this perspective rests. It is called experiential reality. The third moment is made up of everything that has already been constructed (and that is no longer currently being experienced). It includes the broader consensual constructions held by any given society as well as the uniquely individual constructions that are more typically the focus of psychoanalysis. The contents of these moments move cyclically, as is exemplified by memory. Memory exists as a construction (constructed reality) after the moment when its contents were first experienced. After memory leaves consciousness it exists only as a potential (potential reality) in future experience. When it is reexperienced it is, to some extent, a reality constructed anew.

This attempt to imagine a framework on which constructivism might rest has led to the following postulates about construction. These postulates have relevance at the clinical level for a constructivist psychoanalysis: the process of construction in each individual has unique characteristics; the nature of an individual's process of construction is more important than any particular example of it; optimal construction is personally integrative; and, though shared construction literally creates our worlds, sharing construction dilutes its personal aspects as it proceeds. Some additional comments were made regarding the basic concept of mental health from a constructivist perspective and about the nature of the role of a constructivist analysis in an objectivist social world.

Trauma was considered as a test case for a constructivist analysis and was held to involve not so much the idiosyncratic distortion of the construction process as the overwhelming of the capacity to construct. Though forgetting and remembering are forms of construction, parts of trauma are not forgotten so much as never remembered. Consequently, while trauma can be partially defined by the erratic nature of the constructs that are derived from it, it cannot be reliably defined by their content.

Essentially, this perspective holds that we learn about the world only as we help construct it. This is probably never more true for individuals than at birth, but it continues for both individuals and the societies to which they belong as long as they do. It is a view that may have much to offer psychoanalysis.

References

American Heritage Dictionary (1991), New York: Houghton Mifflin.

Arlow, J. A. (1985, March), The structure of memory. Presented at annual Victor Calef, MD Memorial Lecture, University of California, San Francisco.

Auerhahn, N. C., Laub, D. & Peskin, H. (1993), Psychotherapy with holocaust survivors. *Psychotherapy*, 30, 3:434–442.

Bass, E. & Davis, L. (1988), *The Courage to Heal*. New York: Harper & Row.

Berger, P. L. & Luckmann, T. (1966), *The Social Construction of Reality*. New York: Doubleday.

Bergmann, M. S. (1989), Science and art in Freud's life and work. In L. Gamwell & R. Wells, eds., *Sigmund Freud and Art*. Binghamton: State University of New York, pp. 173–183.

Bernstein, R. J. (1983), *Beyond Objectivism and Relativism*. Philadelphia: University of Pennsylvania Press.

Bollas, C. (1987), *The Shadow of the Object: Psychoanalysis of the Unthought Known*. New York: Columbia University Press.

———— (1992), *Being a Character: Psychoanalysis & Self Experience*. New York: Hill & Wang.

Bower, B. (1993a, September 18), Sudden recall. *Science News*, 144, 12:184–186.

———— (1993b, September 25), The survivor syndrome. *Science News*, 144, (13):202–204.

Breuer, J. & Freud, S. (1893–1895), Studies on hysteria, Standard Edition, 2. London: Hogarth Press, 1955.

Bruner, J. (1990), *Acts of Meaning*. Cambridge, MA: Harvard University Press.

173

———— (1993), Loyal opposition and the clarity of dissent: Commentary on Donald P. Spence's "The Hermeneutic Turn." *Psychoanalytic Dialogues*, 3:11–19.

Carstensen, L. L., Gabrieli, J., Shepard, R., Levenson, R. W., Masom, M. A., Goodman, G., Bootzin, R., Ceci, S. J., Bronfrenbrenner, U., Edelstein, B. A., Schober, M., Bruck, M., Keane, T., Zimering, R., Oltmanns, T. F., Gotlib, I. & Ekman, P. (1993), Letters to the editor. *APS Observer*, 6, (2):23.

Coleman, L. (1992), Creating "Memories" of Sexual Abuse. In *Issues in Child Abuse Accusations*, Vol. 4, No. 4, pp. 169–176.

Crews, F., Schimek, J., Hopkins, J., Peyser, H. S., Olds, D. D., Tolpin, M., Ostow, M., Luborsky, L., Blum, H. P., Pacella, B. L., & Rice, J. L. (1994, February 3), The unknown Freud: An exchange. *New York Review of Books*, 41(3):34–43.

Davies, J. M. & Frawley, M. G. (1994), *Treating the Adult Survivor of Childhood Sexual Abuse: A Psychoanalytic Perspective*. New York: Basic Books.

Demause, L. (1991), The universality of incest. *Journal of Psychohistory*, 19:131–132.

DiCenso, J. J. (1990), *Hermeneutics and the Disclosure of Truth*. Charlottesville: University Press of Virginia.

Einstein, A. (1954), *Ideas and Opinions*, trans. S. Bargmann. New York: Wings Books.

Esterson, A. (1993), *Seductive Mirage*. Chicago: Open Court.

Fish, S. (1996, May 21), Professor Sokal's bad joke. *New York Times*, Op-Ed.

Folger, T. (1993, October 14), The ultimate vanishing. *Discover: The World of Science*, No. 10.

Fonagy, P. & Target, M. (1998), Mentalization and the changing aims of child psychoanalysis. *Psychoanalytic Dialogues*, 8:79–87.

Freud, S. (1895), Case histories: Katharina. *Standard Edition*, 2:125–134. London: Hogarth Press, 1953.

———— (1896), The aetiology of hysteria. *Standard Edition*, 3:191–224. London: Hogarth Press, 1963.

———— (1899), Screen memories. *Standard Edition*, 3:299–322. London: Hogarth Press, 1962.

———— (1901), The psychopathology of everyday life. *Standard Edition*, 6. London: Hogarth Press, 1960.

———— (1909a), Family romances. *Standard Edition*, 9:235–244. London: Hogarth Press.

———— (1909b), Analysis of a phobia in a five-year old boy. *Standard Edition*, 10:1–150. London: Hogarth Press, 1955.

———— (1909c), Notes upon a case of obsessional neurosis. *Standard Edition*, 10:151–318. London: Hogarth Press, 1955.

———— (1911), Psychoanalytic notes upon an autobiographical account of a case of paranoia (dementia paranoides). *Standard Edition*, 12:1–84. London: Hogarth Press, 1958.

———— (1913), Totem and Taboo. *Standard Edition*, 13: 1–162. London: Hogarth Press.

———— (1914a), Remembering, repeating, and working through (further recommendations on the technique of psycho-analysis II). *Standard Edition,* 12:145–156. London: Hogarth Press, 1958.

———— (1914b), On the history of the psycho-analytic movement. *Standard Edition,* 14:7–66. London: Hogarth Press, 1957.

———— (1915a), Repression. *Standard Edition,* 14:141–158. London: Hogarth Press, 1957.

———— (1915b), The unconscious. *Standard Edition,* 14:159–204. London: Hogarth Press, 1957.

———— (1917), General theory of the neurosis. *Standard Edition,* 16:241–477. London: Hogarth Press, 1963.

———— (1918), From the history of an infantile neurosis. *Standard Edition,* 17:7–122. London: Hogarth Press, 1955.

———— (1920), Beyond the pleasure principle. *Standard Edition,* 18:1–65. London: Hogarth Press, 1955.

———— (1923), The ego and the id. *Standard Edition,* 19:12–68. London: Hogarth Press, 1961.

———— (1927), The future of an illusion. *Standard Edition,* 14:1–56. London: Hogarth Press, 1961.

———— (1930), Civilization and its discontents. *Standard Edition,* 21:57–147. London: Hogarth Press, 1929.

———— (1933), New introductory lectures on psycho-analysis. *Standard Edition,* 22:5–184. London: Hogarth Press, 1964.

———— (1937), Constructions in analysis. *Standard Edition,* 23:255–270. London: Hogarth Press.

———— (1939), Moses and monotheism. *Standard Edition,* 23:1–138. London: Hogarth Press.

———— (1941), An outline of Psychoanalysis. *Standard Edition,* 23: 141–208. London: Hogarth Press, 1964.

Gadamer, H. (1960), *Truth and Method,* 2nd revised ed., trans. W. Glen-Doepel, rev. J. Weinsheimer & D. G. Marshall. New York: Continuum, 1994.

———— & Wells, R., eds. (1989), *Sigmund Freud and Art.* Binghamton: State University of New York.

Gamwell, L. (1989), The origins of Freud's antiquities collection. In L. Gamwell & R. Wells (Eds.), *Sigmund Freud and Art.* Binghamton: State University of New York, pp. 21–32.

Gay, P. (1988), *A Life for Our Time.* New York: Norton.

Gergen, K. J. (1985), The social constructionist movement in modern psychology. *American Psychologist,* 40, 3: 266–275.

———— (1967), The primary process. In R. R. Holt (Ed.) *Motives and Thought: Psychoanalytic Essays in Honor of David Rapaport.* New York: International Universities Press.

Gill, M. (1994), *Psychoanalysis in Transition: A Personal View.* Hillsdale, NJ: The Analytic Press.

Girard, R. (1986), *The Scapegoat,* trans. Y. Freccero. Baltimore, MD: Johns Hopkins University Press.

Gleick, J. (1987), *Chaos: Making a New Science.* New York: Penguin Books.

Goodman, N. (1978), *Ways of Worldmaking*. Indianapolis, IN: Hackett.

Grayling, A. C. (1988), *Wittgenstein*. New York: Oxford University Press.

Grünbaum, A. (1984), *The Foundations of Psychoanalysis: A Philosophical Critique*. Berkeley: University of California Press.

Habermas, J. (1972), *Knowledge and Human Interests*, trans. J. J. Shapiro. Boston: Beacon Press.

Hanly, C. (1995), On facts and ideas in psychoanalysis. *International Journal of Psycho-Analysis*, 76:901–908.

Hatfield, L. D. (1996, July 2), Repressed memory killing case: No retrial. *San Francisco Examiner*, p. 1.

Hawking, S. W. (1988), *A Brief History of Time*. Toronto: Bantam Books.

Heidigger, M. (1927), *Basic Writings*. New York: Harper & Row, 1977.

Hoffman, I. Z. (1983), The patient as interpreter of the analyst's experience. *Contemporary Psychoanalysis*, 10:389–422.

———— (1987), The value of uncertainty in psychoanalytic practice. *Contemporary Psychoanalysis*, 23:205–215.

———— (1991), Discussion: Toward a social-constructivist view of the psychoanalytic situation. *Psychoanalytic Dialogues*, 1:74–105.

———— (1992), Expressive participation and psychoanalytic discipline. *Contemporary Psychoanalysis*, 28:1–15.

———— (1994), Dialectical thinking and therapeutic action in the psychoanalytic process. *Psychoanalytic Quarterly*, 63:187–216.

———— (1996), The intimate and ironic authority of the psychoanalytic presence. *Psychoanalytic Quarterly*, 65:102–136.

———— (1998), *Ritual and Spontaniety in the Psychoanalytic Process: A Dialectical-Constructivist View*. Hillsdale, NJ: The Analytic Press.

Huizinga, J. (1950), *Homo Ludens: A Study of the Play-Element in Culture*. Boston: Beacon Press.

Israels, H. & Schatzman, M. (1993), The seduction theory. *History of Psychiatry*, Vol. 4, pp. 23–59.

Keller, J. A. (1994), Irwin Hoffman's social-constructivist view of the psychoanalytic situation. *Northern California Society for a Psychoanalytic Psychology Newsletter*, spring: 17–21.

Kelley, G. A. (1955), *The Psychology of Personal Constructs, Vol. 1: A Theory of Personality*. New York: Norton.

Kinston, W. & Cohen, J. (1986), Primal repression: Clinical and theoretical aspects. *International Journal of Psycho-Analysis*, 67:337–355.

Kohut, H. (1971), *The Analysis of the Self*. New York: International Universities Press.

———— (1977), *The Restoration of the Self*. New York: International Universities Press.

———— (1984), *How Does Analysis Cure?* ed. A. Goldberg & P. Stepansky. Chicago: University of Chicago Press.

Krystal, H. (1968), Trauma and the stimulus barrier. In *Massive Psychic Trauma*, ed. H. Krystal. New York: International Universities Press.

Kuhn, T. S. (1962), *The Structure of Scientific Revolutions*, 2nd ed., Chicago: University of Chicago Press, 1970.

Lacey, A. R. (1976), *A Dictionary of Philosophy*. London: Routledge, 1993.

Laplanche, J. & Pontalis, J.-B. (1973), *The Language of Psychoanalysis,* trans. D. Nicholson-Smith. New York: Norton.

Latour, B. (1993), *We Have Never Been Modern,* trans. H. Wheatsheaf & the President and Fellows of Harvard College. Cambridge, MA: Harvard University Press.

Leslie, R. (1990), Must I report adults abused as children: Child abuse reporting law clarified by an attorney. *The California Therapist,* Jan–Feb.:13–15.

Levenson, E. (1991), *The Purloined Self: Interpersonal Perspectives in Psychoanalysis.* New York: Contemporary Psychoanalytic Books.

———— (1983), *The Ambiguity of Change: An Inquiry into the Nature of Psychoanalytic Reality.* Northvale, NJ: Aronson, 1995.

Loewald, H. W. (1960), On the therapeutic action of psychoanalysis. In *Papers on Psychoanalysis.* New Haven, CT: Yale University Press, pp. 221–256.

Loftus, E. F. (1993), The reality of repressed memories. *American Psychologist,* 48:518–537.

Mahoney, P. J. (1987), *Freud as a Writer.* New Haven, CT: Yale University Press.

———— (1989), *On Defining Freud's Discourse.* New Haven, CT: Yale University Press.

Masson, J. M. (1984), *The Assault on Truth.* New York: Farrar, Straus, and Giroux.

———— (ed. and trans.) (1985), *The Complete Letters of Sigmund Freud to Wilhelm Fliess.* Cambridge, MA: Harvard University Press.

Matte-Blanco, I. (1988), *Thinking, Feeling, and Being: Clinical Reflections on the Fundamental Antimony of Human Beings and World.* London: Routledge.

Mitchell, S. A. (1992), Introduction to Symposium: What does the analyst know? *Psychoanalytic Dialogues,* 2:279–285.

Modell, A. H. (1990), *Other Times, Other Realities: Toward a Theory of Psychoanalytic Treatment.* Cambridge, MA: Harvard University Press.

Ofshe, R. & Watters, E. (1993), Making monsters. *Society,* 30(3):4–16.

Ogden, T. (1986), *The Matrix of the Mind: Object Relations and the Psychoanalytic Dialogue.* Northvale, NJ: Aronson.

———— (1988), On the dialectical structure of experience: Some clinical and theoretical implications. *Contemporary Psychoanalysis,* 24:17–45.

Orange, D. M. (1992), Perspectival realism and social constructivism: Commentary on Irwin Hoffman's "Discussion: Toward a social-constructivist view of the psychoanalytic situation." *Psychoanalytic Dialogues,* 2:561–565.

———— Atwood, G. E. & Stolorow, R. D. (1997), *Working Intersubjectively: Contextualism in Psychoanalytic Practice.* Hillsdale, NJ: The Analytic Press.

Otis, L. (1993), Organic memory and psychoanalysis. *History of Psychiatry.* Vol. 4, 349–372.

Polkinghorne, D. E. (1988), *Narrative Knowing and the Human Sciences.* Albany: State University of New York Press.

Popper, K. (1963), *Conjectures and Refutations*. New York: Basic Books.

Rapaport, D. & Gill, M., (1959), The points of view and assumptions of metapsychology. In M. Gill (Ed.), *The Collected Papers of David Rapaport*. New York: Basic Books, 1967.

Renvoize, J. (1993), *Innocence Destroyed: A Study of Child Sexual Abuse*. New York: Routledge.

Ricoeur, P. (1970), *Freud and Philosophy: An Essay on Interpretation*, trans. D. Savage. New Haven, CT: Yale University Press.

Robinson, P. (1993), *Freud and His Critics*. Berkeley: University of California Press.

Rogers, C. (1951), *Client Centered Therapy*. Boston: Houghton Mifflin.

Roiphe, J. (1995), The conceptualization and communication of clinical facts: A consideration of the 75th anniversary edition of the IJPA. *International Journal of Psycho-Analysis*, 76:1179–1190.

Rorty, R. (1996), Something to steer by. *London Review of Books*, 18 (12):7–8.

Sachs, D. (1989), In fairness to Freud: A critical notice of *the foundations of psychoanalysis, by Adolf Grunbaum*. In: *The Cambridge Companion to Freud*, ed. J. Neu., UK: Cambridge University Press, pp. 209–338.

Schafer, R. (1972), Internalization: Process or fantasy? *The Psychoanalytic Study of the Child*, 27:411–438. New Haven, CT: Yale University Press.

——— (1976a), *A New Language for Psychoanalysis*. New Haven, CT: Yale University Press.

——— (1976b), The appreciative analytic attitude and the construction of multiple histories *Psychoanalysis and Contemporary Thought*, 2:3–24.

——— (1980), Narration in the psychoanalytic dialogue. *Critical Inquiry*, 7:29–53.

——— (1983), *The Analytic Attitude*. New York: Basic Books.

——— (1987), Self-deception, defense, and narration. *Psychoanalysis and Contemporary Thought*, 10:319–346.

——— (1989), The psychoanalytic life history. In J. Sandler (Ed.) *Dimensions of Psychoanalysis*. New York: International Universities Press, pp. 13–30

——— (1992), *Retelling a Life*. New York: Basic Books.

——— (1994), The practice of revisiting classics: An essay on Heinz Hartmann's *Psychoanalysis and Moral Values*. *Psychoanalysis and Contemporary Thought*, 17:251–285.

——— ed. (1997), *The Contemporary Kleinians of London*. Madison, CT: International Universities Press.

Scheflen, A. E. (1972), *Body Language and the Social Order*. Englewood Cliffs, NJ: Prentice-Hall.

Schlesinger, H. J. (1995), Facts is facts—or is they? *International Journal of Psycho-Analysis*, 76:1167–1177.

Schutz, A. (1970), *Alfred Schutz on Phenomenology and Social Relations: Selected Writings*. H. R. Wagner (ed.), Chicago: University of Chicago Press.

Schwartz, J. (1995), What does the physicist know? Thraldom and insecurity in the relationship of psychoanalysis to physics. *Psychoanalytic Dialogues*, 5:45–62.

Shapiro, D. (1965), *Neurotic Styles*. New York: Basic Books.

Spence, D. P. (1982), *Narrative Truth and Historical Truth*. New York: Norton.
————— (1987), *The Freudian Metaphor*. New York: Norton.
————— (1993), The hermeneutic turn: Soft science or loyal opposition? *Psychoanalytic Dialogues* 3:1–10.
————— (1994), *The rhetorical voice of psychoanalysis: Displacement of evidence by theory*. Cambridge, MA: Harvard University Press.
Spezzano, C. (1993), *Affect in Psychoanalysis: A Clinical Synthesis*. Hillsdale, NJ: The Analytic Press.
————— (1994), Trauma and fantasy: A commentary on the question of narrative and historical truth in psychoanalysis. In L. Di Donna (Ed.) *NCSPP Newsletter*, The Northern California Society for Psychoanalytic Psychology, San Francisco. Spring: 12–17.
Spiro, A. M. (1976), A philosophical appraisal of Roy Schafer's *A New Language for Psychoanalysis Psychoanalysis and Contemporary Thought*, 2:253–291.
Spitz, E. H. (1989), Psychoanalysis and the legacies of antiquity. In *Sigmund Freud and Art*, ed. L. Gamwell & R. Wells. Albany: State University of New York, pp. 153–172.
Stern, D. B. (1991), A philosophy for the embedded analyst: Gadamer's hermeneutics and the social paradigm of psychoanalysis. *Contemporary Psychoanalysis*, 27:51–80.
————— (1997), *Unformulated Experience: From Dissociation to Imagination in Psychoanalysis*. Hillsdale, NJ: The Analytic Press
Stolorow, R. D. (1988), Intersubjectivity, psychoanalytic knowing and reality. *Contemporary Psychoanalysis*, 24:331–338.
————— & Atwood, G. E. (1992), *Contexts of Being: The Intersubjective Foundations of Psychological Life*. Hillsdale, NJ: The Analytic Press.
————— Brandchaft, B. & Atwood, G. E. (1987), *Psychoanalytic Treatment: An Intersubjective Approach*. Hillsdale, NJ: The Analytic Press.
————— (1995), An intersubjective view of self psychology. *Psychoanalytic Dialogues*, 5:393–400.
Sulloway, F. (1979), *Freud, Biologist of the Mind*. New York: Basic Books.
Taylor, J. (1994), The lost daughter. *Esquire*, 121 (3):76–87.
Tavris, C. (1993, Jan. 3), Beware the incest-survivor machine. *New York Times Book Review*.
Terr, L. (1994), *Unchained Memories: True Stories of Traumatic Memories, Lost and Found*. New York: Basic Books.
Viderman, S. (1979), The analytic space: Meaning and problems. *Psychoanalytic Quarterly*, 48:257–91.
Wachtel, P. L. (1980), Transference, schema and assimilation: The relevance of Piaget to the psychoanalytic theory of transference. *The Annual of Psychoanalysis*, 8:59–76. Chicago: University of Chicago Press.
Warnke, G. (1987), *Gadamer, Hermeneutics, Tradition and Reason*. Palo Alto, CA: Stanford University Press.
Weinberg, S. (1992), *Dreams of a Final Theory*. New York: Vintage Books.
Winnicott, D. W. (1971), *Playing and Reality*. London: Tavistock/Routledge.
Wittgenstein, L. (1953), *Philosophical Investigations*, trans. G. E. M. Anscombe. Englewood Cliffs, NJ: Prentice-Hall, 1958.

Wolf-Man (1971), *The Wolf-man*. (M. Gardiner, ed.). New York: Basic Books.

Wolman, B. W. (1984), *Logic of science in psychoanalysis*. New York: Guilford.

Wright, L. (1993a, May 17), Remembering Satan: Part I. *The New Yorker*, 69, 13:60–81.

——— (1993b, May 24), Remembering Satan: Part II. *The New Yorker*, 69, 14:54–76.

Index

affect attunement, 78
agency, 153–154. *See also* self, as
    structure *vs.* agent
ambiguity, 102, 107, 109–110, 115,
    117, 123, 124
    assumptions regarding, 152
    fundamental, 136
    "Pandora's box" of, 47, 49, 118
The Ambiguity of Change
    (Levenson), 149
analyst(s)
    ability to monitor the influence
        of their unconscious, 64
    attunement, 91–92
    authority, 62–63, 124
        sources of, 161–163
    classical, mediating position
        between psychic and
        historical reality of, 49
    constructivist, 112
    patient's sense of reality and,
        166–167
    patient's experience of motives
        of, 111
    responsibility, 161
    role, 161–164

analytic relationship, 108
    both persons as simultaneously
        subject and object, 108
    overlap of two play areas in, 158
    role in recovery from trauma,
        169–170
analytic space, 92
anarchism, intellectual, 13–14
archeological metaphor of
    psychoanalysis, 30–34, 39,
    50
Arlow, J. A., 142
attunement, 78, 82–83, 92, 121
    rescuing past experiences of
        lack of, 91
Atwood, G. E., 8, 69n, 77–96, 139,
    167
Auerhahn, N. C., 167, 168
autonomy. *See* agency

Bass, E., 5
Berger, P. L., 80, 101, 114, 116, 144
Bergmann, M. S., 31n
Bernstein, R. J., 44
Black, M., 50
"blank screen" model, 121

181